RESOURCES BOOMS AND MACROECONOMIC ADJUSTMENTS IN DEVELOPING COUNTRIES

To my parents Ishaque and Anwara, who taught me to set the goal; and to my love Sarah, Ishraque and Khorshed, who encouraged me to achieve it.

Resources Booms and Macroeconomic Adjustments in Developing Countries

MAMTA BANU CHOWDHURY
University of Western Sydney, Australia

Routledge
Taylor & Francis Group

LONDON AND NEW YORK

First published 2004 by Ashgate Publishing

Reissued 2018 by Routledge
2 Park Square, Milton Park, Abingdon, Oxon OX14 4RN
711 Third Avenue, New York, NY 10017, USA

Routledge is an imprint of the Taylor & Francis Group, an informa business

First issued in paperback 2018

A Library of Congress record exists under LC control number: 2003059569

Notice:
Product or corporate names may be trademarks or registered trademarks, and are used only for identification and explanation without intent to infringe.

Publisher's Note
The publisher has gone to great lengths to ensure the quality of this reprint but points out that some imperfections in the original copies may be apparent.

Disclaimer
The publisher has made every effort to trace copyright holders and welcomes correspondence from those they have been unable to contact.

ISBN 13: 978-0-815-39150-0 (hbk)
ISBN 13: 978-1-138-62039-1 (pbk)
ISBN 13: 978-1-351-15016-3 (ebk)

Contents

List of Tables

List of Figures

Abbreviations and Acronyms

na	Not available
ADF	Augmented Dickey–Fuller
ADL	Autoregressive Distributed Lag
ARMA	Autoregressive Moving Average
A$	Australian Dollar
BCL	Bougainville Copper Ltd.
BOP	Balance of Payments
BPNG	Bank of Papua New Guinea
CPI	Consumer Price Index
CPSF	Commodity Prices Stabilisation Funds
ECM	Error Correction Model
EPI	Export Price Index
GDP	Gross Domestic Product
GNP	Gross National Product
IFS	International Financial Statistics
IMF	International Monetary Fund
IPI	Import Price Index
K	Kina
LSE	London School of Economics
ML	Maximum Likelihood
MRSF	Mineral Resources Stabilisation Fund
MWB	Minimum Wage Board
NEER	Nominal Effective Exchange Rate
NPEP	National Public Expenditure Plan
OLS	Ordinary Least Squares
PNG	Papua New Guinea
PNT	Price of Nontradables
PPP	Purchasing Power Parity
PT	Price of Tradables
RER	Real Exchange Rate
TOT	Terms of Trade

Preface

This book investigates the impact of resources booms on the process of economic adjustment in developing countries. Changes in key macroeconomic variables induced by resources booms, including the real exchange rate, savings and investment, have significant consequences for the performance and structure of an economy. This book contributes to the analytical and empirical research on these issues through an in-depth case study of the economy of Papua New Guinea (PNG) during the period 1970–94. The theoretical framework of the study incorporates an extended version of the core model of 'Dutch disease' and the theory of 'construction boom'. In order to place the policy implication of findings in perspective, PNG's policy responses to booms are compared with those of two other resource-rich countries – Indonesia and Nigeria.

To place the empirical analysis in context, an econometric analysis of the determinants of real exchange rate behaviour has been undertaken. The findings suggest that investment and mineral booms in the early 1970s caused a significant appreciation of the trade-weighted real exchange rate of the country. This adverse effect was compounded by increased government expenditure and excess monetary growth.

Following independence, PNG exercised its most prudent macroeconomic policy and achieved admirable economic stability during the agricultural boom in 1976–77. Commitment to an open trade regime, together with sound income and wage policies and reduced reliance on foreign aid, were instrumental in maintaining macroeconomic stability. Depreciation of the real exchange rate was achieved with expenditure restraint throughout the agricultural export boom, which created a 'reverse Dutch disease' during the height of the agricultural boom in the 1976–77 period. The output of the tradable sector increased significantly during this period. However, the domestic price level began to increase at a substantially faster rate than the domestic equivalent of the world price of tradables from the late 1980s until 1993, greatly reducing the competitiveness of the economy. Real appreciation of the kina was induced by the mineral boom of 1992–93 and aggravated by a persistent expansionary fiscal policy, making it very difficult for the monetary authority to reduce domestic inflation. However, the situation improved greatly as PNG undertook a radical labour market reform and world market prices for PNG's agricultural commodities increased significantly. From 1994, a more restrictive fiscal stance, a large exchange rate devaluation and subsequent flotation and depreciation of the kina, all helped to restore the competitiveness of the economy to a large extent. The second half of the decade, between 1995 and 2000, PNG experienced increasing budget deficits and poor economic performances, followed by a deteriorating standard of living.

The results of the comparative study of the resources booms of PNG, Indonesia and Nigeria suggest that PNG performed much better than the other two countries. PNG was able to maintain a lower level of domestic inflation throughout the 1970s, especially in the second half of the decade. Sensible expenditure and wage restraint policies, and the maintenance of an open trade regime, made it possible for the economy to prevent erosion of the competitiveness of its tradable sector. On average, this outcome was reflected in a depreciation of the real exchange rate over the second half of the 1970s. However, a more restrictive trade regime from the mid-1980s, coupled with undisciplined fiscal policy, contributed to an appreciation of real exchange rates in the early 1990s.

The findings of the study have a number of policy implications. First, fiscal and monetary discipline, combined with reduced reliance on foreign aid and grants, considerably reduces the pressure of a resources boom on domestic price levels and improves competitiveness. Second, and most importantly, a more open trade regime, and flexibility in the labour market, promotes stability of domestic price levels and improves international competitiveness, making the economy more resilient to the adverse effects of external shocks. The resulting depreciation of the real exchange rate has a positive impact on the tradable sector. Finally, perceiving the nature and duration of a resources boom and taking appropriate policy steps accordingly can stretch the economic gain from resources booms and thus enhance long-term economic growth.

Acknowledgments

My greatest intellectual debt in writing this book goes to Professor Ross Garnaut and Professor Premachandra Athukorala. Professor Ross Garnaut provided invaluable advice, guidance and support during the writing of the book. I am greatly indebted to him for his precise and constructive comments and discussions. Many of the ideas that went into forming this book grew out of our discussion sessions.

I am also indebted to Professor Athukorala for his outstanding contribution in improving the structure and presentation of the book, especially in building up the empirical model of the study. His meticulous review of the study, support and encouragements helped me throughout the study.

I was very fortunate to be provided with helpful comments and suggestions on my research from the experts. I thank Professor Max Corden, Professor Warwick McKibbin, Professor Peter Warr, Professor Robert Castle, Professor George Fane, Dr Andrew Elek, Professor Hal Hill, Professor Roger Juchau, Dr Charles Harvie and Dr Khorshed Chowdhury for their contributions in this respect.

I have greatly benefited from the constructive comments and helpful inputs made by my fellow friends and colleagues. I thank them all. My special thanks go to Dr Helal Ahammad for his endless intellectual and moral support when I needed it most. My special gratitude goes to the Australian National University, University of Wollongong and University of Chittagong for their support and help at various stages of the study. I am deeply indebted to the School of Economics and Finance, University of Western Sydney, for their support, encouragements and friendly working environment. My special thanks go to Associate Professor Brian Pinkstone, Professor Raja Junankar, Professor Anis Chowdhury, Mr Verghis George and Dr Girija Mallik for their support and help at various stages of preparation of the book. I also wish to thank AusAID and Borhan Ahmed, Faridul Haq and Habibur Rahman for providing me with useful research materials.

I wish to thank Ms Cat Sparks for her invaluable CRC preparation. I am grateful to Robert Hood for his invaluable editorial contribution and complex diagram drawings. I also wish to thank Ms Trish O'Brien for her friendly assistance whenever I needed it.

I am deeply indebted to my parents for kindling the flame of knowledge in my heart. They are the sources of continuous support, encouragement and inspiration all through my journey. I am grateful to my brothers Mamun, Masum and Litul and my sister Matia who have been supportive from my very childhood. My special gratitude goes to Nurjehan Chowdhury, Idris Akhand, Sandhya Mukhopadhya, D.P. Chaudhri, Dr Abdur Razzaque, Dr Badrul Khan, Dr Tahmina Khan, Dr Abed Chowdhury, Tulip Chowdhury and Professor Hafiz Siddique for their support and encouragement.

Last but certainly not least, I am grateful and wish to thank the members of my family, Khorshed, Ishraque and Sarah, for their endless support and tolerance of my obsession for this study.

Map of Papua New Guinea

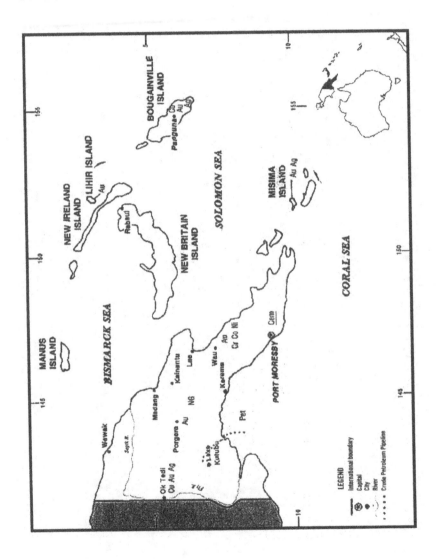

1

Introduction

1.1   Purpose and Scope of the Study

Developing countries are prone to periodic temporary external shocks. Effects of these shocks can be both positive and negative. These can come through a sudden change in the current and capital accounts of the balance of payments or can originate from internal sources. A positive external shock, in the form of a resources boom, enables an economy to attain higher levels of growth, consumption and welfare in the short run through the increased inflow of capital or export revenues. However, a positive shock can be a mixed blessing for a country, because the economic changes triggered by a resources boom will enhance long-term growth prospects only if the government takes appropriate policy measures. Thus a positive external shock also poses a policy dilemma in management of windfall gain.

Using Papua New Guinea (PNG) as a case study, this book investigates the macroeconomic impact of a resources boom and the long-term growth implications of related policy choices. Like many other primary commodity exporting developing economies, PNG has experienced several short-lived export booms over the past two and a half decades. Thus, PNG provides an interesting case study of potential gains from resources booms and the accompanying complex problems of policy management.

For the purpose of the study, four major resources booms experienced by the PNG economy over the period of 1970–94 are identified. The first was in 1971–72, with a large inflow of direct foreign investment by Bougainville Copper Ltd (BCL) in the construction sector. The second was a mineral boom during 1973–74, caused by the increased production of copper and gold after the opening of BCL mine, and by high minerals prices. The third was a major boom in the agricultural sector during 1976–77, induced by increased world market prices for PNG's agricultural commodities. There was then an extended period of slow growth, during the first half of the 1980s, followed by a marked improvement in economic activity, between 1985 and 1988, reflecting the development of the nation's mineral wealth and a recovery in agriculture. The fourth, and presumably, PNG's largest ever mineral boom, was during 1992–93, with the development of an oil field at Kutubu and a new gold mine at Porgera.

All these above-mentioned booms had different origins and the outcomes were strikingly different because of the adoption of different policy measures. The boom associated with the Ok Tedi mine establishment in the second half of the 1980s is not covered in this study because of its similarity to the 1973 mineral boom in terms of underlying causes and hence the related analytical interpretation.

During the twin booms between 1971 and 1974, the construction and mineral sectors' contribution to GDP increased significantly. The prices of tradable goods and services increased due to improvements in the terms of trade (TOT), also improving the competitiveness of the tradable sector during these boom years. At the same time increased government expenditure, excessive money supply and rapid increases in nominal wages, and increased consumer price index (CPI) rose faster than the price of tradables causing the trade-weighted real exchange rate to appreciate significantly.

During the agricultural boom in the mid-1970s, PNG undertook restrictive policy measures to reduce instability in domestic price levels. Loss of competitiveness was also avoided by the use of stricter income and wage-restraint policies and a very open trade regime. In fact, stable domestic price levels, compared with the increased price of tradables during the agricultural boom in 1976–77, depreciated the real exchange rate. In contrast, during the boom years of 1991–93 the government of PNG failed to maintain fiscal discipline. Continuing budget deficits and a more restrictive trade regime exerted enormous pressure on domestic price levels. As a consequence, over the period 1991–93, the real exchange rate appreciated and reduced the competitiveness of the economy.

Although the impact of these resources booms are of paramount importance for the PNG economy, analytical and empirical investigations of the issue are missing. This book aims to fill this void. The central objective of this study is to assess the magnitude of the effects of these resources booms on the real exchange rate, the structure of the economy and overall economic performance in PNG.

1.2   Statement of the Problem

For a small open economy like PNG, which is heavily dependent on a few minerals and primary commodity exports, and which is characterised by a large public sector and significant government intervention, the consequences of a resources boom are likely to be very different to those for a developed economy. Conventionally the issues of macroeconomic adjustment following a resources boom have been addressed in the context of the 'Dutch disease' framework, which treats the windfall as a permanent shock and analyses the consequences in a short-term context only. But most booms in a primary export-dependent country are temporary in nature. Given the less developed nature of the financial sector of a developing economy, such temporary shocks affect capital accumulation through intertemporal choice between consumption, savings and investment. Thus, the intertemporal smoothing of windfall gains and asset behaviour in a developing economy calls for an analysis of long-term adjustment process. The long-term dynamic analysis of a resources boom adds a new dimension to the theory of booming sector literature and is known as the theory of 'construction boom'.

The analytical framework used in this study is developed by extending the core 'Dutch disease' model in terms of three types of openness in the economy. These will be treated as (a) openness in the labour market, (b) openness in the capital market, and (c) openness in the international trade regime. The theory of 'construction boom' is also incorporated with the theory of 'Dutch disease' to capture the long-term dynamic effects of resources booms.

The ideal methodology is to work with a comprehensive macroeconometric model, which captures the key relationships suggested by theory. Unfortunately, this approach was not feasible in the context of the PNG economy given the nature of data availability.[1] Therefore, the methodology that has been chosen is a case study approach bringing together single equation estimates of behavioural relations involving key macroeconomic variables and other relevant information, both quantitative and qualitative, in order to shed light on the key theoretical propositions. A detailed discussion of major resources booms and policy responses in relation to the changes in the sectoral composition and long-term growth of the economy has been presented in Chapter 6 in order to examine the key theoretical propositions postulated in Chapters 4 and 5.

This study also compares the experience of PNG in managing its resources booms with those of Indonesia and Nigeria – two other oil-exporting countries with comparable dependence on volatile mineral exports. This comparison sheds light on the implications of different trade restrictions, labour market conditions and varying macroeconomic policy management issues on the nature of the adjustment process in response to a resources boom. In terms of income per head, size and stages of development, these three countries are quite heterogeneous. They are, however, comparable in terms of a dominant agricultural base and an abundance of mineral resources. These countries are also similar in having a significant primary sector as the chief source of exports and in their use of mineral rents to fund public consumption and capital formation. It will be argued that the main differences are the policy regimes and institutional structures, which brought about different outcomes from resources booms for these economies.

1.3　Organisation of the Study

Chapter 2 provides a review of the literature on the theory of booming sector economics. This review includes the short, medium and long-term static and dynamic models of booming sector economics. Initially, the core model of 'Dutch disease' is discussed. The core model is then extended to incorporate the effects of different institutional and structural rigidities and the effects of various government policies during a boom cycle in the context of a small open developing economy. The extension takes into account the different types of openness in labour and capital markets and international trade regimes in developing countries. Since the intertemporal choice between consumption and savings is important, the theory of 'construction boom' is also discussed in an attempt to capture the long-term dynamic impact of a resources boom.

Chapter 3 presents an overview of the PNG economy. It describes structure, recent development, and changes in the sectoral composition over 1970–94. The movement of key macroeconomic variables, such as domestic price levels, wage rates, the exchange rate, government expenditure, the structure of the financial market, and the balance of payments and trade policy, are also discussed in order to set the stage for the ensuing analysis.

Chapter 4 provides an econometric analysis of the determinants of the real exchange rate. The theory of real exchange rate determination is used to identify the major real and nominal variables that determine the movements of real exchange rate. This extended framework of the real exchange rate model assumes a labour-surplus economy, in the setting of both fixed and flexible exchange rate regime, with different degrees of capital mobility and trade restrictions to make it applicable for a developing economy.

Chapter 5 undertakes an econometric investigation of the sectoral impact of changes in the real exchange rate. The purpose of this chapter is to test the impact on sectoral growth of key macroeconomic variables, suggested by the resources boom literature, in order to provide the empirical basis for the study of each major boom episode in the economy of PNG discussed in the next chapter. This chapter also examines the determinants of savings and investment behaviour in PNG over 1970–95.

Chapter 6 presents a detailed study of major resources booms experienced by PNG and the major macroeconomic policy measures undertaken by the government in the 1970s and 1990s. This chapter also attempts to identify the different nature of these booms, their major beneficiaries and the consequences for changes in the sectoral composition of the economy. The empirical analysis of this chapter makes use of the results of the econometric analysis in Chapters 4 and 5.

Chapter 7 compares the findings of the present study with those of existing studies of the impact of resources booms and macroeconomic adjustment in Indonesia and Nigeria. The basic purpose of this comparison is to shed light on the implications of differences in policy regimes during these resources booms for the structure and competitiveness of these economies.

Chapter 8 summarises the major findings of the study. This chapter draws lessons for developing countries in capturing the maximum benefits from resources booms and avoiding their potential adverse consequences for both short-term stability and long-term growth. Prudent and judicious policies are required to counteract the adverse consequences of resources booms. This chapter also indicates some reservations of the study and makes suggestions for further research on the subject.

Resources Boom and Macroeconomic Adjustment: A Survey[1]

2.1 Introduction

During the 1960s and 1970s, several industrial countries, as well as oil-exporting developing countries, experienced a slump in their traditional export and import competing sectors following resource booms. This phenomenon is known as the 'Dutch disease' and has been the subject of a great deal of discussion and policy debate. The term 'Dutch disease' was first used in the 26 November 1977 issue of *The Economist* to refer to the adverse effects on Dutch manufacturing of natural gas discoveries during the 1960s. While strong growth in the natural gas sector had led to a large surplus in the Netherlands' balance of payments, with an appreciating guilder, the domestic manufacturing sector declined, due to real wage pressure. The unemployment rate also reached record levels. Therefore, the term 'Dutch disease' refers to a boom-induced appreciation of the real exchange rate (a rise in the price of nontradables relative to that of tradables) and a relative decline in the non-booming tradable sector (Garnaut, 1991, p. 19).

The objective of this chapter is to review the core 'Dutch disease' model developed by Corden and Neary (1982) and to discuss some possible modifications to form the basis of an empirical investigation for a developing country like PNG. In particular, the model will be analysed with a focus on both the comparative static and dynamic analysis of resources booms in the short-, medium- and long-term framework. This modification is justified because the core model of 'Dutch disease' is premised on the conditions prevailing in a mature, developed economy.

Essentially, a resources boom produces a temporary shock, as opposed to the permanent shock predicted by the core 'Dutch disease' model. The intertemporal smoothing of a resources boom, and assets behaviour in the case of a boom, calls for an analysis of the dynamic adjustment process. The dynamic analysis of intertemporal choice between consumption, savings and investment adds a new dimension to the theory of resources booms and is known as a 'construction boom' in the literature.

In the following chapter, Section 2.2 reviews the short-, medium- and long-term 'Dutch disease' models and Section 2.3 introduces the 'core model' of 'Dutch disease' to analyse the effects of a resources boom. Limitations of the core model and the need for the intertemporal dynamic analysis of resources booms are also discussed in this section. Section 2.4 discusses some possible extensions of the basic model in the setting of a small, open, developing country. Section 2.5 provides a discussion of the 'construction boom' theory. Section 2.6 concludes with a summary of discussion.

2.2   An Overview of Booming Sector Economics

Over the years a sizeable literature concerning various macroeconomic aspects of resources booms has developed. Gregory's (1976) work is considered to be the first initiative to analyse the adverse consequences of the Australian mineral boom on traditional export and import-competing sectors during the mid-1970s. However, Eide (1973), first described the mechanisms of how a resources boom impacts upon the other sectors of an economy. Since two early papers on the issue remain widely unknown, Gregory (1976) has been credited with the first work on this subject. In a partial equilibrium framework, with a small country assumption, Gregory (1976) indicates that rapid growth in the mineral sector leads to a lower equilibrium price ratio of traded to nontraded goods. He argues that both import-competing industries and pre-existing export sectors shrink due to a mineral boom.

Gregory's (1976) analysis suggests that the growth of mineral exports is comparable with large tariff changes. The empirical findings of his study indicate that the impact of the resources boom in the Australian mineral sector during the early 1970s was approximately equivalent to a doubling of the tariff from the viewpoint of the traditional export sector. Whereas, the effects of resources booms on the import-competing sector were found to be equivalent to the removal of tariffs and the introduction of some form of import subsidies.

Snape (1977) extended Gregory's analysis in a general equilibrium set up and concludes that, though the pre-existing traded sector is expected to shrink due to a mineral boom, the production of some goods in this sector may rise; even if the size of the traditional export sector remains the same, social gain is still possible from growth in the mineral sector; and that, while the price of nontradables can be expected to rise, the output of nontradables may not expand in the short run. Similar studies analysing the consequences of oil discoveries in the UK have been done by Bruno and Sachs (1982) and Forsyth (1982).

There has since been rapid development in the literature on booming sector economics. Among others, the dynamic analysis of a resources boom has been enriched by the contributions of Buiter and Purvis (1982), Eastwood and Venables (1982), Edwards and Aoki (1983), Neary and Wijnbergen (1984), Harvie and Gower (1993) and Harvie (1994). Each of these models makes use of the framework developed by Dornbusch (1976) to analyse the effects of an oil boom during the 1970s and 1980s. In these models economic agents are assumed to possess rational expectations or perfect foresight, financial markets are assumed to be in continuous equilibrium while product markets are subject to downward price stickiness. These models can be classified as being either short-term or long-term. A major contribution of the long-term models is that they give explicit consideration to the accumulation of physical capital stock over time and hence put specific emphasis on the long-term development of an economy.

The short-term dynamic models (Buiter and Purvis, 1982; Eastwood and Venables, 1982; and Neary and Wijnbergen, 1984) assume that windfall gains will affect the spending pattern of an economy. The other assumptions are: windfalls accrue in the first instance primarily to the private sector; the government gets a share by imposing various taxes on the booming sector; the country is a net oil exporter; and the country produces a non-oil traded good which is consumed domestically as well as exported and is an imperfect substitute for imported goods. A fixed exchange rate regime and no restriction on capital mobility are also assumed in these models.

A major shortcoming of these short-term models is that they are incapable of explaining the medium- and long-term adjustments towards steady state. In the short run, the magnitude and the length of the adjustment process is smaller and faster. Developments in the non-oil trade balance and foreign asset stock are not identified from the short-term models. In the context of the long-term models, the incorporation of a fixed exchange rate suggests that there is greater volatility in key macroeconomic variables during the adjustment process in comparison with a flexible exchange rate.

Harvie and Gower (1993) and Harvie (1994) analyse the dynamic adjustment of oil shocks by extending the short-term models to the long-term framework. These models focus on the supply side of the economy with slower quantity adjustment and incorporate the notion of capital stock accumulation, current account and real wealth. The long-term models suggest appreciation of the real exchange rate, unchanged inflation, a rise in real income and a rise in non-oil output. Increases in capital stock, foreign assets stock and private sector real wealth are anticipated with deterioration in the non-oil trade balance.

A new dimension of the study of resources booms has been introduced by Bevan et al. (1990) to analyse the dynamic adjustment between product and assets market and the intertemporal choice between consumption and savings. This dynamic model is known in the literature as the 'construction boom' and is discussed in detail in Section 2.5.

2.3　The Core Model of 'Dutch Disease'

A systematic analysis of 'Dutch disease' was undertaken by Corden and Neary (1982) using a three-sector, two-commodity, medium-term model to identify the consequences of a resources boom. The three sectors are: (a) a booming traded sector, (b) a non-booming or lagging sector, comprising the agricultural and manufacturing sectors, and (c) a nontraded sector, including services, utilities, transportation and construction. These sectors are producing two commodities, one traded internationally at given world prices, the other traded domestically (nontraded) with price determined by domestic demand and supply conditions. This model focuses on the real sectors and ignores monetary considerations. Only the relative price of tradables to nontradables is determined in this model. The model assumes there are no distortions in the commodity or factor markets and assumes labour to be the only mobile factor amongst the three sectors of the economy. The amount of capital is fixed for each sector and is non-shiftable in the short run. All factor prices are assumed to be flexible and factors are not mobile across the geographical boundary of a country.

A boom can be brought about in one of three ways. There can be (a) an exogenous technological improvement in the booming sector, represented by a shift in the production function of the country; (b) a discovery of new resources that is, the increase in the supply of a specific resource; or (c) an exogenous rise in the price of a specific export product. Corden and Neary (1982) considered the first case – a boom induced by a technological improvement in the booming sector.

The initial effect of a resources boom is to raise the aggregate factor income of the booming sector leading to an increase in demand for both tradable and nontradable commodities. Since world price levels determine the price of tradables, a small booming country cannot affect the price of tradables. The excess demand for tradables is satisfied by increased net imports by the booming economy. The increased demand for nontradables is obviously satisfied domestically. Thus, short-term supply constraints in nontradable production increase the relative price of nontradables to tradables to preserve the equilibrium in the nontradable market. The relative price change is induced by two separate effects, a *spending effect* and a *resource movement effect*, which impact upon the output composition of an economy. The spending and resource movement effects can occur independently or in combination with each other.

To the extent that the increased revenue flow generated by the booming sector is absorbed domestically (either directly by the factor owners or by the government which collects this revenue in taxes), the price of nontradables increases, provided that the income elasticity of demand for nontradables is positive. As a result, the nontradable sector becomes more profitable and draws labour from the non-booming traded sector. This is known as the *spending effect* of a resources boom. Substantial resources move into the booming trade sector, based on the assumption that the booming sector is not an enclave but requires increased factor inputs, which must be bid away from other sectors. This situation is known as the *resource movement effect*.

During the boom years the marginal product of labour increases in the booming sector, making the sector more profitable. As a result, nominal wages rise in the economy. Labour mobility allows labour to move out of non-booming sectors to the more profitable booming sector. The labour movement out of the non-booming traded sector into the booming sector is known as 'direct de-industrialisation' and does not require an appreciation of real exchange rate because it does not affect the output of the nontradable sector.

The effects of a resources boom on the output composition of an economy primarily depend upon relative factor intensities among sectors. Corden (1984) demonstrated that if the booming sector is an enclave, that is, the booming sector does not compete with other sectors for its factor inputs, there would not be any 'de-industrialisation'. The key adjustment in this situation is the real exchange rate appreciation through the spending effect. However, when the demand for nontradables increases due to the spending effect, profitability in the nontraded sector also rises. Increased demand for labour, and increased nominal wages in the nontradable sector, pulls labour away from the non-booming traded sector and brings additional real appreciation. Corden (1984, p. 361) terms this effect 'indirect de-industrialisation'.

The output of the nontraded sector would be higher than initial output if the spending effect outweighs the resource movement effect. When both spending and resource movement effects are taken into account, the impact of a resources boom on overall real wages is ambiguous. As the spending effect increases demand and the price of nontradables in the short run, a fall in real wages is more likely if the spending effect is stronger and the share of nontradable goods in the CPI basket is larger. However, real wages may rise if the rate of increase in nominal wages outweighs the rate of increase in domestic price levels.

Capital immobility causes a sharp decline in returns to capital in the non-booming traded sector and raises returns to capital in the nontradable sector. Given supply constraints in the short run, the domestic price level tends to increase and the real exchange rate, relative price of traded to nontraded, must decline. In turn, this appreciation of the real exchange rate erodes competitiveness of the non-booming traded sector by increasing the gap between domestic and international cost-price differences causing the non-booming traded sector to contract. This phenomenon is referred to as *'tradable-squeeze effects'* (Corden and Neary, 1982).

The implication of a resources boom as discussed so far can be illustrated by using the well-known Salter diagram (Figure 2.1), which was developed by Corden (1985) using the original idea of Salter (1959). The vertical axis measures the output of nontradables and the horizontal axis represents the output of tradables. The initial production possibility frontier is represented by the curve NT-T, given the factor endowments and the existing technology of the country. Before the boom, the equilibrium of the economy was determined by the intersection of NT-T with the highest possible attainable social indifference curve, U_0U_0, at point E_0. Hence, prior to the boom, the country produced $0NT_0$ of nontradables and $0T_0$ of tradables. The real exchange rate is represented by the slope of RE, the common tangent to the two curves, NT-T and U_0U_0, at point E_0. The curve $0Y_0$ represents the demand expansion path when the relative prices are held constant at RE and income increases.

A resources boom shifts the production possibility curve to the right to NT-T, while the production possibility frontier for the non-booming traded and nontradables remains at NT-T. After the boom, total production of the economy is at E_1 and comprises NT_0E_0 of nontradable and non-boom tradable output and E_0E_1 of boom output with the real exchange remaining constant at RE_1 (RE_1 is parallel to RE).

At this new equilibrium, desired consumption must expand to the point M along the income expansion path $0Y_0$. As the output of nontradables remains at $0NT_0$, the

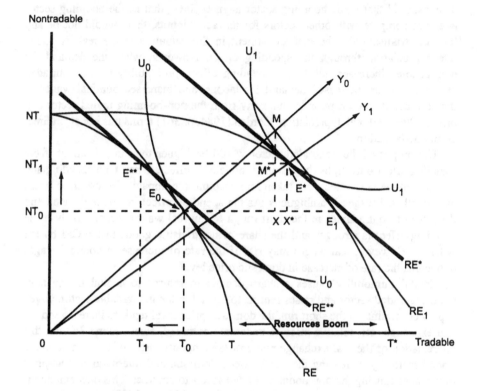

Figure 2.1   The effect of resources boom on the real exchange rate

boom induced increased income flow creates excess demand for nontradables of MX. There is also an excess demand for non-booming tradables equivalent to E_0X with a balance of payments surplus of XE_1.

To restore equilibrium by reducing the excess demand for nontradables, the real exchange rate has to appreciate. This real appreciation arises either from a combination of price increases in non-booming tradables and appreciation of the nominal exchange rate if the nominal exchange rate is floating, or through a price increase for nontradables if the nominal exchange rate is fixed.

The new equilibrium is at E^* along the new income expansion path $0Y_1$ with a new relative price of nontradables to tradables at RE^*. Increased income flow increases the demand for nontradables X to M, but the appreciation of the real exchange rate lowers the demand to M^*, leaving a net increase in demand for nontradables by XM^*. The windfall gain, on the other hand, increases the demand for non-booming tradables from E_0 to X, and appreciation of the real exchange rate expands the demand for them further to X^*.

The appreciation of the real exchange rate increases the profitability of the nontradable sector and draws resources from the non-booming traded sector, reducing profitability in that sector. At the new real exchange rate RE**, which is parallel to RE*, a new equilibrium is at E** with the old production possibility frontier NT-T. At this new equilibrium, with a new real exchange rate RE**, the production of nontradables increases from ONT_0 to ONT_1, but the output of non-booming tradables contracts from OT_0 to OT_1. The increased demand for non-booming tradables is covered by imported non-booming tradables equivalent to E**E*.

When the appreciation of the real exchange rate, induced by windfall revenue, increases the output of nontradables from ONT_0 to ONT_1 and the output of non-booming tradables declines from OT_0 to OT_1 – this effect is known as the 'Dutch disease' effect of a resources boom. The magnitude of the fall in the non-booming tradable sector depends on the initial production possibility frontier and the slope of the initial indifference curve. However, the domestic absorption (welfare) improves, as represented by the movement of the indifference curve from U_0U_0 to U_1U_1.

2.4   Limitations and Extensions of the Core Dutch Disease Model

As discussed, the core 'Dutch disease' model perceives a resources boom to be of a permanent nature and considers some of the consequences of a resources boom in a short-term comparative static framework. It is further assumed that both goods and assets markets adjust simultaneously and there are no imperfections in the labour market. Additionally, the model assumes that the windfall accrues primarily to the private sector and there is no government control over the windfall revenues. However, these assumptions do not hold for most developing countries.

The effect of higher wealth on output composition of an economy is inherently dynamic. The temporary nature of a resources boom and the presence of learning-by-doing externalities, as well as the adjustment between product and assets market, require a dynamic analysis of a resources boom. A temporary shock impacts upon capital stock accumulation and hence on consumption, savings and investment. Thus, intertemporal choice between consumption, savings and investment plays a central role in these analyses, which may have profound, and longer-term developmental effects on an economy. These long-term effects of a resources boom can only be captured by long-term dynamic analysis of resources booms.

The consequences of a resources boom depend upon various key factors. The source, size, and the nature (price and/or production boom) of the boom, the major beneficiaries of windfall gain (government vs. private), income and price elasticity of exports, factor mobility amongst sectors, factor intensity in each sector and the degree of substitutability between the tradable and the nontradable sectors, are the major factors to be considered in the analysis of a resources boom. Economy-wide fiscal, monetary exchange rate and trade policies can also radically alter the effects of a resources boom.

Since some modifications of the 'core' model are necessary to capture the stylised features of a primary commodity-exporting developing country, the Corden-

Neary model will be discussed in terms of three types of openness of a country: (a) openness in the labour market; (b) openness in international trade regime; and (c) increased mobility in capital markets.

2.4.1   Surplus Labour and International Labour Mobility

Unemployment is a prominent feature of the labour market structure of most developing countries. Relaxing the assumption of full employment changes the outcome of a resources boom in a developing country compared with a developed economy. If a developing country has large unemployed resources, both the resource-movement effect and spending effect will be weaker because labour is not a constraint on domestic production. Even if higher productivity and higher wage rates draw labour into the booming sector, the non-booming sectors can satisfy their resource demand from the large unemployed and under-employed labour reservoir. In the short run, these labourers can gain skill by a 'learning by doing' process. In this situation, the resource-movement effect would either be insignificant or not occur at all. Since a labour-surplus economy can increase production without increasing the wage rate, price increases in the nontradable sector would be moderate. Furthermore, in a labour-surplus developing economy, a resources boom causes minimal resource movement if the booming sector is an enclave sector.

Relaxing the assumption of international factor immobility also changes the outcome of the core model. During the oil booms of 1973–82, both labour and capital were internationally mobile. The migrant labour flow can be considered in this context. Migrant labour flow from Asia to Middle Eastern oil-exporting countries is a well-documented phenomenon. The effect of migrant labour flow may have the same consequences as domestic surplus labour in moderating the resource movement effect as well as spending effects. Migrant labourers have a high savings ratio and remit a large share of their income to their home country (Chowdhury and Chowdhury, 1993). This reduces the spending effect, moderates the demand for nontradables and reduces domestic inflation. This, in turn, reduces the real exchange rate appreciation of a booming economy.

2.4.2   International Trade Barriers

All existing models of 'Dutch disease' assume free trade. In reality, it is rarely observed. In most developing countries, government intervention plays a very important role in altering trade flows and thus the structure and composition of domestic production. By imposing price controls, tariffs, and other quantitative restrictions and export subsidies, governments can greatly alter the outcome of a resources boom. By imposing various restrictions and subsidies, the government can moderate the adverse effects of a boom on the non-booming traded sector by protecting this sector from world-market competition and enhancing the production of this sector. In fact, following a boom, the output of the manufacturing sector in most developing countries was significantly altered by existing quantitative import restrictions, and high tariff and price controls during the 1970s and 1980s. However, such trade restrictions have adverse impact on domestic price level and competitiveness of the country.

During the height of a resources boom, the growth of the manufacturing sector in a developing country may also be explained by relaxing the assumption of perfect substitutability of domestically produced traded goods and imported traded goods. Given qualitative trade restrictions, most manufacturing goods in a developing country are only semi-traded or partially traded. As in the case of nontraded goods, the domestic price of these traded goods is determined by domestic demand and supply rather than international prices. The imperfect substitutability of importable to import moves these traded manufacturing goods to the nontradable category and results in an expansion of the manufacturing traded sector. Thus, contrary to the prediction of the core model, the manufacturing traded sector can expand as well. As the agricultural export sector is usually less protected than the manufacturing sector, the agricultural traded sector contracted in the developing countries during the resources booms of 1973–82. The agricultural sector may be hit twice, once by real appreciation and then by direct resource loss to the import-substituting manufacturing sector (Corden, 1984). Therefore, the degree of openness in the international trade regime plays a significant role in this context. On the other hand, the output of non-booming tradables declines due to domestic price and cost increase and also loses their competitiveness in the world market.

2.4.3   Domestic and International Capital Mobility

The nature of restrictions on international capital mobility also changes the outcome of the core model. If capital is mobile within the economy, capital-intensive production will be more profitable during the boom period. In this case, both the resource movement and the spending effects need not occur. Relaxing the assumption of capital immobility leads to another dimension to the study of booming sector economics. The theory of 'construction boom' (Bevan et al., 1990) takes into account not only the intertemporal choice between consumption and savings but also the possibility of capital movement between domestic nontradable sectors and across national boundaries.

The 'Dutch disease' theory treats a resources boom as a permanent shock and explains the consequences of shocks essentially in a comparative static framework. However, most resources booms are temporary in nature, and last for only a few years, making short-term dynamic effects important in assessing the consequences of these shocks. If these booms are perceived to be temporary the increase in domestic savings may be greater than expenditure, and the spending effects of 'Dutch disease' would be minor. Part of the windfall savings that comes to the domestic financial sector reduces the pressure on the domestic interest rate. Thus, increased domestic savings reduces the cost of funds for investment. In this case, a resources boom is likely to lead to higher investment instead of consumption of nontradables and the 'spending effect' may not occur at all.

In the absence of a developed capital market, in most developing countries, both government and private agents would try to invest their savings on nontradable capital goods. This, in turn, transmits encouraging price signals to nontradable assets such as buildings and construction, and raises the price of these assets, generating a 'construction boom'.

2.5   The Theory of Construction Boom

The intertemporal choice between consumption and investment, due to the temporary nature of a resources boom, is systematically analysed by Bevan et al. (1990). They disaggregated the nontradable sector into nontradable capital and nontradable consumption goods sub-sectors. The nontradable capital goods sector includes a range of activities, which may vary between economies, but the most common activity in this sector is 'construction'. The major emphasis in this theory is the relationship between a resources boom and domestic investment in nontradable capital goods.

A resources boom increases the demand for both tradable and nontradable goods and thus increases investment demand. A construction boom is usually induced by two routes: (a) through permanent increases in consumption; and (b) through temporary increases in savings. A boom usually increases consumption via increases in windfall income. The increased demand for nontradable consumption goods increases the production of the nontradable capital goods sector. This, in turn, raises construction activities and generates the construction boom.

An increase in savings is a rational outcome of a resources boom where the boom is perceived as short-lived and temporary. If the capital market is perfect, and future prices are known, the windfall gain will increase temporary savings but not investment. Thus, when a boom is perceived to be temporary, the increased revenue gain is seen to be transient and has virtually no impact on changing the sectoral composition of domestic production. However, in the absence of a developed capital market and capital mobility in most developing countries, a temporary boom provides incentives to smooth consumption over the longer period, which raises savings. Increased domestic savings reduce the cost of funds by increasing the base money, thereby stimulating domestic investment due to a lower cost of availability of funds. Unless tradable and nontradable capital are perfect substitutes in the production process, the increased propensity to invest out of the windfall revenue flow increases demand for nontradable capital goods, such as 'construction', relative to consumer goods. This sector becomes more profitable and draws resources from other sectors. With a given level of capital in the nontradable sector, a resources boom raises the marginal physical product of capital while labour moves into the nontradable sector. This increases the efficiency of capital and directs post-shock investment to the nontradable capital sector. Thus, the allocation of capital goods between productive sectors affects relative prices by altering the supply conditions of capital (Bevan et al., 1990).

The intertemporal choice between consumption and savings, and their impact on the relative price of nontradables to tradables, can be illustrated using Figure 2.2. The nontradable sector is disaggregated into nontradable capital (NK) and nontradable consumption (NC) goods to analyse the effects of a temporary resources boom on domestic investment. The relative price of the nontradable capital to the tradable goods, P_{NK}/P_T, is given in the vertical axis. The horizontal axis measures the relative price of nontradable consumption goods to tradable, P_{NC}/P_T. The NC locus depicts the equilibrium for nontradable consumption goods (such as services)

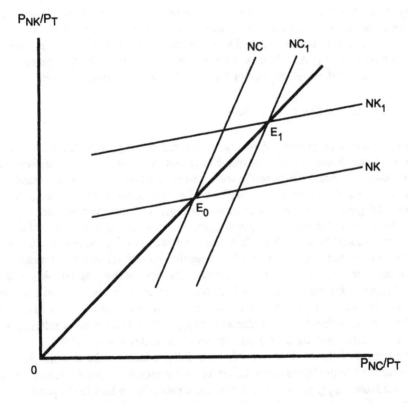

Notes: NC = nontradable consumption goods; NK = nontradable capital goods; P_{NK} = price of nontradable consumption goods; P_{NK} = price of nontradable capital goods; P_T = price of tradables.

Source: Adapted from Bevan et al. (1990), figure 4.2, p. 102.

Figure 2.2   The effects of temporary boom on the nontradable sector

and the NK locus shows the equilibrium for nontradable capital goods (an example could be the stock of buildings).

Along a ray from the origin, the price of the nontradable capital goods relative to tradable would rise more and the price of the nontradables consumption good stays constant relative to the price of the tradables. Therefore, the NC locus must be steeper and the NK locus must be flatter than the ray through the origin.

The initial equilibrium, E_0, combines the pre-boom price loci NC and NK. A temporary positive shock increases the demand for, and the price of, the nontradable and shifts both NC and NK to the right. Due to correct perception of the temporary nature of a resources boom, and imperfections in the capital market in most developing countries, the propensity for a rise in demand for nontradable capital goods is higher than the propensity for a rise in demand for nontradable consumption goods. Thus, the demand for nontradable capital goods, such as buildings, rises relative to nontradable consumption goods, such as services. This raises the NK locus proportionately upward more than the rightward shift of NC locus and shifts the equilibrium to E_1. At this new equilibrium, P_{NK}/P_T increases more than P_{NC}/P_T and raises the relative price of P_{NK}/P_{NC} higher than pre-boom level.

2.5.1   Effects of a Construction Boom

The rise in the price of nontradable capital to tradable (P_{NK}/P_T) relative to price of the nontradable consumption to tradable (P_{NC}/P_T) has significant distributional effects besides the usual effects on domestic demand and supply. The initial spending out of the windfall comes to the suppliers of nontradables as rent. Thus, part of the windfall gain, in the form of increased income, is transferred to other agents within the economy through the spending effect. As a consequence, the incidence of gain distributed between the urban and rural sectors of an economy changes. The increase in the relative price of nontradable capital relative to nontradable consumption reduces the quantity demanded for nontradable capital. When the price of nontradable capital goods is fully accounted for by rents, there will not be an economy-wide income effect, since the purchasing power of the windfall of the initial recipients is already being reduced. On aggregate, therefore, the windfall from asset accumulation will have only substitution effects (Bevan et al., 1990).

The impact of the relative price increase fully reflects on the upward-sloping supply curve of nontradables due to increased resource cost and income effect. Since the nontradable supply in the short run is less elastic, due to lags in the production process, and administrative difficulties in absorbing rapid changes, it would be costly to attempt to absorb a windfall gain into the domestic economy too quickly. At the same time, it might also be too costly to invest a windfall gain too slowly, since they can only earn a relatively low lending rate of interest if they are held in the form of foreign financial assets over a long period (Bevan et al., 1990).

The role of foreign assets is another major building block of the theory of construction boom. If there is no impediment to international capital mobility, it will be efficient to invest the windfall gain in foreign assets instead of investing in the domestic economy. The price of domestic capital goods rises sharply during a construction boom, since capital goods are partly nontradable. If there is no imperfection in the capital-market, the domestic rate of return will exceed the world deposit interest rate, making it optimal to invest the windfall savings domestically. However, there are capital market imperfections in most developing countries and the price of capital goods rises during a construction boom. Therefore, investing in foreign assets would be optimal, as the real value of the windfall gain is protected by holding foreign assets and repatriating them when the capital goods price drops at the end of the boom period. Thus, the investment boom can be spread out over a longer period and building up foreign financial assets during the boom years can moderate the relative price of 'construction'. Repatriated foreign assets can also be used in the post-boom period to finance a higher level of consumption. Hence, access to the world capital market raises welfare compared to a closed capital model in two ways. First, domestic investment is subject to diminishing returns while the interest rate on foreign assets is constant. Second, it offers the possibility of postponing investment until the price of domestic capital goods has fallen, reducing the spending effect,[2] and dampening the symptoms of 'Dutch disease' as well as 'construction boom'.

2.5.2   Private Versus Public Savings

In most economies, the government plays a central role in determining the overall response to a resources boom. As a result, the consequences of a boom are borne differently by different agents in an economy. In many developing countries private agents are not allowed to hold foreign financial assets directly. They can either match their savings to domestic capital formation continuously or they can hold foreign assets indirectly, by acquiring financial claims on government, which then effectively holds foreign assets on their behalf. Even if windfall revenue does accrue directly to the private sector, the government is likely to control this by various policy measures, thus altering the consequences of a resources boom. Governments can sterilise the foreign exchange flow by increasing the required reserve ratio of the banking system, thereby eliminating excess demand for money. Governments can also invest the revenue gain in foreign financial assets received from private agents in exchange of domestic currency. These actions can moderate the effects of a construction boom, stretching the investment boom into a *savings boom* (Bevan et al., 1991, p. 107).

Even where the windfall accrues to private agents, in the absence of government intervention to manage it, a change in tax and public expenditure management is an obvious passive participation of government in response to a positive trade shock. As national income increases permanently following a resources boom, tax revenues also increase, lowering the public sector's deficit. Public expenditure is expected to rise if the elasticity of 'desired' public expenditure is positive with respect to permanent national income. Governments can choose to spend the windfall on capital goods and thus increase capital formation. They can also choose to spend the windfall earnings on consumer goods, which tends to reduce the propensity to save as well as invest.

In many developing countries the government is the major 'shareholder' of the booming sector and the windfall assets automatically accrue to the government. In this case, the government has to decide how to share the gain between the private and public sectors. The government can reduce taxes; give subsidies to private production or consumption, or purchase goods and services on behalf of the private sector. In the case of production subsidies, private suppliers can share the benefit through higher income and enjoy lower prices, in the case of price subsidies given by government in an attempt to transfer the windfall gain. When government purchases goods and services for the public sector, the benefit to the population depends partly upon whether they desire it and partly upon the nature of the goods (Bevan et al., 1991). The population can enjoy the benefit of the windfall if increased government expenditure leads to greater availability of public goods, such as medical facilities, education, roads etc, through which a higher factor incomes and higher standard of living can be provided.

2.6   Summary and Conclusion

The study of the effects of a booming sector, which was initiated by Gregory and subsequently developed by various economists in short-, medium- and long-term contexts, was formally integrated by Corden and Neary and is known as the 'core' model. The major prediction of the model is that appreciation of the real exchange rate induced by a resources boom reallocates productive resources and changes the structure of an open economy. However, the outcomes of the core 'Dutch disease' model may not materialise in a developing country with unemployed resources and a restricted trade regime. Therefore, some modifications have been suggested to deal with the various inadequacies of the 'core' model of 'Dutch disease'. These amendments are likely to generate different outcomes in the process of economic adjustment towards long-term equilibrium.

While this extended version of the 'Dutch disease' model shows the linkage between movements of the real exchange rate and macroeconomic adjustment, the 'construction boom' theory analyses the dynamic adjustment of the goods and assets market in response to a resources boom. As in the static case, the resulting 'construction boom' does not constitute a 'disease', if the nature of the shock is correctly perceived, and if agents are free to adjust their portfolio of foreign and domestic assets. Just as the so-called 'Dutch disease' is not a disease, so a 'construction boom' may be the appropriate response to a trade shock in a developing country.

The main objective of this study is to analyse the outcomes of a resources boom in a developing country context, given a condition of openness in labour, capital and the international trade regime, by studying the PNG experience over the past two and a half decades. It incorporates the extended version of the 'Dutch disease' model, and the theory of 'construction boom', in an attempt to analyse macroeconomic adjustment with emphasis on the major linkages between the real exchange rate movement, sectoral transformation and the long-term growth of PNG in response to resources booms over the study period.

Notes

1. Unless otherwise stated data used in this study are taken from the Quarterly Economic Bulletin, Bank of Papua New Guinea, Port Moresby.
2. Cameroon provides an example of avoiding the spending effects of a resources boom by investing abroad (Benjamin et al., 1989).

3

An Overview of the Papua New Guinea Economy

3.1 Introduction

This chapter provides information about the resources base, structure of the economy, institutional settings, characteristics of the labour market, importance of foreign trade and the major macroeconomic policies.

The chapter is organised into ten sections. Section 3.2 discusses political background; Section 3.3 sketches economic performance; Section 3.4 presents the structure of the economy; Section 3.5 discusses the characteristics of the labour market; Section 3.6 describes the role of the public sector; Section 3.7 provides a financial sector overview; Section 3.8 describes external trade patterns; Section 3.9 discusses macroeconomic policies; and Section 3.10 summarises the economy's key features.

3.2 Political Background

Papua New Guinea (PNG) comprises the eastern half of the island of New Guinea, called the mainland, the Bismarck Archipelago, and the northern part of the Solomon Islands, together with hundreds of small offshore islands between the Coral sea and South Pacific ocean. PNG was colonised at various times by Australia, European powers and Japan.

A Papua New Guinean-controlled central government was formed in 1972. The territories of Papua and New Guinea became a self-governing country on 1 December 1973. PNG became fully independent from the Australian administration on 16 September 1975, although the ties between PNG and Australia remained very close. The British monarch, represented by a Governor-General, is head of state, but the real leadership is exercised by the Prime Minister. The country consists of twenty provinces with a central government in Port Moresby. The National Parliament, a Westminster-style structure, consists of one hundred and nine representatives, democratically elected every five years.

3.2.1 Geography and Resource Base

New Guinea is located in the second largest island in the world, with a land area totalling 462.8 thousand square kilometres and a sea area of 3.1 million square kilometres. Most of its total land area is situated on the eastern half of the island of New Guinea. The main island is divided between PNG and Indonesia.

PNG is in the humid tropics and displays little variation in temperature. Its land-mass is dominated by rugged mountainous terrain which means that many villages and clans are isolated from each other. Approximately 30 per cent of the total land area of 460,000 square kilometres is classified as suitable for agricultural development but only about one quarter of this is regularly used for agriculture, representing about 7 per cent of the total land area. Nearly 360,000 square kilometres of forested area covers about 78 per cent of the country (AIDAB, 1991).

The total population of PNG was around 5.13 million in 2000, is predominantly Melanesian, rural-based, and growing at about 3.1 per cent per annum between 1990 and 2000. More than 700 different local languages and dialects are spoken with allegiances closely tied to villages. English, Tok Pisin and Motu are the official PNG languages. The education system is controlled by the government but primary education is not compulsory. As a result primary school enrolment is much lower (only 70 per cent in 1992) compared to other lower-middle income countries (100 per cent in 1992) as shown in (Appendix Table A3.1).

PNG is abundantly endowed with renewable and non-renewable natural resources. This abundance of natural resources has given the country considerable developmental potential in agriculture, forestry, fisheries, tourism, minerals and petroleum, and agro-processing activities. PNG has some of the world's richest gold and copper deposits, and became a producer of oil from the early 1990s. PNG also has good potential for the supply of liquefied natural gas and methanol (AIDAB, 1994, p. 183).

3.2.2 Stages of Social Development

According to the Human Development Report 1995, published by the United Nations Development Program (UNDP), PNG ranked 126th out of 174 countries, based on a human development index, a composite measure of income per capita, life expectancy and literacy rates (AusAID, 1996). PNG's rank worsens to 133 in 2002 in the UNDP Human Development Index compared to 122 in 2001. Apparently, about a fifth of PNG's population are currently living in poverty. With a GNP per capita estimated at US$810 in 1999, Papua New Guinea is ranked as a lower-middle income developing country (World Bank, World Development Indicators, 2002a). Its middle income status is somewhat misleading, however, in terms of some basic social indicators, PNG more closely resembles countries which are classified as low-income economies (GNP per capita of $650 and below).

Life expectancy at birth is about 59 years, the adult literacy rate is 65 per cent, and primary-school enrolment rose to about 84 per cent in 2000. These social indicators are substantially below those seen in PNG's major neighbouring countries in the South Pacific and South-east Asia (for example, Fiji, Tonga, Thailand and Malaysia). However, PNG has achieved reasonable improvement in some key social indicators, compared with other low-income countries, including female and male life expectancies, infant mortality rates, and crude birth and death rates (Appendix Table A3.1).

PNG faces enormous economic and social problems in its efforts to develop its physical and human resources. PNG is characterised by its poor infrastructure. Only two thirds of the population is within the reach of a road. The rugged terrain, widely dispersed population centres, and low level of market oriented activities of the country present barriers to effective and low-cost transport and communications. As a consequence, fragmentation of the domestic market has increased production costs. The short supply of basic human skills, capital and entrepreneurship has resulted in a heavy dependency on external investment and highly paid foreign skilled workers.

The concept of private property is not well established. The traditional redistribution system of 'Wantok' provides a valuable safety net for the community in times of sickness and distress, but also reduces individual incentive, in terms of entrepreneurship and wealth accumulation. About 97 per cent of land is owned in the traditional manner with the remainder owned by the government. The availability of land is limited because of the disorganised administration of land tenure arrangements. Traditional owners of land have only agreed to a small portion of land in the major cities being converted from customary ownership to a leasehold form. There is no formal market for small pieces of land. As lenders prefer secure collateral, the insecurity of land tenure also limits access to finance. There is under-utilisation and under-investment in improving the productivity of land due to major divergence between private and social value of land (Jarrett, 1985). In addition to these limitations, increased social tensions and serious law and order problems remain a major impediment to both private investment and development in general. The provision of law and order services suffer from lack of proper management, poor training and skills, inadequate supervision, poorly articulated policies and implementation of policies in a timely fashion. Thus lack of law and order condition escalates the cost of providing other critical services. The problem of lawlessness is not only confined to the towns. Increased incidence of robberies on the High Land's highways during the harvest season also directly reduce the income of rural people (Jarrett and Anderson, 1989).

3.3   Economic Performance

Prior to independence, the economy of PNG achieved an average annual growth rate of 6.7 per cent of Gross Domestic Product (GDP) between 1965 and 1973, spurred by rapid growth in aid-financed public expenditure and by the establishment of the BCL mine. In the first few years after independence real GDP growth was moderate and PNG maintained a stable macroeconomic environment. The growth of per capita GDP was slow during the late 1970s and early 1980s. According to Jarrett and Anderson (1989) this poor performance of PNG economy was greatly influenced by the incidence of expatriates leaving the country taking their savings and skills.

However, Garnaut and Baxter (1984) indicated a substantial increase in the share of market GDP accruing to the nationals in the late 1970s and by the end of the 1970s, nationals' share of production was stabilised at a high level. However, PNG experienced an appreciable increase in growth from the mid-1980s, owing particularly to strong world market prices for its mineral resources and a marked improvement in the agricultural commodity export sector. The country faced an enormous setback in 1989, through the forced closure of the BCL mine, due to the secessionist rebellion, and a significant decline in world market prices for its major agricultural and tree crops exports. A nine year secessionist revolt on the island of Bougainville ended in 1997.

The gloomy scenario was somewhat mitigated by strong growth in the petroleum and mineral sectors from the early 1990s. During the early 1990s, substantial expansion in the mineral and petroleum sector contributed to a relatively large growth in GDP. In 1993, PNG's per capita GNP amounted to an estimated US$1,130. Over the period 1991 to 1994, an average annual growth rate of 10.6 per cent was achieved (Appendix Table A3.2). However, the growth rate of GDP and GNP both deteriorated over the second half of the decade due to poor economic performance and continuous laxity of fiscal policy.

Table 3.1
Economic growth in PNG and lower–middle income economies, 1970–2001

	Papua New Guinea			Lower–middle income economies		
	1970– 80	1981– 94	1995– 2001	1970– 80	1981– 94	1995– 2001
Annual % growth in GDP	2.2	3.1	0.3	5.1	1.6	3.6
GNP per capita (US$)ᵃ	260	1130	580	170	1590	430
Annual % growth in GNP per capitaᵃ	6.6	2.1	0.3	1.4	–0.5	2.8

Notes:
a.   GNP is calculated using the World Bank Atlas method, which adjusts the standard measure for recent changes to the exchange rate.

Sources: The World Bank Group (2002), AusAID (1996), Table A3, World Bank (1981).

3.3.1   Investment and Savings

PNG's ratio of gross investment to GDP has been comparable to other lower middle-income countries over the years. Investment is dominated by the mining sector, most of which comes through foreign companies. The mining sector's contribution to gross capital formation averaged between 19.6 per cent and 56.8 per cent over 1984–94 and remained buoyant, although it fluctuated considerably over the years. Over 1970–94, gross domestic investment (GDI) accounted for about 26 per cent of GDP on average.

During the early 1970s, high investment activities were associated with mining and construction-sector investment. The sharp drop in aggregate investment in the mid-1980s was mainly due to the completion of major construction activity at the

Table 3.2
Investment and savings, 1970–99
(current prices and percentage of GDP, kina million)

	1970	1975	1980	1985	1990	1991	1993	1999
Gross domestic investment	187.9	221.9	456.3	500.7	751.9	1017.4	1018.0	1439.3
Gross fixed capital formation	182.4	186.5	395.2	466.9	772.9	1032.4	943.0	1062.7
Changes in stocks	5.5	35.4	61.1	33.8	−21.0	−15.0	75.0	376.6
Gross national savings	19.8	164.2	321.9	299.9	8.6	485.2	1434.0	1545.3
Domestic resource gap	−168.1	−57.7	−134.4	−200.8	−743.3	−532.2	416.0	406.0
Gross domestic savings	105.8	238.0	381.1	299.8	638.9	266.1	1575.0	1898.6
Percentage share of GDP								
Gross domestic investment	35.4	22.1	26.3	21.9	24.6	29.9	18.8	13.0
Gross national savings	3.7	16.4	18.5	13.1	18.7	19.4	44.0	17.6
Gross domestic savings	19.9	23.7	21.9	13.1	20.9	23.4	31.4	20.9

Source: The World Bank Group (2002), World Bank (1995), AusAID (1996), Bank of Papua New Guinea, *Quarterly Economic Bulletin*, various issues.

Ok Tedi mine, but gross domestic investment increased sharply from 1990 onwards (Figure 3.1), due to an upsurge in construction activity on the Kutubu and Porgera projects.

The share of non-mining investment fell from about 14 per cent of GDP in 1981 to 8 per cent in 1991. However, since the early 1990s forestry has been attracting significant foreign investment. Investment in forestry and construction has greatly influenced the present steady performance in non-mining private investment. Higher investment in the construction sector also resulted from mineral booms during the early 1990s. Investment in the manufacturing sector is not high except in some protected industries. A large portion of PNG's investment has been financed by foreign sources.

The performance of public savings in PNG has been very poor. Lower public savings is one of the major reasons why total domestic savings stays at a low level, averaging 13 per cent of GDP from the mid-1980s to the early 1990s. Despite a large capital outflow in 1992–93, as a result of openness in the capital market, private saving's contribution to investment was remarkably high and averaged around 30 per cent of GDP over the 1991–93 period. As measured by the resource gap, PNG's dependence upon foreign savings dropped sharply in 1993, as a result of strong growth from the early years of the 1990s (Table 3.2). However, the real gross fixed

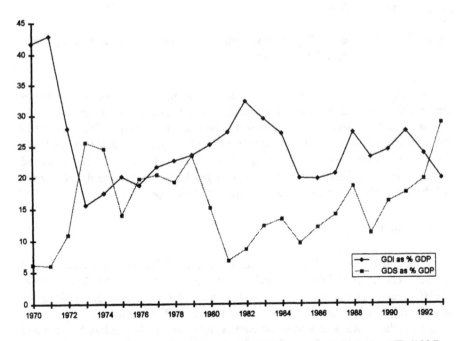

Source: Constructed from various tables in World Bank (1995), (1991), AusAID (1996).

Figure 3.1   Gross domestic investment and gross domestic savings, 1970–93 (percentage of GDP)

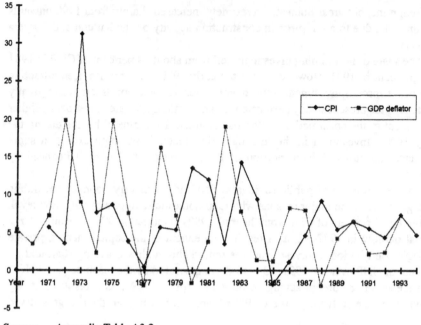

Source: Appendix Table A3.2

Figure 3.2   Inflation in Papua New Guinea, 1970–94 (percentage change in CPI and GDP-deflator)

capital formation fell down to 13.7 per cent of GDP in 1998 compared with 21 per cent in 1984 mainly due to outflow of foreign capital since 1994 (Curtin, 2001) .

Australia is the largest foreign investor in both mining and non-mining sectors of PNG. Development of new mines such as Ok Tedi (copper and gold), Hides (gas), Kutubu (oil), Lihir (gold), Porgera (gold) and Misima (gold) have also attracted USA, UK and Canadian mining interests. Malaysia has become a significant investor in fisheries, timber and other trade and construction sub-sectors.

3.3.2   Inflation

From the mid-1970s, PNG was a low-inflation country. The average annual rate of inflation between 1975-79 was around 4.7 per cent, which was well below the level of PNG's major trading partners. Appendix table A3.2 and Figure 3.2 indicate the trend of inflation over two and a half decades in the PNG economy.

During the 1980s, a moderate increase in inflation was due mainly to increased prices for food, raw materials and petroleum products, and a weaker kina. Between 1990 and 1994, the average annual CPI-based inflation rate was around 5 per cent.

Favourable external factors also contributed positively to the decline in inflation, including low international inflation, particularly in Australia, the major source of

PNG's imports (imported products carrying a weight of 50 to 60 per cent in the CPI). However, annual average rate of inflation between 1995 and 2001was 11 per cent. CPI and GDP deflator annual change jumped to a double digit figure of 16.4 per cent and 10.8 per cent respectively in 2000 from its previous year. Both the figures dropped considerably in 2001, mainly because of the exclusion of large upward piece movements in seasonal CPI categories and the imposition of a selected excise tax on the subgroup of cigarettes and tobacco.

3.4   Structure of the Economy

Data on sectoral growth and the changing composition of GDP are given in Table 3.3. The exploitation of abundant natural resources has led to the development of a dualistic economic structure dominated by a significant agricultural and forestry sector, and a capital intensive oil and minerals sector. Agriculture accounts for approximately one third of GDP,[1] and virtually all non-mineral exports, as well as providing the livelihood for about 80 per cent of the population. There are two types of cash crop grown; those grown specially for the export markets and food crops grown for sale in the local market. Food crops consist mostly of vegetables and fruit, and constitute about half of this sector's output. In the early 1960s, the agricultural

Table 3.3
Sectoral composition of GDP, selected years
(as percentage of GDP)

	1970	1975	1980	1985	1990	1993	2000	Average annual growth rate 1991– 2001
Agriculture	40	30	33	33	29	27	26	3.2
Minerals and Petroleum	0.1	13	13	10	15	30	33	12.1
Manufacturing	5	7	10	12	9	9	8	3.7
Construction	13	7	4	5	5	4	3	5.5
Services	42	43	40	40	42	30	30	2.7

Source: Constructed from The World Bank Group (2002), AusAID (1996), AIDAB (1991), Bank of PNG, *Quarterly Economic Bulletin*, various issues.

sector accounted for more than 50 per cent of GDP. The GDP share of agriculture (including forestry and fishery) declined from 40 per cent in 1970 to about 27 per cent in 1993. The share of forestry accounted for about 8 per cent of GDP in 1993.

In terms of investment, exports, and net contributions to the balance of payments and government's fiscal revenues, the mineral sector consisting of copper, silver, gold and oil production, is the dominant sector of the PNG economy. Data on sectoral growth indicates spectacular growth in the mining sector over the past two and a half decades.

The mining sector's share (copper and gold) of GDP increased from 0.1 per cent in 1970 to about 30 per cent in 1993. Mineral and oil exports constituted over 73 per cent of total export earnings in 1992 compared with 18 per cent in 1972. The sector is represented by four active establishments,[2] consisting of the copper and gold mine at Ok Tedi in Western Province and the gold mines at Misima, Milne Bay and at Porgera in Enga Province. Ok Tedi, Misima and Porgera have more than made up for the closure of Panguna. Although the mineral sector is overwhelmingly foreign owned, the government has reserved the right to acquire a 30-per-cent equity in mining projects and 22.5 per cent in petroleum (AIDAB, 1991). The Kutubu oil project was the first oil development in PNG and its first exports were shipped in July 1992. Further developments are occurring in the Gobe Main and Southeast Gobe fields.

The manufacturing sector includes food, soft drinks, beer, food canning and tobacco processing. Furniture making has been a minor feature of the sector. Small-scale engineering and metal processing, clothing and other light industries are also included. The sector is dominated by capital-intensive activities and is foreign owned and managed. The share of the manufacturing sector in the economy is small and has been stagnant over the past two decades. The expansion of manufacturing has been hampered by the shortage of entrepreneurial, managerial and labour skills, especially by the high cost of labour relative to productivity (Goodman et al., 1985). Over the period 1970–95, its contribution to GDP has varied in the range of 5 to 12 per cent.

Over the 1970s and the 1980s, the services sector accounted for more than 40 per cent of GDP on average and declined to 31 per cent in 1995. This sector includes all economic activities such as electricity, gas and water, transport and communications, trade, finance, insurance, real estate, community, social business and personal services.

The construction sector grew rapidly in the early 1970s, with the establishment of BCL, followed by a declining trend over the 1980s. The major cause of this fall was the failure to implement infrastructure projects. The contribution of the construction sector settled at around 5 per cent of GDP during the first half of the 1990s. Contribution of all sectors' output to GDP remained constant at the end of the decade.

3.5   Labour Market

Data on employment are very scarce as there is no comprehensive reliable series of wage employment data in PNG. Major studies (Garnaut et al., 1977; Lodewijks, 1987; McGavin, 1993, 1991, 1986; Levantis, 1997) on PNG's labour market indicate that the concept of employment is of limited relevance in PNG, since the majority of the population works in the non-monetised economy.

According to the 1971 census, less than one third of the population above the age of ten was in the work force, and less than one quarter of the labour force worked mainly in money-earning activities. In 1979, formal employment was about 15 per cent of the total economically active population. The labour force grew at about 1.5–2.2 per cent per annum over the 1980s. The 1990 census estimated the total labour force at 1.6 million, or 46 per cent of total population. The total increase in unemployment between 1980 and 1990 grew at an annual compound rate of 16.3 per cent, and was 27 per cent for males in 1991 (McGavin, 1993, p. 59). Lack of formal job opportunities in the rural area and the large wage disparity between rural and urban minimum wages until 1992 induced large scale rural to urban migration and increased urban unemployment which was 29.3 per cent according to 1990 Census (Levantis, 1997). A detailed discussion of wage structure in PNG is presented in Section 3.4.3.

The predominance of self-employment in the agricultural (35.5 per cent of total labour force in 1980) and subsistence sector (41.2 per cent of total labour force in 1980) indicates that wage employment in rural areas of PNG is relatively unimportant (AIDAB, 1991). Agriculture is the main source of employment, employing nearly 80 per cent of the total labour force. In the formal sector,[3] the private sector is the largest employer, providing almost 60–70 per cent of all formal jobs. Available data on employment over the period 1968–95 (Appendix Table A3.6) indicate no growth in formal-sector employment in the non-agricultural and mining sectors, although agricultural employment grew by 3.7 per cent per annum between 1980 and 1991 (McGavin, 1991, p. 66). After the labour market reforms in 1992, employment in the private sector grew about 8 per cent by 1994 (AusAID, 1997). Employment in all sectors except retail and manufacturing fell considerably at the end of the decade.

PNG suffers from short supply with regards to high skilled labour. This short fall is normally satisfied by recruiting skilled expatriates. Expatriate labourers mainly come from Australia. Naturally, the wages and salaries to such high skilled labour are considerably high. However, the domestic supply of skilled labour has increased over time in response to high returns. As a result, the expatriate labour supply in formal wage employment has fallen from 7.3 per cent in 1980 to 3.6 per cent in 1990 (Levantis, 1997).

Over the past three decades the growth rate in formal-sector employment has not kept pace with labour-force growth. Between 1970 and 1993, the annual growth rate of the labour force was 2.3 per cent, whereas the growth rate of formal wage employment was estimated at only 0.7 per cent. The breakdown of formal wage employment indicates that the share of public-sector employment declined from

26.6 per cent of total wage employment in 1975 to 24 per cent in 1991 (Appendix Table A3.6).

Employment in the mining sector has remained at about 3 per cent of total formal employment since independence. Several other industry groups, mainly finance, communication and social service, and building and construction registered significant employment growth in the 1990s. However, despite high economic growth, urban employment fell in the 1990s, adding to the number of unemployed persons in urban areas and increased incidents of crimes.

3.6   Public Sector

PNG inherited a relatively large public sector from the colonial era which occupies a prominent position in the economy. Between 1970 and the early 1990s, government expenditure constituted about one third of total GDP on average and about 40 per cent of non-mining GDP. The government's share in total non-mining investment was 41 per cent of GDP over the 1970s and 1980s, which is high compared with other low middle-income developing countries. The public sector provides more than 40 per cent of all jobs in the formal sector.

Despite its large size, the public sector has not been able to contribute much to sustainable economic growth in PNG. A major share of government expenditure has been directed towards consumption rather than investment, with nearly 85 per cent of total expenditure absorbed by wages and salaries and various kinds of administrative activities. Capital expenditure represents a small proportion of total expenditure (see Appendix Table A3.3), resulting in a failure to meet the basic infrastructure needs of the private sector. Expenditure on operations and maintenance of capital and basic institutions has been neglected, resulting in a perpetual reduction in the efficiency of infrastructure, investment and public services.

3.7   Financial Sector

PNG's financial system is controlled by the Bank of Papua New Guinea (BPNG). The sector consists of five commercial banks, five merchant banks, sixteen active savings and loan societies, four financial companies, government-controlled pension and investment companies, nine insurance companies, a merchant bank and the Central Bank. The five commercial banks own over 80 per cent of the sector's assets. Since independence, development in the financial-services sector has remained limited, and access to financial services in rural areas is particularly poor. Only the savings and loan societies function with some degree of effectiveness. The Rural Bank was established in 1994 from an old Development Bank and is targeted at the rural sector's financial facilities. In recent years, the PNG government has undertaken various measures to deepen capital markets and create a more favourable climate for the financial sector to diversify and extend its reach to the rural population. Although the financial sector of PNG is relatively small, contributing less than 1 per cent of total non-mining GDP, the modern monetary economy has grown strongly with the mining sector's development.

3.8 Foreign Trade

The economy of PNG is highly dependent on international trade. Merchandise exports account for about 40-50 per cent of GDP, and are concentrated around a small number of mineral and agricultural commodities. In the mid-1960s, coffee was the major export. In the 1970s, the main sources of export earnings were mineral and agricultural commodities, among which palm oil became a significant export earner. Agricultural exports are dominated by tree crops, such as coffee, copra, cocoa, coconut and palm oil and palm kernel, which constitute over 95 per cent of agricultural export earnings. From the early 1990s, the combination of higher prices and volumes increased the value of log exports more than five-fold and accounted for almost 20 per cent of the export value in 1994.

From the early 1990s, the dominance of mineral exports in total exports continued to increase, from 53.0 per cent in 1985 to 72.0 per cent in 1995 and 78 per cent in 2000. The mineral and petroleum sector accounted, on average, for more than 35 per cent of GDP per annum during 1992–95.

Australia is the major trading partner, accounting for 47 per cent of total trade. Japan is another significant trading partner, accounting for 27 per cent of total trade in 1990. Over 40 per cent of PNG's imports come from Australia. Japan and the United States are also important sources of imports.

Non-mineral exports

Non-mineral exports, which include exports from agriculture, forestry, fishery and others, contributed significantly to total exports in 1977–80. The share of agricultural exports in total export earnings was depressed over the first half of 1980s due to low world market prices for PNG's major agricultural export crops. Total export revenues from the agricultural sector improved significantly in the mid-1980s and accounted for about 36 per cent of total exports but declined after 1985 because of a decline in production and falling prices (Table 3.4). The situation began to improve after 1992, due to an improvement in world prices for PNG's agricultural exports and a 10 per cent nominal devaluation of the kina in 1990. (For detailed information, see Appendix Tables A3.4 and A3.5.)

Agricultural exports increased almost 30 per cent in 1994 from the 1990 level in real terms and accounted for 33 per cent of total exports. Since 1992, the export volumes of all major agricultural commodities increased significantly, with the exception of copra, rubber and tea.

Table 3.4
Minerals and agricultural exports of PNG, 1970–2000
(current prices, kina million)

	Mining exports	Agriculture exports	Non-mining exports[a]	Total exports
1970	—	75.3	92.8	99.0*
1975	240.1	131.2	162.5	402.6
1980	322.4	230.3	319.4	704.2*
1985	489.9	330.2	436.3	926.2
1990	758.0	205.0	365.0	1123.0
1991	1005.4	204.6	384.6	1390.0
1992	1371.5	224.0	491.1	1862.6
1993	1767.8	270.0	759.2	2527.0
1994	1783.0	375.0	899.0	2682.0
1995	2435.0	498.0	965.0	3400.0
2000	4494.6	955.5	342.5	5792.0

Notes:
a.   Non-mining exports include the export value of agriculture, forestry, marine and other re-exports.
*   Some total export entries are not equal to the sum of mining exports and non-mining exports because of omission of other minor exports items and re-exports.

Source: The World Bank Group (2002), AusAID (1996, 1997), Bank of Papua New Guinea, *Quarterly Economic Bulletin*, various issues.

Mineral exports
Both the volume and value of minerals exports have grown significantly since the early 1970s after the establishment of the BCL mine. The mineral sector's contribution to total exports increased dramatically from virtually nothing in 1970 to nearly 60 per cent of total export earnings in 1975. From the mid-1980s, the share of exports as a proportion of GDP grew rapidly (Table 3.4 and Appendix Table A3.5).

In 1989, copper, gold and coffee alone generated 72 per cent of total sales. In 2001 mineral exports accounted for 80.5 per cent of total merchandise exports compared to 73.5 in 1992 and 53 per cent in 1985. The increase was due to the combined effects of the commencement of crude oil exports in June 1992 and increases in the value of gold exports, reflecting increased production at the Porgera and Misima mines. In 1993, export revenues from minerals and petroleum accounted for 35 per cent of GDP and 70 per cent of total merchandise exports. Total exports accounted for 52 per cent of GDP between 1993–95 and 56 per cent in 1999.

Terms of trade
The prices of PNG's export commodities exhibited a great deal of volatility in the world market. PNG's terms of trade remained at a high level during the 1970s and then fell substantially over the early years of the 1980s. TOT improved greatly in 1984 as the world market prices of PNG's export commodities improved from the depressed situation of the early 1980s. TOT started to fall from the mid-1980s (with an exception in 1988) and remained low until 1992. The situation improved in 1993, with increased world market prices for agricultural commodities. TOT fell by 2.9 per cent in 2001 compared to its previous year due to relative price increase in PNG's imports.

3.8.1   The Balance of Payments and International Reserves

In the 1970s, PNG's balance of payments (BOP) was generally in surplus. During 1983–85, a positive BOP was achieved, but this deteriorated in 1989, following the closure of the Bougainville mine and a drastic decline in PNG's agricultural commodity prices. From 1992, both the trade and current account went dramatically into surplus, due largely to the contribution from the Kutubu petroleum project and increased gold and log exports. The share of imports fell from over 53 per cent in 1984 to 45.5 in 1998. In 2001, the overall BOP surplus was K708 million, compared to a surplus of K359 million in 2000. Current account recorded a surplus of K935 million whereas the capital account incurred a deficit of K262million in 2001.

International reserves
PNG's international reserves, which include actual holdings of gold, SDRs and foreign exchange assets, plus the reserves position at the IMF, have fluctuated sharply over the years. Due to an unfavourable external situation, international reserves for PNG fell to K272.2 million at the end of 1982. The reserve position improved substantially in 1985 and covered 5.8 months of total import bills. The large growth in liquidity created a continual decline in the international reserve level between 1990 and 1994. However, the level of international reserves improved at the end of 1995 to K357.4 covering 2.6 months import bill (Table 3.5). The level of gross foreign exchange reserves was K1617 million at the end of 2001, sufficient for 6.1 months of total import cover and 8.7 months of non-mineral imports cover (Quarterly Economic Bulletin, 2001).

3.8.2   Foreign Aid

Foreign aid (including grants) plays an important role in PNG's economy. The country has always had access to international sources of finance and generous

Table 3.5
International reserves and import ratio, 1975–2001
(selected years, kina million)

	1975	1980	1985	1990	1991
International Reserves[a]	140.1	300.4	464.3	377.9	309.0
Import Ratio[b]	4.1	4.8	5.8	4.3	2.4

	1992	1993	1994	1995	2001
International Reserves[a]	244.0	137.9	112.4	357.4	1617.0
Import Ratio[b]	2.5	1.6	1	2.6	6.1

Notes:
a   Reserves are the actual holdings of gold, SDRs and foreign exchange assets plus the reserves position at the IMF, which are available to the monetary authorities to meet balance of payments needs.
b   The import ratio shows the number of months of import that the international reserves could purchase using the previous three months imports as the base.

Source: Bank of Papua New Guinea, *Quarterly Economic Bulletin*, various issues.

concessionary finance for public-sector activities. The contribution of foreign aid averaged about 11 per cent of GDP between 1977 and 1993. In 1997, the net official development assistance to PNG was $292 million which increased to $400 million in 1999.

The major share of foreign aid to PNG comes from Australia. However, the share of Australian aid to total foreign aid declined from 85 per cent in 1982 to 73 per cent in 1993, compared with 100 per cent of total aid in 1970 (Appendix Table A3.7).

Net official assistance declined sharply from 24 per cent of GDP in 1975 to 14.5 per cent of GDP in 1977 and then continued to fall more steadily until 1990. The share of total aid accounted for only 5.9 per cent of GDP in 1993, with a significant decline in budget support from Australia. This decline in the share of foreign assistance to GDP was offset by increased gains from export revenues and taxes from external trade during the early 1990s. Other major donors are the Asian Development Bank (ADB), the Overseas Economic Cooperation Fund of Japan, the European Union and Germany.

Table 3.6
Foreign aid to PNG, 1970–94

	Total aid (US$, million)	Aid per capita (US$)	Share of aid to GDP (%)
1970	112.4	46.1	17.3
1971	135.2	54.5	18.8
1972	148.6	58.5	17.4
1973	208.6	80.2	15.9
1974	307.2	115.1	20.8
1975	322.1	118.0	23.7
1976	283.9	101.8	18.7
1977	238.0	83.2	14.5
1978	263.5	89.9	13.6
1979	270.6	90.2	11.8
1980	326.0	106.2	12.8
1981	336.0	107.0	13.4
1982	310.7	96.8	13.2
1983	333.0	100.9	12.9
1984	324.3	95.9	12.6
1985	259.2	74.9	10.7
1986	263.9	74.3	10.0
1987	321.9	88.7	10.3
1988	374.7	101.8	10.3
1989	336.5	89.5	12.4
1990	413.1	107.6	12.9
1991	397.2	101.1	10.5
1992	443.4	110.3	10.4
1993	303.2	73.8	5.9
1994	326.0	77.6	6.3

Sources: Constructed from World Bank (1981), World Bank (1995) and AusAID (1995, 1996, 1997).

3.9   Macroeconomic Policies

The objectives of macroeconomic policies can be described as the establishment and maintenance of external balance and internal balance (including price stability), with an efficient allocation of resources. The most difficult task confronting policy makers is to achieve several goals simultaneously. Thus, the common practice is to identify particular instruments which are most effective in achieving particular desired goals. Economic theory suggests that in a small open economy the instrument of expenditure policy could be assigned to the external-balance objective, the wages policy to the internal-balance objective and the exchange rate to the price-stability objective (Garnaut and Baxter, 1984). Trade and exchange rate policy can also play a powerful role in determining relative prices, profitability and production of traded goods, as well as providing incentives to domestic producers in external trade. PNG pursued active macroeconomic policies for stabilising the economy. These policies are discussed in the following sub-sections.

3.9.1   Fiscal Policy

PNG's administration earned a reputation for prudent macroeconomic management during the second half of the 1970s and the 1980s. Cautious policies were pursued with respect to external borrowing, domestic absorption and the exchange rate.

Throughout the period 1976-82 fiscal restraint was the most important instrument through which external balance was sought. As a result, the budget deficit, as a ratio to GDP, declined to 2 per cent in 1975-79 from a budget deficit of 4 per cent in 1970–74 (Table 3.7). The declining trend in the budget deficit continued until the mid-1980s when the deficit was only 1 per cent of GDP.

From 1989–90, the fiscal deficit rose significantly to a new peak of 6 per cent of GDP due to the closure of the Panguna mine in Bougainville and the subsequent fall in PNG's agricultural-commodity export prices in the world market. The fiscal deficit widened considerably due to indiscreet fiscal actions. As a result, the budget deficit averaged 4.75 per cent of GDP per annum over the 1990–93 period. However, due to fiscal restraint the budget deficit declined to 2.3 per cent of GDP in 1994.

Stabilisation funds
Cushioning the economy against the destabilising effects of external shocks has been an important objective of government policy. Two types of stabilisation fund were established to deal with the impact of fluctuating mineral and commodity prices. The Mineral Resources Stabilisation Funds (MRSF), established in 1974, receives all government revenues from the minerals sector. Originally it released them to the government budget, according to a formula designed to reduce fluctuations that would otherwise occur. In the early 1980s with the depressed world prices for PNG's exports, the MRSF contributed between 16 to 21 per cent of the central government's internal revenue. In 1992, the MRSF contribution declined to 7 per cent of government internal revenue. Legislative changes in the mid-1990s allowed more direction in the flow of funds to the budget and the MRSF taxes accounted for 18 per cent of total revenue and grants in 1997.

Operated by the Commodity Boards, the Commodity Price Stabilisation Funds (CPSF) for three major agricultural export commodities aims to stabilise the prices along a moving long-term average export price. The major objective of CPSF is to provide price support to producers during difficult periods. CPSF receives the

Table 3.7
Central government revenues and expenditures, 1970–99
(percentage share of GDP)

Share of GDP (%)	1970–74	1975–79	1980–84	1985–89	1990–94	1995–99
Total revenue and grants	31	37	35	34	29	29
Internal revenue	13	16	21	23	23	25
MRSF	na	5	5	4	1	2
Foreign grants	18	16	9	7	5	4
Total expenditure	35	35	36	32	32	30.5
Current expenditure	26	31	30	30	28	29.5
Capital expenditure	9	4	6	2	4	1.0
Overall surplus/ deficit	–4	–2	–1	2	–3	–1.5

Note: na = not available

Sources: Constructed from AusAID, 1996 and 1999 and World Bank (1991), various tables.

levies paid by exporters and holds these deposits, returning them to producers during periods of low prices.

3.9.2   Monetary Policy

The Bank of Papua New Guinea is responsible for the conduct of monetary and financial policies. Monetary policy has been geared towards financial stability, by neutralising the impact of temporary fluctuations in liquidity originating from external shocks, whilst ensuring the availability of sufficient liquidity and credit to assist the growth of the non-mining sector. The use of open-market operations is not a viable option, as the market for government securities is too small. In the absence of open-market operations, the BPNG relies on credit ceilings, changes in liquidity requirements and moral suasion on interest rates.

During the 1970s, monetary policy was somewhat passive, because of constraints imposed by the fixed exchange rate regime. Through tight monetary policy, monetary stability was achieved over the 1980s and the money supply remained stable, at around 33 per cent of GDP, well below the 44-per-cent average for comparable low middle-income countries (AIDAB, 1993).

Between 1991 and 1993, the money supply grew much faster than GDP (Table 3.8). A deterioration in fiscal management was mainly responsible for monetary growth in the early 1990s. Domestic debt rose to K1606 million or around 26 per cent of GDP in mid-1994, 32 per cent of GDP in 1998 due to a high level of government borrowing from the domestic banking system.

Interest rates were below Australian levels through the period of price stability in the 1970s and middle of the 1980s, rose sharply through the exchange rate crisis of the early 1990s, and subsequently eased but remained substantially above international levels.

Table 3.8
Monetary conditions (selected years, 1982–98)

	1982	1985	1990	1991	1992	1993	1994	1998
Volume of Money (kina million)								
Total Money supply (M3)	568	814	1082	1273	1432	1812.5	1853.6	3218
Growth rate of M3 (%)	2.4	8.7	4.3	17.7	12.5	26.6	2.3	4
Interest Rates (% per annum)								
Commercial lending rate (weighted average)	na	16.1	16.0	15.2	13.8	10.7	10.0	20
182 day Treasury Bills	11.7	12.25	10.50	10.5	6.50	6.02	8.75	24
Term deposits (weighted average)	na	16.4	9.90	9.6	6.6	4.6	4.5	9
Liquid Assets Ratios (all commercial banks)								
Actual	19.4	13.9	15.0	13.5	19.2	28.9	31.7	34
Minimum	16.0	12.0	11.0	11.0	11.0	11.0	26.0	0

Note: na = not available

Sources: Bank of Papua New Guinea, *Quarterly Economic Bulletin*, September 1991, June 1993 December 1994 and December 2001.

After flotation of the kina in 1994, the conduct of monetary policy changed substantially. Under the floating exchange-rate regime the BPNG has greater control over the conduct of monetary policy as there is no direct link between money supply and international reserves.

3.9.3 Wages Policy

The concept of paid labour and cash were introduced in PNG with the establishment of plantation in the nineteenth century. PNG has a long history of official intervention in the labour market, primarily through the setting and indexation of minimum wages, public-sector wages and employment policies. During most of the colonial period, the main objective of labour-market intervention was to attract and protect new entrants in the formal sector (primarily in plantations), leading eventually to the introduction of a system of cash wage employment and a legal minimum wage.

Wages in the formal sector are set by the Minimum Wage Board (MWB), formally established in 1972,[4] based on a tripartite board of employers, employees and government, in contrast to the Australian system of compulsory arbitration (AIDAB, 1994). In 1974, the MWB was institutionalised, following the Australian practice of six-monthly automatic cost-of-living indexation. This system of full and automatic indexation to the cost of living continued until 1983.

Between 1972 and 1975, minimum urban wages increased three-fold, in nominal terms, and 50 per cent in real terms. Consequently, rural-urban wage differentials increased sharply, creating unrealistic expectations about job prospects in urban centres. The consequent influx of population to city centre increased the urban unemployment rate as well as contributing to a deterioration in law-and-order. The PNG government froze urban wages temporarily in 1976. From 1983, partial indexation has been followed which has served to moderate real wage increases. Despite the worsening employment situation, real minimum wages remained remarkably constant until 1994 and after that show a declining trend until 1998.

There is a large gap between wages in the formal and informal sectors. Limited data on informal market wages were available, prior to a 1990 urban survey, which found that average weekly wages for the informal market was 62 per cent of the minimum hourly rate and 84 per cent of the minimum weekly rate for urban wages, and average earnings for the self-employed was 52 per cent of the minimum weekly wage (AIDAB, 1993).

The urban wage rates were also much higher in PNG compared to other developing countries. The urban minimum wage in the late 1970 in PNG was double than that in Malaysia and Western Samoa, four times that in the Philippines and Thailand and about ten times that in Indonesia and Sri Lanka (McGavin, 1986:152). This high minimum wages contributed largely to an unemployment problem and hindered the development of manufacturing sector (Goodman et al., 1985).

In August 1992 the centralised wage-fixing system was abandoned in favour of a system whose focused on productivity, which unified the dual system of rural and urban minimum wages and introduced a national youth wage set at 75 per cent of

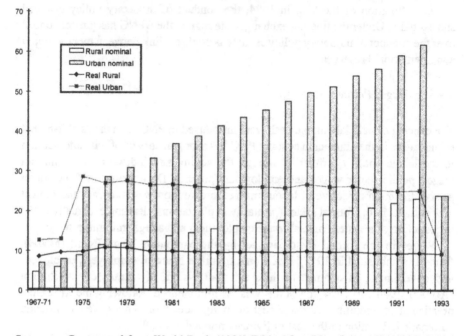

Sources: Constructed from World Bank (1991) Table 4.2, p.75 and AusAID (1995) Table A22.

Figure 3.3   Nominal and real urban and rural minimum wages, 1967–93 (weekly wages, real wages are at constant 1977 prices)

the new national minimum. In 1993, this resulted in a 4.7 per cent decline in real wages, followed by a further decline of 2.8 per cent in 1994 and 14.7 per cent in 1995 (AusAID, 1996).

3.9.4   Trade Policy

During the 1970s and early 1980s, PNG had a fairly liberal trade regime. Taxes on imports were quite low on average, at about 5 per cent, during the 1970s. In the early 1980s, a protective tariff of 10 per cent was provided to import-competing industries. Since the mid-1980s, increased protection in the form of tariff and import bans has been prominent. These interventions were motivated by an assortment of revenue collection and distributional objectives to discourage imports and encourage domestic production (import substitution).

The 10 per cent tariff was subsequently increased to 17.5 per cent in the mid-1980s, and raised again to 30 per cent in the early 1990s, for all goods where there was domestic production. Import taxes on luxury goods and other consumer goods were imposed at higher rates of 50 to 80 per cent. A few other items, such as tobacco, wine, beer and spirits, soft drinks, motor vehicles and petroleum products were subjected to even higher import taxes and sometimes even to penal import duties. Poultry, pork, sugar, flour, animal feed, canned meat, fruit, vegetables, honey, toilet soap, matches, wooden doors and plywood were protected by quotas or by a complete ban on imports.

From the early 1990s, the protection accorded sugar and cement, for example, led to higher consumer prices and a reduction in general welfare. Import taxes on essential consumer items, such as canned fish and rice, and other non-competing inputs to domestic production, were exempted or reduced. Effective protection for the agricultural sector, especially for food items exports, is low or negative. While inputs to domestic production of food items are taxed substantially, imports of canned fish and cereals are exempt from duty and the domestic production of luxury and 'special' items – such as cigarettes, soft drinks, spirits, beer, and tobacco – has been given major incentives.

In the early 1990s, the effective rate of protection on most locally manufactured goods ranged between approximately 60 to 160 per cent (AusAID, 1996). Final products were protected at rates of 30 to 80 per cent. The protection rate for imports of non-competing inputs was zero, which accounts for about one-half of the value of imports.

3.9.5   Exchange Rate Policy

Before independence, PNG was a part of the Australian monetary system and had no foreign-exchange requirements of its own. The Central Bank of the country was established and a set of exchange regulations was formulated and introduced prior to independence. The BPNG issued PNG's first currency, the 'Kina', on 19th April 1975 on a par with the Australian dollar. PNG's monetary system became independent from the Australian monetary system on 1 January 1976.

Between Independence and the end of 1981, the kina was revalued by 30 per cent against the Australian dollar, by 15 per cent against the import-weighted basket, and by about 9 per cent against a trade-weighted basket (Garnaut and Baxter, 1984, p. 15). The method of setting the exchange rate daily, and quoting daily to some variant of a trade-weighted basket, by the BPNG against the Australian and US dollar, was actively introduced after 1980.

The movement in the nominal effective exchange rate (NEER) over time is shown in Figure 3.4. In the 1970s, PNG pursued a 'hard kina' policy to maintain a fixed exchange rate, while utilising appropriate monetary and fiscal policies to achieve external and internal balance.

The major aim of the 'hard kina' policy was to maintain a strong balance of payments with manageable levels of foreign debt through restraint on the real level of domestic expenditure and wages (Garnaut and Baxter, 1984:1). Until the mid-1980s, PNG maintained a convertible currency and reasonably low inflation by world standards. The policy of 'hard kina' had been pursued actively until fiscal policy became lax from the early 1980s.

There was a significant policy shift with a 10 per cent devaluation against the Australian dollar in March 1983, followed by another 10 per cent in January 1990. By the beginning of 1994 foreign exchange reserves had been under persistent pressure and were rapidly depleted due to widening of current account deficit which was mostly reflection of unsustainable fiscal policy. In October 1994, in the face of the worsening foreign exchange crisis, and after a brief suspension of convertibility, the government decided to float (managed float) its currency.

3.10   Summary and Conclusion

PNG is a developing country with substantial economic potential. Abundant precious natural resources, and a small population, provide opportunities for

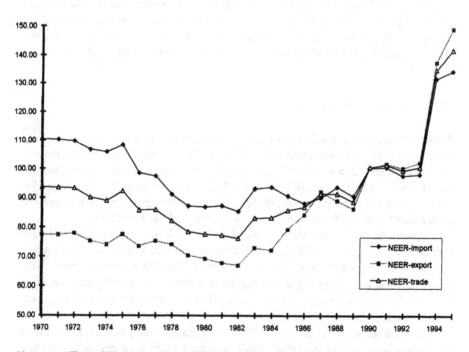

Note: Three different nominal effective exchange rate indices are constructed by using import share, export share and trade share as weights. The three measures show a similar pattern in their movements.

Source: Appendix Table A4.1.

Figure 3.4   Nominal effective exchange rate in PNG, 1970–94 (1990 = 100)

economic development, provided there is prudent economic management coupled with political stability. The sectoral composition of GDP indicates structural changes have taken place in the economy from the early 1970s. The economy is dominated by the agricultural and mineral sectors with the manufacturing and services sectors declining over time and the minerals and petroleum sector's contribution to GDP on the increase.

Overall, PNG's growth has been marked by periods of high and low (even negative) growth. Gross domestic investment accounted for about 26 per cent of GDP on average over 1970–94 and the average annual contribution of gross domestic savings was more than 20 per cent of GDP between 1970 and 1994. Low inflation was maintained until the mid-1980s but increased substantially thereafter.

Population growth is moderate but unemployment is on the rise, due to the non-expansion of wage employment. Wages in PNG were subject to a large degree of centralisation, with wage rates for the formal private sector determined by the MWB. The large urban-rural wage differential that existed for a long time but reduced by the wage policy reform of 1992 when PNG abandoned its centralised wage-fixing arrangements for a more flexible, productivity-based market-determined wage system which improved labour-market conditions and the competitiveness of the economy to a large extent.

In the 1970s and the first half of the 1980s, PNG followed a cautious fiscal stance. However, in the later part of the 1980s and early 1990s, fiscal indiscretion resulted in budget deficit blowouts. In terms of monetary policy, to a large extent, the BPNG has been able to maintain stability in monetary aggregates and contain interest rates and inflation.

Following a foreign exchange crisis in 1994, PNG moved away from the fixed exchange-rate regime to a managed float system. Trade policy was liberal until the early 1980s when it began to be slowly replaced by quantitative trade restrictions and higher tariffs. The current government has reaffirmed its commitment to broad-based tariff reform. In recent years, PNG has attempted to reduce its reliance on foreign assistance, which is expected to reduce instability in the domestic price level by reducing the spending effect on the domestic nontradable sector.

Notes

1   As Levantis (1997) indicated, the reliability of this figure is poor since information on aggregate subsistence production and production marketed in the informal domestic markets is largely non-existent and hence this is an underestimate.
2   A large new gold company, the Lihir Gold Ltd, commenced production in 1997.
3   The formal sector comprises agriculture and plantation, the public services, mining, manufacturing and services.
4   Governmental interventions in the labour market by introducing the minimum wages was first set in 1945. The structure now in place was established between 1972 and 1975 (World Bank, 1981, p. 19).

Determinants of Real Exchange Rate in Papua New Guinea

4.1 Introduction

As discussed in Chapter 2, the real exchange rate – the price ratio of tradable to nontradable goods – is the key link between resources booms and their impact on the performance of an economy. Like other relative prices, real exchange rates are affected by real and nominal disturbances, which may be either long lasting or transient. A real exchange rate reacts to a series of real and nominal disturbances, including international terms of trade (TOT) shocks, government expenditure patterns, trade restrictions, net capital inflow and technological progress, as well as to domestic credit creation and nominal devaluation.

The objective of this chapter is twofold: to construct a real exchange rate index and to identify the major determinants of real exchange rate behaviour using a dynamic model of real exchange rate determination. Section 4.2 of this chapter presents the general concept of the real exchange rate; Section 4.3 constructs several series of real exchange rates for PNG, discusses the problems of constructing such indices, and offers alternative measures to overcome the problems; Section 4 develops a dynamic model of real exchange rate determination to analyse how the long-term equilibrium real exchange rate reacts to a series of real disturbances, and also attempts to develop a monetary model incorporating variables determining the movements of the actual real exchange rate; Section 4.5 presents an empirical model of the real exchange rate using the theoretical model developed in Section 4.4; Section 4.6 presents the data sources and the different measures of variables employed; Section 4.7 shows the econometric procedures used; Section 4.8 presents the empirical results; and Section 4.9 summarises conclusions.

4.2 Concept of Real Exchange Rate

The real exchange rate (RER) can be defined as the ratio of relative price of tradables (PT) with respect to nontradables (PNT). This ratio, which is also known as the 'Salter ratio', can be written symbolically as follows:

$$RER = \frac{\text{Price of Tradables}}{\text{Price of Nontradables}} = \frac{P_T}{P_{NT}}$$

It is clear from the above definition that real exchange rate is a concept that measures the relative price of two goods as opposed to the nominal exchange rate, which is a measure of two monies (Edwards, 1988b). International competitiveness is usually measured in terms of real exchange rate movements. The definition of RER focuses on the rate at which tradables are exchanged for nontradables, or the cost of domestically produced tradables (Edwards, 1988b). A fall in this ratio represents an appreciation of RER, induced by an increase in the price of nontradable goods, and/ or by a reduction in the relative price of tradables to nontradables. Real exchange rate appreciation is synonymous with a deterioration in a country's international competitiveness, as it increases the profitability of the nontraded sector and attracts resources from other traded sectors, as well as increasing the domestic cost of producing tradable goods. By contrast, an increase in this ratio represents a real depreciation, or an improvement in the international competitiveness of tradable production.

It is important to recognise a fundamental notion about the concept of RER. RER is not unique for every sector of an economy. Within the tradable sectors, different real exchange rates can be observed for import substitutes and for exportables. For example, an exporter's real exchange rate can be significantly different from the real exchange rate for an importer, due to costs and productivity differences in these sectors. For these reasons different RER indices are used separately to identify the changes in the competitiveness of importable and exportable sectors of an economy.

4.3 Real Exchange Rate Indices

Construction of a RER index is difficult, since the exact counterpart of the price of tradables (PT) and nontradables (PNT) is not directly observable. Furthermore, in the presence of quantitative trade restrictions, some potentially tradable sectors behave as nontradable sectors. Thus, disaggregation between these sectors becomes less meaningful. Empirical study to examine the theory of the real exchange rate in the tradable and nontradable spheres has always lagged behind due to the limitations of precise variable measurement and difficulty in obtaining data along tradable and nontradable lines.

Disaggregating GDP between the tradable and nontradable sectors and deriving the price ratio of these two sectors to observe RER movements can construct the most direct measure of the RER. GDP and imports of goods and services are divided into two broad divisions of tradables and nontradables. Tradable goods are defined as goods and services that are either traded internationally or could be traded at some 'plausible range of variation in the relative prices' (Goldstein and Officer,

1979, p. 415). Therefore, tradable goods have a wider scope than traded goods and their prices are determined by world prices and exchange rates. Nontradables are those goods and services that, for reasons (such as transport costs) cannot be traded internationally. Their prices are determined by the interaction of domestic demand and supply conditions. Goldstein and Officer (1979) suggest three criteria to draw the distinction between tradable and nontradable goods. First, tradable goods have a higher degree of foreign trade participation rate than nontradables. Secondly, correlations of price changes for tradables are much higher across countries than for nontradables, and finally, tradables are closer substitutes for traded goods than are nontradables.

The method of disaggregating GDP into tradable and nontradable sectors has two fundamental drawbacks. First, in most developing countries this disaggregation of GDP between tradables and nontradables is too broad to compare across sectors. Second, in the presence of quantitative trade restrictions, some tradable sectors behave as nontradable sectors and, in this case, the existing disaggregation between tradable and nontradable sectors does not provide a meaningful comparison.

A more practical proposition is to construct the real exchange rate index by disaggregating the components of the CPI into tradable and nontradable categories. Housing, rent and power components of domestic CPI can be commonly used as proxies for nontradable prices.[1] This method also has some drawbacks, because, although this price index of nontradables includes most of the nontradable elements, it also incorporates some tradable items such as fuel and household equipment in production. Another problem with this index is in selecting appropriate weights to be attached to each component of this proxy. Furthermore, with very few exceptions, disaggregated CPI data are not readily available on an annual basis in most developing countries, including PNG.

Given the practical limitations of direct measures, RER is usually proxied by the following measure:

$$RERppp = \frac{eP_T{}^*}{P}$$

where e is the nominal exchange rate defined as a domestic currency price of foreign currency, $P_T{}^*$ is the foreign price, and P is the domestic price level. The PT is a composite price measure of exportables and importables and the domestic price level, P, measures the domestic price of nontradables (PNT). Therefore, the real exchange rate is the ratio of foreign prices measured in domestic currency to the domestic price level.

The problem with constructing the above index starts with the choice of an appropriate nominal exchange rate. Should the nominal exchange rate be with respect to a single foreign currency, that is, a bilateral exchange rate, or does the nominal exchange rate have to be a weighted average of bilateral exchange rates of major trading partners? Then comes the problem of choice of weights. Traditionally trade weights are popularly used to capture the trading pattern of a country. Corden

(1984) conjectures whether services and remittances should be included alongside the merchandise trade weights. The problem is further complicated by the existence of multiple exchange rates systems in some developing countries.

Several alternative price indices for the PT and PNT have been suggested as possible candidates for the construction of a PPP-based RER. The popular and common practice is to construct a real exchange index by deflating the trade-weighted nominal exchange rate adjusted for foreign price by a proxy for domestic nontradable price. The most widely used proxy for tradable and nontradable price is CPI. This measure is popular, since almost every country publishes CPI on a regular basis.

But the foreign CPI index has a major drawback as a fair proxy for the PT. The deficiency of using this index is that CPIs include large elements of nontradable prices. If, for example, the price of foreign nontradables increases relative to the price of tradables, then this increase in the PNT will reflect on the foreign CPI. Therefore, foreign CPI, as a proxy for tradable prices, is not appropriate as it may overstate the relevant foreign inflation and thereby overstate the depreciation of the real exchange rate (Little et al., 1993, p. 259).

Because of the problem associated with the use of CPI as a proxy for the PT, the use of the foreign wholesale price index as a proxy of PT to measure the RER is the most common practice. We used this measure of trade-weighted real exchange rate (RER1) for our study. Therefore, the trade-weighted real exchange rate is defined as:

$$RER1 = e_{TW} \frac{WPI^*}{P}$$

where WPI* is the foreign wholesale price index proxied for the world price of tradables, e_{TW} is the trade-weighted nominal effective exchange rate and P is the domestic price level representing the price of domestic nontradables. Using average trade-weighted WPI*s as proxy for tradables solves some of the problems arising from using foreign CPIs. WPI* is heavily weighted with tradable items and does not include services. There may arise some possibility of double counting while using WPI as a proxy for the price of tradable, since WPI measures commodity prices at varying stages of production. Despite this minor limitation, WPI is considered to be the most reasonable proxy for the world price of tradables.

Domestic CPI is the standard proxy for the PNT since the major components of the domestic CPI basket comprises nontradable goods and services. The price deflator for GDP is another common proxy that is used for the PNT. Neither CPI nor the GDP deflators are appropriate indicators of the price of nontradables, since both of these indices measure the price movement as an aggregate of tradable and nontradable goods and services and do not just represent independently the separate price movement for nontradables. The GDP deflator has one advantage over the CPI index as it captures all domestic price movements on a value added basis (Goldstein and Officer, 1979). To overcome the limitations of CPI and GDP deflators as a proxy for the PNT, some authors disaggregate the CPI components into tradable and nontradable goods and services and then take the weighted average of the nontradable components of CPI to construct a price index for nontradables. This index, represents the proper price movements for nontradables, and is the most appropriate method if data is available.

So far, the PT has been considered as a composite price of importables and exportables as in Salter's (1959) dependent economy model. But a distinction between the price of importables and the price of exportables is necessary as different trade controls and changes in international prices can affect the price movements in exportables and importables quite differently. Moreover, domestic quantitative trade restrictions can affect the price of importables more than exportables and may change some import substitutes into nontradable categories. Therefore, it has been argued that it is more appropriate to use the export price index (EPI) and import price index (IPI) separately as proxies for the world price of exportables and importables. This division of EPI and IPI clearly reflects the price movements of goods and services that are actually traded.

Therefore, two other commonly used direct measures of the real exchange rate can be defined as the relative price of exportables to nontradables (proxied either by the domestic CPI or GDP deflator or by the weighted average of nontradable components of CPI):

$$RER2 = \frac{P_{EXP}}{P_{NT}}$$

and the relative price of importables to domestic nontradables,

$$RER3 = \frac{P_{IMP}}{P_{NT}}$$

which can serve as direct measures of competitiveness in the tradable sectors of an economy. But the use of these indices to proxy the world price of tradables has also faced some criticism. It is argued that these indices (EPI, IPI) have well known deficiencies as measures of price of heterogeneous commodity groups and are generally expressed in unit value terms. It is, therefore, not surprising that there exists quite a number of different measures of the real exchange rate, given that there could be several possible proxies used to represent the PT and nontradables.

The next sub-section attempts to construct the three indices – RER1, RER2, RER3 – for PNG.

4.3.1   Real Exchange Rate Indices for Papua New Guinea

Three alternative measures of real exchange rates have been constructed namely RER1, RER2 and RER3. RER1 is reported in Tables 4.1. In Table 4.1 the trade-weighted nominal effective exchange rate (NEER) of PNG has been multiplied by the weighted average of the wholesale price indices of PNG's major trading partners (Australia, Japan, UK, US and West Germany). As discussed earlier, this measure represents the index of trade-weighted world price of tradables (PT-trade) converted in terms of PNG's domestic currency (kina) value. With respect to the domestic price of nontradables, PNG's consumer price index has been used as an approximate measure of the PNT. The world price of tradables is then deflated by the domestic CPI to construct the index of the trade-weighted real exchange rate (RER1) for PNG. Trade shares[2] of major trading partners in 1990 have been used as weights in the calculation.

Some substantial exchange rate movements, as reflected in the trade-weighted NEER, resulted from discretionary exchange rate policy measures.

The NEER index for PNG indicates a significant appreciating trend in the post-independence period between 1975 and 1982. This nominal appreciation reflects PNG's 'hard kina' strategy to insulate the domestic economy from imported inflation by revaluation of the kina several times after monetary independence in 1976. Discretionary depreciations of the kina by 10 per cent in 1983 and 10 per cent in 1990 are reflected in the overall depreciation of the NEER during this period. Then a gradual appreciation from 1991 to 1993 occurred before 1994's sharp depreciation of the NEER, which mostly resulted from official devaluation of the kina by 12 per cent followed by the subsequent floating of the kina.

Over the 1970s and the 1980s, the price index of tradables moved very close to the domestic CPI (Figure 4.1). During the 1970s, the PT was on average higher than the price of domestic nontradables. However, the domestic CPI started to rise from the early-1980s and continued until the early-1990s. During this period the change in the PT remained lower than domestic inflation. In 1994, the PT started to rise higher than the domestic price level and to a large extent the economy regained its competitiveness in the world market, as seen in Figure 4.1.

The trend in the real exchange rate of PNG is shown in Figure 4.2. During the construction boom and minerals boom in 1971–73, the domestic wage-price increased faster than the price increase in tradables, which is clearly evident in the real exchange rate appreciation in 1973. The index of RER declined sharply by about 18 per cent in 1973 from the previous year.

The commodity boom of 1976–77 had more moderate effects on real exchange rate movements, due to cautious macroeconomic policies and a gradual reduction in foreign aid flows. Foreign aid fell by about 26 per cent in 1977 from the period of independence (Appendix Table A3.7), which helped to depreciate the RER. This real depreciation in 1977 indicated a 'reverse resources boom' in PNG.

While the RER1 of PNG appreciated during 1973 because of relatively high inflation in PNG compared with its major trading partners, the rate depreciated significantly in 1977, due to virtually imperceptible domestic inflation maintained by prudent macroeconomic policy. A more stable real exchange rate movement from the mid-1970s to the late 1980s was consistent with the objectives of macroeconomic policies intended to control inflation and ensure a stable macroeconomic environment.

Table 4.1
Trade-weighted real exchange rate (RER1) index, 1970–94 (1990 = 100)

	NEER (trade- weighted)	WPI* (trade-weighted)	PT (trade-weighted)	CPI	RER1
1970	93.29	32.72	30.52	24.97	122.25
1971	93.19	33.45	31.17	26.37	118.24
1972	92.98	34.36	31.95	27.29	117.07
1973	89.82	38.41	34.49	35.78	96.41
1974	88.71	47.00	41.69	38.47	108.36
1975	92.01	50.55	46.51	41.77	111.34
1976*	85.53	53.98	46.16	43.34	106.51
1977	85.65	56.80	48.65	43.52	111.79
1978	81.85	58.30	47.72	45.93	103.89
1979*	78.21	64.12	50.15	48.35	103.71
1980	77.33	73.53	56.87	54.82	103.74
1981	76.94	77.75	59.82	61.33	97.55
1982	75.94	81.58	61.95	63.42	97.69
1983#	82.92	83.66	69.38	72.36	95.88
1984	83.03	85.96	71.37	79.07	90.27
1985	85.50	88.13	75.35	77.55	97.17
1986	86.64	86.79	75.19	78.35	95.97
1987	91.09	88.52	80.63	81.87	98.49
1988	91.03	92.43	84.15	89.30	94.23
1989	88.37	96.29	85.09	94.02	90.51
1990#	100.00	100.00	100.00	100.00	100.00
1991	101.07	101.55	102.64	105.42	97.36
1992	99.09	102.22	101.29	109.91	92.16
1993	100.22	102.61	102.83	117.82	87.28
1994#	134.27	102.78	138.00	123.20	112.01

Notes: * = discretionary revaluation and # = discretionary devaluation; NEER = nominal effective exchange rate; WPI*= world wholesale price index; PT= price of tradable; CPI= domestic consumer price index; RER1 = Trade-weighted real exchange rate.

Sources: Author's computation using data from World Bank World Tables, IMF International Financial Statistics, Bank of PNG *Quarterly Economic Bulletins*, various issues.

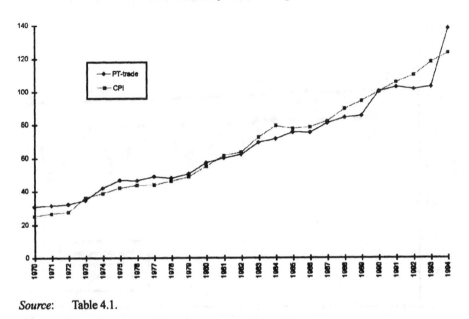

Source: Table 4.1.

Figure 4.1 Price index of tradables and domestic CPI in PNG (1990 = 100)

The real appreciation from 1990 to 1993 was due to a combination of several external and internal factors. PNG's inflation rate increased rapidly relative to its major trading partners' inflation rates during the early-1990s. The resources boom in PNG's mining sector over this period also impacted upon the PNT, which was fuelled by expansionary fiscal stances. This relative increase in PNT to the PT was quite rapid and appreciated the trade-weighted real exchange rate (RER1) during this period (Table 4.1 and Figure 4.2).

The export price index (EPI) and import price index (IPI) have been deflated by the price index of nontradables (constructed by taking only the weighted average of nontradable items in the CPI basket) to construct the real exchange rates for exportables (RER2) and for importables (RER3) for PNG. These direct measures are reported in Table 4.2 and shown in Figure 4.4. In general, all indices of the real exchange rate (RER1, RER2, RER3) moved quite differently over 1970s. Then the rest of the period they followed a similar pattern (Figure 4.4).

Between 1972 and 1979, the RER2 and RER3 indices show strong depreciation (with an exception in 1975) whereas the trade-weighted real exchange rate (RER1) indicates a significant real appreciation during 1973. RER1 appreciated due to the rate of increase of domestic CPI being higher than the PT, whereas RER2 and RER3 depreciated because export and import price indices were higher than the domestic price of nontradables in the early-1970s (Table 4.2). Over the 1980s, all measures of the RER appreciated on average, due to a declining trend in PNG's export price

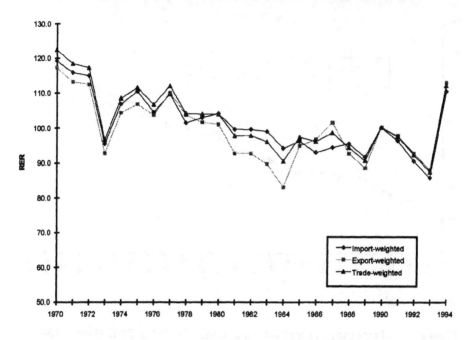

Note: Three different real effective exchange rate indices are constructed by using import share, export share and trade share as weights. The three measures show a similar pattern in their movements.

Sources: Author's computation using data from World Bank World Tables, IMF International Financial Statistics, Bank of PNG Quarterly Economic Bulletins, various issues.

Figure 4.2   Real Exchange Rate (RER1) indices of PNG, 1970–94 (1990 = 100)

index and rapid growth in the domestic price level. After 1992, PNG's export price index increased significantly and brought about a real depreciation of RER2 over 1993–94 and improved competitiveness for the export sector. But RER1 and RER3 appreciated between 1991–93 before starting to depreciate in 1994, due to flotation and a large depreciation of kina and increase in price of tradables relative to domestic price level (Figure 4.2 and 4.4).

Now we proceed to develop a theoretical model in order to shed light on the possible determinants of the real exchange rate, which might have impacted upon the movement of PNG's real exchange rate.

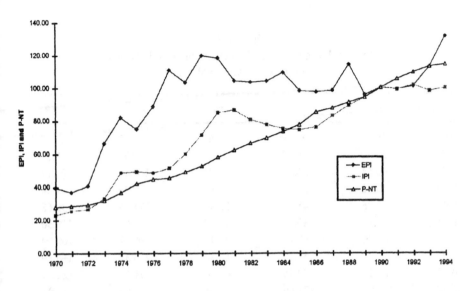

Source: Table 4.2

Figure 4.3 **Export price index, import price index and price of nontradables (1990 = 100)**

4.4 Theoretical Framework

The basic theoretical framework used in this study has been adopted from Edwards' (1989) model of real exchange rate determination. The model captures most of the stylised features of a small open developing economy, including the existence of exchange and trade controls. This model allows only the 'fundamentals' or real variables to play a role in determining the long-term equilibrium real exchange rate, whereas both real and nominal factors influence the actual real exchange rate in the short term.

The model assumes a small, open economy, which produces and consumes two goods – tradables and nontradables. Importables and exportables are aggregated into one tradable category. The government sector consumes both tradables and nontradables and finances its expenditures by non-distortionary taxes and domestic credit creation. The country holds both domestic money and foreign money. At a later stage of the study it is assumed that there are no capital controls, and that there are some capital flows in and out of the country. The nominal exchange rate of the economy is fixed with a basket of currencies of its major trading partners. It is also assumed that there is a tariff on imports. The price of tradables in terms of foreign currency is fixed and equal to unity that is, $P_T = 1$. Finally perfect foresight is assumed in this model.

Table 4.2
Real exchange rate indices for export and import
competing sector (1990 = 100)

	EPI	IPI	PNT	RER2	RER3
1970	39.36	22.82	27.65	142.37	82.55
1971	36.70	25.23	28.28	129.78	89.21
1972	40.54	26.22	29.08	139.39	90.17
1973	66.22	33.03	31.63	209.39	104.44
1974	81.96	48.38	36.46	224.78	132.68
1975	74.98	49.21	41.88	179.02	117.50
1976	88.46	48.46	44.43	199.11	109.09
1977	110.70	51.29	45.31	244.31	113.19
1978	103.12	59.75	48.84	211.12	122.33
1979	119.55	71.45	52.56	227.46	135.94
1980	118.17	84.98	57.82	204.40	146.98
1981	104.20	86.47	62.18	167.58	139.07
1982	103.41	80.66	66.47	155.58	121.35
1983	104.00	77.68	69.51	149.63	111.75
1984	109.22	75.35	73.45	148.70	102.59
1985	98.20	74.52	77.53	126.67	96.13
1986	97.51	76.02	85.23	114.41	89.19
1987	98.40	82.99	87.54	112.40	94.80
1988	114.17	89.05	91.03	125.42	97.82
1989	95.72	94.02	94.11	101.71	99.91
1990	100.00	100.00	100.00	100.00	100.00
1991	99.10	99.00	105.39	94.04	93.94
1992	100.89	101.66	109.42	92.20	92.90
1993	112.83	98.17	113.00	99.58	86.88
1994	131.56	99.92	114.36	115.04	87.37

Notes: EPI = price index of exportable; IPI = price index of importable; PNT = price index of nontradable; RER2 = real exchange rate for export industry; RER3 = real exchange rate for import competing industry.

Sources: Author's computation using data from World Bank World Tables, IMF International Financial Statistics, Bank of PNG Quarterly Economic Bulletins, various issues.

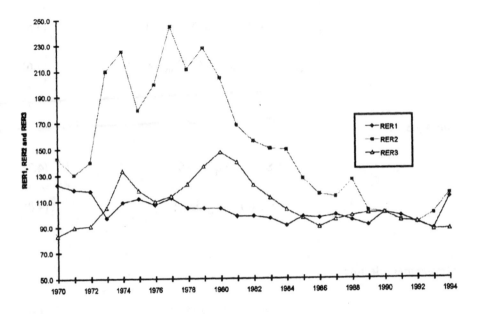

Sources: Table 4.1 and Table 4.2.

Figure 4.4   Real exchange rate indices for export and import competing sectors, 1970–94 (1990 = 100)

The model is represented by the following equations:

Portfolio Decisions:

$$A = M + FM \tag{4.1}$$

$$a = m + fm \text{ where } a = A/E, m = M/E, fm = FM/E \tag{4.2}$$

$$\dot{FM} \neq 0 \tag{4.3}$$

Demand Side:

$$e = E^*P_T/P_{NT} \tag{4.4}$$

$$C_T = C_T \text{ (e, a) } \delta C_T/\delta e < 0; \delta C_T/\delta a > 0 \tag{4.5}$$

$$C_{NT} = C_{NT} \text{ (e, a); } \delta C_{NT}/\delta e > 0; \delta C_{NT}/\delta a > 0 \tag{4.6}$$

Supply Side:

$$S_T = S_T \text{ (e) ; } \delta S_T/\delta e > 0 \tag{4.7}$$

$$S_{NT} = S_{NT} \text{ (e) ; } \delta S_{NT}/\delta e < 0 \tag{4.8}$$

Government Sector:

$$G = P_{NT} G_{NT} + E*G_T \tag{4.9}$$

$$g = g_T + g_{NT;} \text{ where } g = G/E; g_T = G_T ; g_{NT} = P_{NT}G_{NT}/E = G_{NT}/e \tag{4.9'}$$

$$E*G_T/G = \lambda \tag{4.10}$$

$$G = t + DC \tag{4.11}$$

External Sector:

$$CA = S_T \text{ (e) - } C_T \text{ (e, a) - } G_T \tag{4.12}$$

$$KA = f \text{ (i - i}_f) \tag{4.13}$$

$$\dot{R} = CA + KA \tag{4.14}$$

$$\dot{M} = \dot{DC} + E\dot{R} \tag{4.15}$$

Equation (4.1) defines the total assets, *A*, as the sum of domestic money M and foreign money FM. Equation (4.2) defines real assets (*a*) in terms of tradables, where E is the nominal effective exchange rate (foreign currency value in terms of domestic currency). Domestic money (m) and foreign money (fm) are also defined in terms of the nominal exchange rate in this equation. Equation (4.3) shows there is international capital mobility, therefore, FM ≠ 0.

The demand side of the economy is given by equations (4.4) to (4.6). The real exchange rate (e) is defined as the ratio of foreign price in terms of domestic currency to the price of domestic nontradables in equation (4.4). Demand for tradables and nontradables is determined by the real exchange rate and the level of real assets. Asset level positively affects demand for both tradables and nontradables whereas real depreciation reduces the domestic demand for tradables but increases the demand for nontradables, which is shown in equation (4.5) and (4.6).

Equations (4.7) and (4.8) summarise the supply side of the economy. The supply of tradables and nontradables is solely determined by the real exchange rate. An appreciation of the real exchange rate reduces the supply of tradables and increases the supply of nontradables. To keep the model simple the tax function is not included (equations 4.5–4.8) in the demand function and the tariff function is not included in the demand for importables.

Government sector is summarised by equations (4.9) to (4.11), where G_{NT} and G_T are government consumption of nontradables and tradables, respectively. Equation (4.9) is the real government consumption of tradables and nontradables in terms of tradable. Equation (4.10) defines the share of government consumption of tradables to the total government expenditure as λ, which is equal to (g_T/g) in real terms. Equation (4.11) represents the government budget constraint where government consumption is financed by taxes (t) and domestic credit creation (DC).

The external sector is represented by equations (4.12) to (4.15). Equation (4.12) defines the current account as the difference between the output of tradables and both private and public consumption of tradables expressed in foreign currency. Equation (4.13) indicates that there is inflow and outflow of capital. The capital account is defined as a function of interest rate differentials between domestic and foreign economies. Equation (4.14) defines the change in stock of international reserves. Finally the model is closed with equation (4.15), which shows that the change in domestic money ($\dot{m}$) is determined by changes in domestic credit creation and changes in international reserves.

Long-term equilibrium is attained when the nontradable goods market and external sector are simultaneously in equilibrium – which implies that the current account is equal to the capital account in the long term. However, in the short and medium term, there can be departures from CA = K, which will result in the accumulation and decumulation of international reserves. Therefore, the long-term steady state is attained under four scenarios, which can be summarised as follows:

(1) there is internal equilibrium or equilibrium in the nontradable sector;
(2) there is external equilibrium so that $\dot{R} = 0 = CA = KA = \dot{m}$;
(3) the government runs a balanced budget such that G = t and DC = 0, that is, fiscal policy is sustainable; and

(4)   portfolio equilibrium holds.

The real exchange rate attained under these steady-state conditions is known as the long-term equilibrium real exchange rate, ERER, that is,

$$ERER = e^* = E^*P_T/P_{NT} \tag{4.16}$$

The nontradable market clears when

$$C_{NT}(e, a) + g_{NT}(e) = S_{NT}(e) \tag{4.17}$$

The real government consumption of nontradables in terms of tradables has been defined as g_{NT}. Thus, the PNT can be expressed as a function of a, g_{NT}, P_T and τ (trade restrictions).

$$P_{NT} = n(a, g_{NT}, P_T, \tau) \tag{4.18}$$

where, $\delta n/\delta a > 0$; $\delta n/\delta g_{NT} > 0$; $\delta n/\delta P_T > 0$, $\delta n/\delta \tau > 0$

Equilibrium in the external sector requires that $\dot{m} = 0$. The following equation can be derived from earlier equations as

$$\dot{m} = \{S_T(e) - C_T(e, a)\} - KA + g_{NT} - t/E \tag{4.19}$$

When government expenditures are fully financed with taxes, the $\dot{R} = 0$ will coincide with the $\dot{m} = 0$.

From (4.18) and (4.19) it is possible to find an equilibrium relation between e, a, g_{NT} and τ.

$$ERER = e^* = x(a, g_{NT}, P_T \text{ and } \tau), \tag{4.20}$$

where $\delta x/\delta a < 0$; $\delta x/\delta g_{NT} < 0$; $\delta x/\delta P_T > 0$; $\delta x/\delta \tau < 0$

An increase in m, domestic money in terms of foreign currency, results in higher real wealth and a current account deficit. To restore equilibrium real wealth, the price of nontradables will rise (4.18). Thus, an increase in the value of real assets increases the price of nontradables and appreciates the RER to maintain long-term equilibrium. Increases in government expenditure on nontradables (g_{NT}) have the same effects on the equilibrium RER. A rise in the PT (through an improvement in TOT due to an increase in the price of exportables) generally depreciates the RER, given that the price of nontradables and the nominal exchange rate remain constant. However, if the increase in the PT increases export earnings, and is spent in the nontradable sector, the demand for and price of nontradables increases more than the PT causing a RER appreciation. The total effect of an import tariff depends on the initial expenditure on domestic nontradables and importables. An increase in the tariff on importables worsens the current account by increasing import bills, lowers the demand for tradables, raises the demand and price for nontradables and tends to appreciate the long-term real exchange rate. But if an increase in tariff worsens the current account balance without any substitution effects, it will increase the composite PT alone and may depreciate the real exchange rate. It is therefore, possible to observe, simultaneously, a real depreciation and a worsening of the current account. So the increase in the PT and changes in trade policies can have either positive or negative impacts on the RER.

Equation (4.20) stipulates that the long-term equilibrium RER is a function of real variables only. The value of real assets, government consumption, price of tradables and trade restrictions in this equation are normally influenced by changes in other real variables such as TOT shocks, changes in government expenditure, technological progress, and changes in trade and capital restrictions. Changes in these real variables can cause the actual RER to deviate from its equilibrium level. However, changes in nominal variables, such as domestic credit expansion, and changes in the values of the nominal exchange rate, also affect the path of the actual RER in the short term. The impacts of real and monetary disturbances on the RER, both in the short- and long-term are discussed in the next section.

4.4.1   *Real Disturbances and Misalignment of Real Exchange Rate*

Changes in the long-term sustainable values of real variables have important effects on the equilibrium real exchange rate (ERER) and can cause it to deviate from its equilibrium level. This is commonly known as *structural misalignment* of the real exchange rate. In fact, the movement of the ERER from its sustainable long-term position has significant consequences for policy evaluation as it can imply either gain or loss of external competitiveness. According to the purchasing power parity version of the real exchange rate, this movement of ERER is considered a disequilibrium situation. But according to recent developments in the theory of the real exchange rate this movement of ERER does not necessarily reflect disequilibrium, since the change in ERER is induced by changes in fundamentals, that can represent a new long-term equilibrium for the real exchange rate (Edwards, 1988b). This section attempts to analyse the ways in which the equilibrium RER reacts to a number of real disturbances.

Real exchange rate fundamentals are often categorised as external and domestic fundamentals. Domestic fundamentals can be divided into policy-related and non-policy-related fundamentals. The most important external fundamentals, which affect the RER in the long term, include international terms of trade, and international transfer, including foreign aid and world real interest rates. Included among policy-related domestic fundamentals are import restrictions, export taxes or subsidies, exchange and capital controls, and government consumption expenditure. Technological progress and productivity improvement are the two most important domestic non-policy fundamentals. The role of these fundamental factors is discussed below.

Terms of trade disturbance
International TOT is one of the most important external real exchange rate fundamentals and is often included as one of the major determinants of RER in the literature, since foreign price shocks have accounted for large fluctuations in RERs of both developed and developing countries. The overall effect of TOT on the real exchange rate is ambiguous. The price of tradables is a weighted average of the price of exportables and importables. TOT may have two different effects on the real exchange rate, namely, substitution and income effects. The income effect results when an increase in export prices, or a fall in import prices, raises the income of an economy and increases demand for nontradables. This, in turn, tends to reduce the relative price of tradables to nontradables and so appreciate the RER. On the other hand, the substitution effect can be observed due to relative cheapness of nontradables. Thus an improvement in TOT due to an export price increase brings about a RER depreciation for given levels of nominal exchange rate and nontradable prices. However, if the improvement in TOT is brought about by a fall in the price of imports alone, then the improvement in the current account balance would increase aggregate income and the PNT and cause an appreciation of the RER. The income effect would be more prominent in this case. Because of the ambiguity about the final effects of a TOT shock on the RER, the price of importables and exportables should be regarded as two separate variables in determining real exchange rate behaviour.

Government expenditure
Government expenditure is another fundamental real variable, which can cause the real exchange rate to deviate from its equilibrium value. Increases in government expenditure increase the demand for nontradables if the major portion is spent on nontradable goods and services. In the short term this excess demand for nontradables bids up their price and results in RER appreciation. However, there will be depreciation of the RER if the larger share of government expenditure is spent on the tradable sector rather than on consumption of nontradables. Thus, the sign of this variable can be either positive or negative in determining behaviour of the equilibrium real exchange rate.

Trade restrictions
Trade restrictions in the form of tariff generally cause a RER appreciation. If tariff worsens the current account position and increases the demand for and price of nontradables, the RER appreciates. An increase in binding quantitative trade restriction (import quota) also increases the demand for import substitutes, which behave as nontradables due to imposition of quantitative trade restrictions during a boom period (Warr, 1986). This results in higher prices and profitability for nontradables and leads to a long-term equilibrium real appreciation. In these cases, the increase in the PNT due to trade restrictions is higher than the increase in the composite PT. However, if trade restrictions lead to a worsening of the current account deficit and reduce the demand for nontradables, there will be

RER depreciation. In this case negative income effect will overweight the positive substitution effect.

Exchange and capital controls

Relaxation of capital controls may affect the movement of RER in either way. If liberalisation of capital control increases net capital inflow, it leads to expansion in the monetary base. This raises current expenditure over income and increases the demand for nontradables, resulting in an appreciation of the equilibrium RER. A fall in world real interest rates or a rise in international transfers, such as aid flows, also affects the equilibrium RER in a similar way to net capital inflow. If the major share of foreign aid is spent on nontradables, the demand for and price of nontradables increases relative to tradables, which tends to appreciate the RER.

Technological and productivity improvement

The non-policy domestic fundamental variable, namely, technological advancement (growth rate of real GDP), generally increases the efficiency and productivity of the tradable sector. Increased productivity induced by technological progress increases factor availability. By reducing the cost and price of tradables, increased productivity makes the tradable sector more competitive and tends to depreciate the RER of the sector. In this situation, supply effects of technological progress offset the demand effects according to the Rybczynski principle (Edwards, 1989, p. 48). But if the advancement in technology increases income, which, in turn, increases demand for and price of nontradables relative to tradables, there will be a real appreciation. In this case, the demand effects of technological progress are greater than the supply effects and this is known as the Ricardo-Balassa effect (Edwards, 1989, p. 136).

4.4.2   Nominal Determinants and Real Exchange Rate Misalignment

The real exchange rate often departs from its equilibrium values influenced by macroeconomic pressures, which is commonly known as *macroeconomic policy induced misalignment* of the real exchange rate. The effects of macroeconomic policies and changes in the nominal exchange rate on the real exchange rate will now be discussed.

In order to maintain a sustainable macroeconomic equilibrium in an open economy, fiscal and monetary policies must be consistent with the exchange rate regime. Misalignment of the real exchange rate occurs due to inconsistencies between macroeconomic policies and the official exchange rate policy. Under a fixed exchange rate regime, expansionary monetary or fiscal policy raises the real stock of money, increasing demand for both tradable and nontradable goods and financial assets. The excess demand for tradable goods results in a higher trade deficit and loss of international reserves, whereas the increased demand for nontradables raises their price and tends to deviate the actual RER further from its equilibrium value. The over-valuation of the RER, which is a fall in the actual real exchange rate from its long-run equilibrium, will be short-lived and the economy adjusts through reduction of the money stock. The higher demand for nontradables induced by the higher stock of money, would require a higher (actual) RER to re-establish equilibrium in the nontradables market. The stock of international reserves will fall by the decline of the real domestic money. The actual RER will continuously depreciate through reductions in the price of nontradable goods and revert towards the long-term sustainable equilibrium RER position in the long term.

The time involved in the readjustment of a misaligned RER to its long-run equilibrium depends on the original stock of money as well as a number of other variables. Adjustment of the nominal exchange rate (devaluation/revaluation) could be one possible strategy to speed up this readjustment. In the case of an over-valued real exchange rate, a nominal devaluation reduces the stock of money since m=M/E and thus reduces the real value of financial assets. This induces expenditure reducing effects, by reducing expenditures on both tradable and nontradable goods. A nominal devaluation also induces expenditure-switching effects by reducing expenditure on tradables. It also tends to increase the production of tradables, since the PT is relatively higher and the exportable sector is more competitive following devaluation. This depreciates the RER resulting in an expansion of the export sector. Expenditure switching effects tend to increase the demand for nontradables but expenditure reducing effects may reduce their price. Therefore, following a nominal devaluation, the demand for nontradables increases and the price falls to re-establish equilibrium in the nontradable market, and this induces a real depreciation.

Following a nominal devaluation a number of policies can lead to an increase in the price of nontradables, most obviously expansionary monetary and/or fiscal policy and wage indexation policy. However, if a nominal devaluation is accompanied by restrained fiscal and monetary policies in the absence of wage indexation, the nominal devaluation will probably succeed in generating a real devaluation and achieving competitiveness in the tradable sectors. Simultaneous imposition of an import tariff and an export subsidy can affect the RER in the same way as devaluation. While export subsidies increase demand for and domestic price of exportables, a tariff increases the price of importables, so that the composite price of tradables as a group will increase in this situation. The relative price of exportables and importables will not be affected as long as the rate of tariff and subsidy is the same, but the price of tradables (as a composite measure of exportables and importables) will rise relative to nontradables as in the case of devaluation. However, while devaluation does not affect fiscal policy directly, a tariff with subsidy policy has a direct impact on the government budget. Furthermore, while a tariff with subsidy policy only affects the domestic price of tradable goods and services, devaluation affects the domestic price of both tradable goods and tradable assets. Accordingly, while the expectation of further devaluation may affect the domestic interest rate, the tariff with subsidy policy, does not have any direct effect on the domestic interest rate (Edwards, 1988b, p. 31).

4.5   Empirical Model

The purpose of this section is to analyse empirically the relative importance of real and nominal variables in explaining the real exchange rate movements in PNG, as reported in Tables 4.1 and 4.2. In an attempt to estimate the dynamics of the real exchange rate, it is necessary to specify an empirical equation for the equilibrium real exchange rate e_t^*. Based on the theoretical model developed in Section 4.4, the equilibrium real exchange rate is exclusively determined by real variables. According to the discussion in Section 4.4, the most important 'fundamentals' in determining the RER are:

1. international terms of trade;
2. government expenditure;
3. trade restrictions;
4. exchange and capital controls; and
5. technological progress and productivity gain.

Incorporating the above-mentioned 'fundamentals' a model of equilibrium real exchange rate was formulated in the following equation.

$$\log e_t^* = \beta_0 + \beta_1 \log (TOT)_t + \beta_2 \log (GEX)_t + \beta_3 (NKI)_{t-1} + \beta_4 \log (AID)_{t-1}$$
$$+ \beta_5 \log (OP)_t + \beta_6 \log (TECP)_t + u_t \qquad (4.21)$$

The following notations have been used in the above model:

e_t^* : equilibrium real exchange rate
TOT : barter terms of trade, defined as Px^*/Pm^*
GEX : share of government expenditure to GDP
NKI : net capital inflow (proxied for capital control)
AID : foreign aid and grant
OP = (X+M)/Y : trade restrictions substituted by the openness of an economy[3]
TECP : measure of technological progress
u_t : error term

The actual RER is a function of both real and nominal variables. Three major factors determine the dynamics of actual RER and are specified by the following equation:

$$\log e_t = \alpha\{\log e_t^*\} - \lambda\{MP_t\} + \gamma\{\log E_t - \log E_{t-1}\} \qquad (4.22)$$

where, e is the actual real exchange rate, and e* is the equilibrium RER, which is a function of real variables as specified in equation (4.21). The second determinant of the actual RER in equation (4.22) is MP_t, which states that if macro policies were unsustainable in the long term under a fixed rate, there would be a tendency for the RER to appreciate. A large λ represents a large over-valuation of the actual RER from its long-term equilibrium value. Finally, RER movements are affected by the changes in the nominal exchange rate ($\log E_t - \log E_{t-1}$). A nominal devaluation has a short-term positive impact on an over-valued RER in restoring a misaligned real exchange rate towards its equilibrium value. The actual magnitude of a short-term depreciation of the RER depends on the parameter γ. The long- and medium-term effects of changes in the nominal exchange rate would depend on the initial condition of the equilibrium real exchange rate, $\log e_t^*$, and on the accompanying macroeconomic policies of credit creation. The parameters α, λ, γ are positive and capture the most important dynamic aspects of the adjustment process.

The term, MP_t in equation (4.22) indicates the role of macroeconomic policies in determining real exchange rate behaviour. If macro policies were unsustainable in an expansionary direction, the real exchange rate would tend to appreciate, given that the other variables remain constant. To capture the impacts of macro policies, macroeconomic policy behaviour was proxied in two ways. Firstly, by the excess supply of domestic credit, measured as the rate of growth of domestic credit minus the rate of growth of real GDP.

$$\text{EXMS} = [\Delta \log \text{domestic credit} - \Delta \log \text{GDP}_t]$$

Secondly, the rate of growth of domestic credit is used to measure the macroeconomic policy impacts on real exchange rate movements.

By successive substitution for $\log e_t^*$, the macroeconomic policy variable by excess supply of domestic credit, the rate of growth of domestic credit and the change in nominal devaluation by NDEV in equation (4.22), the following estimable equation for the actual RER is given by:

$$\log e_t = \theta_1 \log (\text{TOT})_t + \theta_2 \log (\text{GEX})_t + \theta_3 (\text{NKI})_{t-1} + \theta_4 \log(\text{AID})_t$$
$$+ \theta_5 \log (\text{OP})_t + \theta_6 (\text{DTR})_t + \theta_7 \log (\text{TECP})_t - \lambda_1 \text{EXMS}_t$$
$$- \lambda_2 \text{DCR}_t + \gamma \text{NDEV}_t + u_t \qquad (4.23)$$

where θs are the combination of αs and βs.

The above model incorporates the real and nominal factors affecting the observed RER both in the short and long term. The "fundamentals" or the real variables affect the equilibrium RER in the long term whereas the nominal variables impacts on the RER only in the short term. An improvement in TOT can result in either real depreciation or real appreciation, and so is the outcome of an increase in government spending. Relaxation in exchange and capital controls tends to increase capital inflow given the political and economic stability of a country. It will appreciate the RER, if the major share of this capital flow is spent on the domestic nontradable market, thus raising the price of nontradables relative to tradables. Increased openness in international trade policy tends to depreciate the RER if the changes in trade policies reduce the price of nontradables. Moreover, if openness in the trade regime brings more competition in the tradable sector by reducing the domestic price of tradables in line with the world price level, a real depreciation will occur. But outwardness in international trade policies may appreciate the RER if it improves the trade account and increases demand for and price of nontradables relative to tradables.

Since a resources boom can be reflected in an increase in TOT, government expenditure or capital inflow, a positive change in any of these 'fundamentals' under the most plausible conditions will increase the relative price of nontradables to tradables and tend to appreciate the RER, as postulated by the discussion of booming sector economics in Chapter 2. A more restricted trade regime would worsen the situation by increasing demand for and price of semi-traded and import substitutes, since they behave as nontradables and their prices are determined by domestic demand and supply conditions during the boom years.

The model predicts that an expansionary macro policy associated with domestic money creation would widen the current account deficit, deplete international reserves and cause a RER appreciation. A restrictive wage and income policy can slowdown the appreciation of the RER by reducing demand for and price of nontradables. A change in the nominal exchange rate can help to restore the misaligned real exchange rate towards its equilibrium value. A nominal devaluation helps to prevent erosion of competitiveness in the export sector by reducing the foreign currency price of exports in the world market. The effectiveness of a change in the nominal exchange rate correcting a misaligned real exchange rate would be more powerful and long lasting if they are accompanied by appropriate macroeconomic policies. These two assumptions of nominal determinants of the real exchange rate portray most of the stylised features of macroeconomic policy options available for a small open developing economy such as PNG to correct a misalignment of the real exchange rate.

4.6 Variable Definition and Measurement

The real exchange rate model in equation (4.23) is estimated over the sample period 1970–1994 using annual data. In this section, data sources are listed and the method of data transformation adopted and its key limitations are discussed. All variables, except net capital inflow, are measured in natural logarithms.

The real exchange rate series presented in Tables 4.1 and 4.2 have been constructed from the available secondary data sources in the absence of ready-made data for the key dependent variable, the real exchange rate (log e_t). The explanatory variables are extracted from a variety of sources including The World Bank, *World Tables*, IMF, *International Financial Statistics*, Bank of PNG, *Quarterly Economic Bulletin* and from the National Centre for Development Studies International Economic Data Bank.

Before estimating equation (4.23), a number of issues relating to data availability should be mentioned. One of the major obstacles faced was the non-availability of annual data for most of the real exchange rate fundamentals. External TOT is the only real variable for which data are readily available. Therefore, some proxies had to be constructed to estimate the real exchange rate equation (4.23). Government expenditure is included in the model as a ratio of GDP (GEX). It is possible for this ratio to increase with a reduction in government consumption on nontradables.

Thus, the actual sign of GEX in relation to RER can be either positive or negative depending on its share in the nontradable or tradable sector.

Exchange and capital mobility is represented by the lagged long-term net capital inflow (NKI). Net capital inflow is defined in the World Tables as 'residents' long-term foreign liabilities less long-term assets'. Changes in capital control affect the flow of capital and any relaxation of capital controls increases the inflow of capital in principle. This, in turn, an increase in international reserves would be expected to appreciate the RER. For PNG, as in most developing countries, resources boom, direct foreign investment or international grants induce capital inflow and aid flows. Therefore, foreign aid flows have been included as a separate variable in equation (4.23) since they are not included in the long-term capital inflow. Foreign aid generally increases the expenditure on nontradable sector and is expected to appreciate the RER.

It is difficult to find a good proxy for trade policy due to the non-availability of consistent and longer period data on tariff rates or tariff revenues as a proportion of imports. The standard practice in the literature is to proxy exchange and trade controls by the degree of openness of the economy. This is given by the expression [(X+M)/Y] and used as an indicator of trade policy restrictions such as tariffs and quotas. It should not be overlooked that a less restrictive trade regime is only one of the major factors of openness, as international trade is also determined by other factors affecting imports and exports, including the RER itself (Cottani et al., 1990). For example, an increase in import quotas reduces openness and is usually expected to lead to an appreciation of the RER, whereas more openness in the trade regime tends to depreciate the RER by reducing the price of nontradables to tradables. A dummy variable has also been included to capture the effects of broad trade policy responses. This dummy variable, dummy for trade restriction (DTR), takes a value of 1 for years 1983–94 for increased trade restrictions and 0 for 1970–82 when PNG had virtually no restrictions in its trade regime.

Technological progress (TECP) has been used as an explanatory variable to capture the Ricardo-Balassa effect on the equilibrium RER and is proxied by the rate of growth of real GDP.[4] According to this hypothesis, productivity improvement in rapidly growing economies tends to be concentrated in the tradable sector and usually accounts for an appreciation of RER through increasing the income and PNT (Balassa, 1964).

Regarding the dependent variable, the trade-weighted real exchange rate (RER1) and real exchange rates for the export sector (RER2) and import competing sector (RER3) are used as alternative measures.

4.7   Econometric Procedure

The conventional approach to time-series econometrics is based on the implicit assumption of stationarity of time-series data. A recent development in time-series econometrics has cast serious doubt on the conventional time-series assumptions.

There is substantial evidence in recent literature to suggest that many macroeconomic time-series may possess unit roots, that is, they are non-stationary processes. A time-series integrated of order zero, I(0), includes a white-noise series and a stable first-order autoregressive AR (1) process, while a random walk process is an example of time-series integrated of order one, I(1). Thus, a time-series integrated of order zero, I(0), series is stationary in levels, while a time-series integrated of order one, I(1), is stationary in first differences. Most commonly, series are found to be integrated of order one, or I(1). The implication of some systematic movements of integrated variables in the estimation process may yield spurious results. In the case of a small sample study, the risk of spurious regression is extremely high. In the presence of I(1) or higher order integrated variables, the conventional t-test of the regression coefficients generated by conventional OLS procedure is highly misleading (Granger and Newbold, 1977).

Resolving these problems requires transforming an integrated series into a stationary series by successive differencing of the series depending on the order of integration (Box and Jenkins, 1970). However, Sargan (1964), Hendry and Mizon (1978) and Davidson et al. (1978) have argued that the differencing process loses valuable long-term information in data, especially in the specification of dynamic models. If some, or all, of the variables of a model are of the same order of integration, following the Engle-Granger theorem, the series are cointegrated and the appropriate procedure to estimate the model will be an error correction specification. Hendry (1986) supported this view, arguing that error correction formulation minimises the possibilities of spurious relationships being estimated as it retains level information in a non-integrated form (Hendry, 1986, p. 203). Davidson et al. (1978) proposed a general autoregressive distributed lag model with a lagged dependent variable, which is known as the 'error-correction' term. Hendry et al. (1985) also advocated the process of adding lagged dependent and independent variables up to the point where residual whiteness is ensured in a dynamic specification. Therefore, error correction models avoid the spurious regression relationships.

Mindful of these considerations, the estimation process was begun by testing the time-series properties of the data series. Many test procedures are available for testing non-stationarity in a time-series. In this study, the Dickey-Fuller procedure was used with Augmented Dickey-Fuller test statistics to test the null hypothesis of a unit root against the alternative of stationarity of data series. The results from these tests suggested that all the variables used in this model do not have the same order of integration. The key dependent variable (RER) and some of the explanatory variables are found to be stationary. The test results are reported in the Appendix Table A4.2.

To guard against the possibility of estimating spurious relationships in the presence of some nonstationary variables, estimation was performed using a general-to-specific Hendry-type error correction modelling (ECM) procedure. This procedure begins with an over-parameterised autoregressive distributed lag (ADL) specification of an appropriate lag. The decision on lag length is determined by the consideration of the available degrees of freedom and type of data. With annual data, one or two lags would be long enough, while with quarterly data a maximum lag of four can be taken. Under this ECM procedure, the long-term relationship is embedded within the dynamic specification. Therefore, the general model of real exchange rate can be specified as follows:

$$Y_t = \alpha_0 + \Sigma \, \alpha_i Y_{t-i} + \Sigma \, \beta_i X_{t-i} + u_t \tag{4.24}$$

where α_0 is a vector of constants, Y_t is a $(n \times 1)$ vector of endogenous variables, X_t is a $(k \times 1)$ vector of explanatory variables, and α_i and β_i are $(n \times n)$ and $(n \times k)$ matrices of parameters. As annual data are used for the model, one period lag is assumed. When the lag length is one, the general model can be written as:

$$Y_t = \alpha_0 + \alpha_1 Y_{t-1} + \beta_1 X_t + \beta_2 X_{t-1} + u_t \tag{4.25}$$

Now we can consider the error correction version of the model as:

$$\Delta Y_t = \alpha_0 - (1-\alpha_1) \, Y_{t-1} + \beta_1 \, \Delta X_t + (\beta_1 + \beta_2) \, X_{t-1} + u_t \tag{4.26}$$

The above equation can be reparameterised in terms of differences and lagged levels so as to separate the short-term and long-term multipliers of the system:

$$\Delta Y_t = \beta_1 \Delta X_t - (1-\alpha_1) \, [Y_{t-1} - \gamma_1 - \gamma_2 X_{t-1}] + u_t \tag{4.27}$$

where the new parameters

$$\gamma_1 = \alpha_0 / (1 - \alpha_1)$$

$$\gamma_2 = \beta_1 + \beta_2 / (1 - \alpha_1)$$

In equation (4.27) short-term relationships are captured by the coefficients on differenced variables, while long-term relationships are captured by the coefficients on lagged level variables, namely by γ_1 and γ_2.

The error correction specification for the different versions of the real exchange rate model can be represented by the following equations with one period lag as annual data has been used for the model estimation:

$$\Delta RER1 = f \, (\Delta TOT, \Delta GEX, \Delta NKI, \Delta OP, \Delta AID, \Delta EXMS, \Delta NDEV,$$

$$TOT_{t-1}, \, GEX_{t-1}, \, NKI_{t-1}, \, OP_{t-1}, \, AID_{t-1}, \, EXMS_{t-1}, \, NDEV_{t-1},$$

$$DTR, RER1_{t-1}) \tag{IV.4.1}$$

$$\Delta RER2 = f \, (\Delta TOT, \Delta GEX, \Delta NKI, \Delta OP, \Delta AID, \Delta EXMS, \Delta NDEV,$$

$$TOT_{t-1}, GEX_{t-1}, NKI_{t-1}, OP_{t-1}, AID_{t-1}, EXMS_{t-1},$$

$$NDEV_{t-1}, DTR, RER2_{t-1}) \tag{IV.4.2}$$

$$\Delta RER3 = f(\Delta TOT, \Delta GEX, \Delta NKI, \Delta OP, \Delta AID, \Delta EXMS,$$

$$\Delta NDEV, TOT_{t-1}, GEX_{t-1}, NKI_{t-1}, OP_{t-1}, AID_{t-1}, EXMS_{t-1},$$

$$NDEV_{t-1}, DTR, RER3_{t-1}) \qquad (IV.4.3)$$

The following notations have been used in these above equations:

Dependent variables:

RER1 = Trade-weighted real exchange rate
RER2 = RER for export sector (EPI/PNT)
RER3 = RER for importable sector (IPI/PNT)

Independent variables:

TOT = international terms of trade (1990 =100)
GEX = government expenditure to GDP
NKI = net capital inflow
OP = (X+M)/Y : index of trade restrictions substituted by the openness of an economy
AID = flow of foreign aid and grant
EXMS = excess supply of domestic money supply
NDEV = nominal devaluation
DTR = a dummy variable which takes 0 for the years (1970–82) of an open trade regime and 1 for years 1983–94 with increased trade restrictions.

All variables, except NKI, which takes negative values in some years, are measured in natural logarithms. NKI is in terms of millions of kina.

The above equations are 'tested down' using OLS by dropping statistically insignificant differenced and lagged terms. The testing procedure continues until a parsimonious error correction representation is obtained which retains the *a priori* theoretical model as its long-term solution. The selection of final equations is made after careful diagnostic tests on the OLS error process.

4.8   Results

The estimates of parsimonious dynamic Error Correction Models are reported in Table 4.3 together with the most common diagnostic tests. The long-term elasticities relating to the key explanatory variables and their t-ratios are reported in Table 4.4. While the long-term elasticities are derived from the short-term estimated equations, their respective standard errors are derived by using Kmenta's (1986) formula.[5]

The adjusted R^2 is quite high and suggests the model has a fairly good fit. The model is also statistically significant in terms of the standard F-test. The lagged error correction term for the real exchange rate equation (IV.4.1) is statistically significant at the 5-per-cent level and has the expected negative sign. The computed value for the Jarque-Bera test for normality of the residuals is $JBN-\chi^2(2) = 0.05$ and is much smaller than the critical value of $JBN-\chi^2(2) = 9.21$ at a 1-per-cent significance level, indicating normality of the residual errors. The computed value for Lagrange multiplier test of residual serial correlation is $LM-\chi^2(6) = 3.99$ in equation (IV.4.1), which is smaller than the critical value of $LM-\chi^2(6) = 16.81$ and indicates no serial correlation among the residuals in the real exchange rate model. A residual correlogram of up to six years was estimated for each equation, with no evidence of significant serial correlation in the error terms. The equations also comfortably passed the CUSUM test on recursive residuals and the CUSUM test on backward recursive residuals. The ARCH$-\chi^2$ test for error variance shows that the computed value of ARCH$-\chi^2(1)$=0.95 is smaller than the tabulated value ARCH$-\chi^2(1)$=6.63 at a 1-per-cent significance level. Thus, the results suggest the error variances are not correlated in equation (IV.4.1).

The equation also passed the specification choice in terms of joint variable deletion tests against the maintained hypothesis of the theory of the real exchange rate. Ramsey's RESET test for specification error indicates that the calculated F value F(1, 13)=0.32 in equation (IV.4.1) is much smaller than the critical value F(1,13)=9.07 at a 1-per-cent significance level. Hence, the computed RESET-F value for the equation is not significant, indicating the equation is not misspecified. The equation passed the Chow tests for parameter stability as the computed F-value of Chow-test for the equation is CHOW$-$F(11,12)=0.67 for equation (IV.4.1) is smaller than the critical value CHOW$-$F(11,12)= 4.22 at a 1-per-cent significant level which indicates parameter stability for the model.

Equations (IV.4.2) and (IV.4.3) in Table 4.3 are also statistically significant in terms of the standard F-test. The adjusted R^2 are fairly high (ranging between 0.72 to 0.80) for both real exchange rate models suggesting that the models have a fairly good fit. They also perform well by all other diagnostic tests. The Jarque-Bera test statistic for residual normality for the equations are less than the critical value for a chi-square distribution with 2 degrees of freedom, indicating normality of residuals of the models of the export sector real exchange rate (equation IV.4.2) and real exchange rate for the import-competing sector (equation IV.4.3). ARCH$-\chi^2$ test for error variance shows that in both models computed values of ARCH$-\chi^2(1)$ are smaller than the tabulated value of ARCH$-\chi^2(1)$=6.63 at a 1-per-cent significance level. Thus the computed statistics suggest that error variances are not correlated in these equations.

Both models passed the specification choice in terms of joint variable deletion tests against the maintained hypothesis of the theory of the real exchange rate. Ramsey's RESET test for specification error indicates that calculated F values are much smaller than the critical value at a 1-per-cent significance level. Hence, computed RESET-F values for the equations are not significant, indicating the equations are not misspecified. A residual correlogram of up to six years was estimated for each equation, with no evidence of significant serial correlation in the error terms. The equations comfortably passed the CUSUM test on recursive residuals and the CUSUM test on backward recursive residuals. The Lagrange multiplier LM–χ^2 test for residual serial correlation also indicates the calculated χ^2 values in equation 4.2 and 4.3 are much smaller than the tabulated value. The calculated LM–χ^2 value=2.37 and 11.0 are much smaller than the tabulated value LM–χ^2=16.81 at a one per cent significance level, indicating no serial correlation in residuals. Both equations passed the Chow tests for parameter stability as the computed F-values of Chow-test are insignificant. The coefficients of the technological progress variable (TECP), the openness in trade regime (OP) and the growth of domestic credit (DCR) were consistently insignificant in experimental runs and dropped from the final equations.

Equation IV.4.1 indicates an improvement in external TOT does not have any significant long-term impact on the trade-weighted real exchange rate. Although the coefficient indicates a positive sign in relation to RER, but it is not statistically significant both in the short term as well as in the long term at the conventional 5-per-cent level.

The coefficient of the government expenditure variable (GEX) has the expected negative sign with respect to the trade-weighted real exchange rate in equation (IV.4.1) but does not have any significant short-term or long-term effect at the conventional 5-per-cent level.

The net long-term capital inflow significantly affects the trade-weighted real exchange rate. The sign of the coefficient is negative as expected in the theoretical model. A 1-per-cent increase in capital inflow appreciates the RER by 0.35 per cent in the long term. Foreign aid and grant flows have the expected negative sign with respect to the RER in equation (IV.4.1) but do not have any significant long-term effect at the 5-per-cent significance level.

Trade restrictions, as measured by the dummy variable (DTR), has a significant negative effect on the trade-weighted real exchange rate. The dummy variable for trade restriction indicates that the introduction of restrictive trade policies from the mid-1980s appreciated the RER of PNG in the long term. Trade restrictions tend to have appreciated the RER of PNG by 0.08 per cent in the long term. Thus, the trade regime had an important bearing on the movement of the real exchange rate in PNG.

The role of macro policy, as proxied by the excess growth of money supply over the growth rate of real GDP (EXMS), was found to be significant in affecting the real exchange rates of PNG in equation (IV.4.1). A 1-per-cent excess money supply over the growth of GDP appreciated the RER by 0.05 per cent in the long term. Unsustainable macropolicy, in terms of excess money supply, raised the domestic price of nontradables and appreciated the RER of PNG, confirming the theoretical analysis of the real exchange rate discussed earlier in this chapter.

The coefficient of the nominal exchange rate variable (NDEV) is statistically significant with positive sign as expected by the theoretical model. The econometric

Table 4.3
Determinants of real exchange rates in Papua New Guinea, 1970–94

Trade-weighted real exchange rate (Equation IV.4.1)

$$DRER1 = 3.28 + 0.61\ DNDEV + 0.10\ TOT_{t-1} - 0.28\ NKI_{t-1} - 0.23\ AID_{t-1}$$

$$\qquad\qquad (3.57)\qquad\quad (1.56)\qquad\quad (1.73)\qquad\quad (1.85)$$

$$- 0.01 GEX_{t-1} - 0.03\ EXMS_{t-1} - 0.06\ DTR + 0.63\ NDEV_{t-1}$$

$$(1.12)\qquad\quad (1.68)\qquad\qquad (1.92)\qquad\quad (3.92)$$

$$- 0.81\ RER1_{t-1}$$

$$(3.90)$$

Adjusted $R^2 = 0.82$ $F(8,14) = 13.5$ $JBN-c^2(2) = 0.05$ $LM-c^2(6) = 3.99$
$ARCH-c^2(1) = 0.95$ $RESET(2)-F(1,13) = 0.32$ $CHOW-F(11,12) = 0.67$

Real Exchange Rate for Export Sector (Equation IV.4.2)

$$DRER2 = 2.63 + 0.66\ DTOT + 0.39\ TOT_{t-1} - 0.27\ AID_{t-1} - 0.09\ EXMS_{t-1}$$

$$(4.57)\qquad\quad (2.01)\qquad\qquad (2.11)\qquad\quad (1.88)$$

$$- 0.20\ GEX_{t-1} - 0.15\ DTR + 0.12\ NDEV_{t-1} - 0.64\ RER2_{t-1}$$

$$(1.93)\qquad\qquad (2.12)\qquad\quad (1.94)\qquad\qquad (4.52)$$

Adjusted $R^2 = 0.80$ $F(8,14) = 15.6$ $JBN-c^2(2) = 0.58$ $LM-c^2(6) = 2.37$
$ARCH-c^2(1) = 0.29$ $RESET(2)-F(1,13) = 0.65$ $CHOW-F(11,12) = 2.80$

Real Exchange Rate for Import Competing Sector (Equation IV.4.3)

$$DRER3 = 3.53 - 0.30\ DTOT - 0.17\ TOT_{t-1} - 0.09\ DTR - 0.09\ GEX_{t-1}$$

$$(2.93)\qquad\qquad (2.25)\qquad\quad (2.08)\qquad\quad (1.79)$$

$$- 0.12\ EXMS_{t-1} - 0.20\ AID_{t-1} - 0.17\ NDEV_{t-1} - 0.53\ RER3_{t-1}$$

$$(2.12)\qquad\qquad (3.20)\qquad\qquad (2.97)\qquad\qquad (5.49)$$

Adjusted $R^2 = 0.72$ $F(7,15) = 9.06$ $JBN-c^2(2) = 0.86$ $LM-c^2(6) = 11.0$
$ARCH-c^2(1) = 0.24$ $RESET(2)-F(1,14) = 1.74$ $CHOW-F(11,12) = 1.91$

Notes:
1. Figures in parentheses are t-statistics.
2. The F statistic is against the null that all coefficients = 0. The Durbin Watson for first order serial correlation is not reported for these models since it is strictly not valid in these models with lagged dependent variables.
3. LM is the Lagrange multiplier general test for residual serial correlation. ARCH is the test for Autoregressive Heteroscedasticity, RESET is the Ramsey's RESET test for functional mis-specification, residual normality test for skewness and excess kurtosis is given by Jarque Bera Normality (JBN) test.

results indicate that there is a close link between the two variables in PNG. A 1-per-cent nominal devaluation depreciated the RER by 0.61 per cent in the short term and 0.8 per cent in the long term.

Equations (IV.4.2) and (IV.4.3) indicate the major factors affecting the RER in PNG's export and import competing sectors. An improvement in TOT significantly depreciates the RER for the export sector in the short term as well as in the long term as price effect overweights the income effect of increased TOT. A 1-per-cent increase in TOT depreciates the real exchange rate for the export sector by 0.66 per cent in the short term and 0.61 per cent in the long term. However, the change in TOT has significant negative effects on the real exchange rate for the import-substitute sector in the short term as well as in the long term which indicates that the income effect is much greater than the price effect. A 1-per-cent improvement in TOT appreciates the real exchange rate of the import competing sector by 0.3 per cent in the short term and 0.16 per cent in the long term. The coefficient of government expenditure has a significant negative impact on the real exchange rate for the export and import substitute sectors (RER2 and RER3) in the long term.

The impact of net capital inflow (NKI) is found to be insignificant with respect to the real exchange rate for the export and import competing sectors and was dropped from the final equations. However, it is found that foreign aid has a significant negative impact on the real exchange rate of PNG's export- and import-competing sectors. A 1-per-cent increase in foreign aid flows appreciate the real exchange rate for exportable sector by 0.41 per cent and real exchange rate for import competing sector by 0.37 per cent in the long term. As expected by the theoretical proposition, that increased aid and grant flows are usually spent mostly in the nontradable sector, real exchange rate appreciation was generated in the economy.

Trade restrictions measured by the dummy variable, DTR, had significant negative impacts on the real exchange rate for the export and import competing sectors' real exchange rates (RER2 and RER3). From the mid-1980s, trade protection for selected industries appreciated the real exchange rate for the export sector by 0.15 per cent in the short term and 0.23 per cent in the long term. The real exchange rate for import-competing industries also appreciated by 0.09 per cent in the short term and 0.16 in the long term, due to an increase in trade restrictions.

Nominal devaluation improved the competitiveness of the export sector by 0.18 per cent in the long term. But nominal devaluation seems to have a significant negative impact on the import-competing sector's real exchange rate in the long term, a result which is not consistent with the theoretical prediction. A 1-per-cent devaluation of the nominal exchange rate appreciated the real exchange rate of the import competing sector by 0.23 per cent in the long term.

4.9   Summary and Conclusion

The purpose of this chapter has been to examine real exchange rate behaviour in PNG and evaluate whether the movements in the real exchange rate follow the theoretical

Table 4.4
Estimates of long-term elasticities of RERs
in Papua New Guinea, 1970–94

| Dependent Variable | RER1 | RER2 | RER3 |
Independent Variables	(IV.4.1)	(IV.4.2)	(IV.4.3)
TOT	0.12**	0.61**	–0.16**
	(1.45)	(2.56)	(2.77)
NKI	–0.35**		
	(1.76)		
GEX	–0.01	–0.3	–0.17
	(0.12)	(1.97)	(1.79)
DTR	–0.08**	–0.23	–0.16**
	(2.20)	(3.05)	(2.77)
EXMS	–0.05	–0.14	–0.22
	(1.76)	(1.96)	(2.17)
AID	0.28	–0.41**	–0.37**
	(0.67)	(2.03)	(2.75)
NDEV	0.77**	0.18*	–0.23*
	(2.45)	(1.95)	(3.17)

Notes: Figures in parentheses are t-statistics. ** denotes significant at 5%, * denotes
significant at 10 %.

Source: Long run multiplier values are computed from the long-term steady state solutions
to the estimated models reported in Table 4.3.

expectations postulated by the framework of the study in Chapter 2. The theory of
real exchange rates states that, while the long-term equilibrium value of the real
exchange rate is determined by real variables, the actual or observed real exchange
rate is influenced by both real and nominal variables in the short term. Movement
of the equilibrium RER from its original position does not necessarily represent
disequilibrium since the long-term equilibrium is affected by the real variables. This
chapter has examined the extent to which real and nominal determinants can explain
the behaviour of the real exchange rate in PNG.

Resources booms can be brought by change in any of the real variables, which
may change the relative PT to PNT and shift the equilibrium RER from its original
position. As discussed in the extended version of the theoretical framework of
resources booms in Chapter 2, policy-induced real (trade policy) and nominal (fiscal

and exchange rate policy) variables can rectify misalignment of the exchange rate if implemented properly and in time. The results suggest that a resources boom brought about by an improvement in the external TOT seems to have no long-term effect on the trade-weighted RER in PNG, whereas increased net capital inflow and foreign aid flows appreciated the RER. Increased trade restrictions from the early-1980s appear to have adversely affected the traded-goods sector through RER appreciation. It was found that the nominal variables also significantly affected the real exchange rate of the economy over the study period. In particular, expansionary fiscal policy resulted in an increased domestic price of nontradables and led to an appreciation of the real exchange rate, whereas a nominal devaluation helped to re-establish the real exchange rate in the short term, as well as in the long term. Nominal devaluation had a significant positive impact on the trade-weighted real exchange rate and real exchange rate for the export-competing sector in the long term, indicating that a nominal devaluation can be a powerful device to correct real exchange rate misalignment. However, the result is negative for the import-competing sector.

Notes

1   Warr (1986) computed the index of the relative PT to PNT for Indonesia, taking the ratio of the wholesale price of imported commodities to the Indonesia-wide CPI component, which belongs to nontradable categories.

2   Shares of export and import of major trading partners in 1990 have also been used separately as weights. The calculation (Appendix Table A4.1) shows that there is very little difference between export, import and total trade-weighted series and they follow a similar trend.

3   The limitations of this measure are discussed in p. 66.

4   This is admittedly a weak proxy because factor accumulation itself can increase GDP with little technical progress.

5   As Kmenta (1986, p. 486) writes "The formula refers to the general case where an estimator, say α, is a function of k other estimators such $\beta_1, \beta_2, \dots \beta_k$; that is,

$$\alpha = f(\beta_1, \beta_2, \dots \beta_k)$$

Then the large sample variance of α can be approximated as

$$Var(\alpha) = \Sigma[\delta f / \delta \beta k]^2 Var(\beta k) + 2 \Sigma[\delta f / \delta \beta j] [\delta f / \delta \beta k] Cov[\beta j, \beta k]$$
$$(j, k = 1, 2 \dots \dots k)(j < k)$$

(The approximation is obtained by using Taylor's expansion for $f(\beta_1, \beta_2, \dots \beta_k)$ around $\beta_1, \beta_2, \dots \beta_k$ dropping terms of the order two or higher and then obtaining the variance by the usual formula)".

5

Determinants of Sectoral Output, Savings and Investment in Papua New Guinea

5.1   Introduction

The previous chapter examined the determinants of the real exchange rate and identified the major sources of real exchange rate movements in the PNG economy. The major changes in key macroeconomic variables, including changes in the RER and changes in aggregate demand and domestic policy variables all greatly influence the structure of an economy. This chapter focuses on the impact of the real exchange rate and domestic policy decisions on savings and investment behaviour and sectoral output growth in PNG, in order to examine the theoretical propositions of the 'theory of booming sector' discussed in Chapter 2.

A resources boom, can be a mixed blessing for a mineral and primary commodity producing developing economy. While the influx of export revenue and capital inflow relaxes the foreign exchange constraint on economic growth by improving the balance of payments and raising national income, some sectors can be affected adversely as output and factor incomes decline. The extended version of this analytical model predicts that, with huge unemployed resources and adopting a more open trade regime, a small open developing economy might not experience the classical problems of 'Dutch disease' associated with booming sector theory.

This chapter is organised as follows: Section 5.2 presents a model based on the analytical framework developed in Chapter 2 to estimate the effects of a resources boom and the real exchange rate on sectoral growth; Section 5.3 presents the empirical model and discusses data sources, variable definitions and measurement; Section 5.4 presents and interprets the results of the study; Section 5.5 contains a discussion on savings and investment behaviour and assesses the macroeconomic policy impacts on the long-term growth of the economy over the study period and Section 5.6 summarises findings of the chapter.

5.2   Determinants of Sectoral Output

Sectoral growth of an economy is determined by several real, nominal and policy variables. To quantify the impact and extent to which macroeconomic variables affect the sectoral output of PNG, the output of each sector has been modelled as a function of anticipated profitability for that sector, which is assumed to be a function of the following variables:

1. real exchange rate (RER);
2. government expenditure (comprising government consumption and government investment) (GEX);
3. domestic absorption net of government expenditure (DA); and
4. openness (OP) of an economy (proxied by X+M/Y).

Summed up, the determinants of sectoral output can be expressed as follows:

$$\text{Output} = f\,(\text{RER, GEX, DA, OP}) \qquad (5.1)$$

Note that GEX and OP were among the explanatory variables in the RER equation developed in Chapter 4. These two variables and DA are included as additional explanatory variables because they can impact on output directly, over and above the impact operating through RER is discussed below.

The change in the RER, and its impact on general inflation, is one of the major factors affecting the composition of sectoral growth in an economy. The theory of booming sector postulates that sectoral growth is influenced not only by the relative price of tradables to nontradables but also by other direct demand effects. Thus, all other variables used in this model are control variables, to capture the impact of the macroeconomic environment over and above the impact of the RER on sectoral output growth. These variables may be partially correlated with the movements of the real exchange rate, since they also affect the changes of the real exchange rate. The effects of these policy variables on sectoral growth will be analysed separately.

Real exchange rate
Real exchange rate plays a key role in determining sectoral growth of an economy. An expected increase in the domestic price level indicates predicted short-term profitability and tends to increase the output of nontradables since the income effect of resources boom is very high during the boom years. However, an increase in the domestic price level lowers the marginal product of labour and capital of the tradables sector making the sector less competitive than its trading partners and reducing the output of the tradables sector. Therefore, the expected sign[1] for the RER in relation to sectoral growth is positive for tradables and negative for nontradables, given that the RER is defined as the price ratio of tradables to nontradables.

As discussed in the extension of the theoretical model in Chapter 2 the imposition of trade restrictions may completely change the effects of the RER on sectoral output. In most developing countries, various forms of trade restrictions shelter the manufacturing sector, so that manufacturing output may expand, since this sector behaves as a nontradable sector during the boom period. Therefore, given the limited size of an indigenous capital goods sector and low levels of industrialisation, together with high levels of protection towards import substitute industries, a windfall gain and subsequent appreciation may increase demand, price and output for the domestic manufacturing sector of a developing country like PNG. However, protection of the manufacturing sector negatively taxes the agricultural export sector and the output of this sector falls as the price of exportable declines relative to the price of domestic nontradables. Further, due to imperfect substitutability between some import-competing goods and imports in most developing countries, an appreciation tends to increase profitability and expand output of the import-competing sector during the boom years. Thus, in the presence of some form of trade restrictions, an appreciation expands manufacturing output, while a depreciation of the RER reduces the profitability of the nontraded sector by reducing the price and output of nontradable goods and services.

Government expenditure
Government expenditure, either in the form of consumption, investment or subsidies (protection), greatly influences the output of an economy. Increased government consumption of nontradable goods and services raises the demand for and prices of nontradables and leads to an expansion of output of the nontradable sectors. Increased spending on government investment and subsidies contributes to the expansion of nontradable construction as well as the agricultural traded sector. Thus, the anticipated sign for this variable is positive for both the traded and nontraded sectors, depending on the relative share of government expenditure spent on a specific sector. Since the nontradable component in government spending is generally higher in the nontradable sector than that of private spending, increased government spending expands nontradable output and adversely affects tradable output.

Domestic absorption
An increase in domestic absorption (less government spending) tends to increase the output of nontradables as well as both import substitutes and agricultural tradable products through an increase in private consumption and investment demand. The expected sign for domestic absorption is positive for the agriculture and import substituting tradable sector as well as for the nontradable sector. However, the increased demand for domestically produced goods and services raises competition for factors of production amongst the sectors. Increased domestic absorption eventually increases the domestic price level compared to tradables and reduces competitiveness of tradables in the world market. Thus, the anticipated sign for domestic absorption is negative in terms of the exportable sector.

Openness in the trade regime
Both developed and developing countries attempt to protect some specific sectors or an industry by several quantitative and qualitative trade restrictions (proxied by

the degree of openness in the trade regime). In a developing country, an import-competing sector is generally protected by trade restrictions. While trade restrictions reduce demand for imports, they may improve the current account position and increase demand for and output of the importable sector. Increased protection also raises the output of nontradables and import substitutes due to imperfect substitution between imports and import substitutes during the boom years.

Trade protection for a sector acts as a trade tax for other tradable sectors. The cost of production increases in the non-protected tradable sector, as a result of a general cost increase caused by salary and wages pull from the protected sector and the nontradable sector. On the other hand, a more outward oriented trade policy reduces taxes on the non-protected tradable sectors and reduces the price of essential imported inputs used in domestic production. By increasing competition in the domestic market, greater openness in the trade regime also introduces new strategies for cost effective production and increases the output of exportables and importables. Openness in a trade regime reduces the domestic price level and makes the export sector more competitive in the world market. Hence the expected sign for openness in a trade regime is positive for the tradable sector. The sign can be either positive or negative for the nontradable and import substitute sectors.

5.3 The Empirical Model

The general error correction model to determine sectoral impact can be presented by the following equations. This general model of sectoral growth is specified with one lag on all of the variables as annual data has been used for model estimation.

$$\Delta AVA = f(\Delta RER, \Delta GEX, \Delta OP, \Delta DA, GEX_{t-1}, OP_{t-1},$$
$$DA_{t-1}, RER_{t-1}, AVA_{t-1}) \dots \tag{5.2}$$

$$\Delta MVA = f(\Delta RER, \Delta GEX, \Delta OP, \Delta DA, GEX_{t-1}, OP_{t-1},$$
$$DA_{t-1}, RER_{t-1}, MVA_{t-1}) \dots \tag{5.3}$$

$$\Delta MIN = f(\Delta RER, \Delta GEX, \Delta OP, \Delta DA, GEX_{t-1}, OP_{t-1},$$
$$DA_{t-1}, RER_{t-1}, MIN_{t-1}) \dots \tag{5.4}$$

$$\Delta NT = f(\Delta RER, \Delta GEX, \Delta OP, \Delta DA, GEX_{t-1}, OP_{t-1},$$
$$DA_{t-1}, RER_{t-1}, NT_{t-1}) \dots \dots \tag{5.5}$$

$$\Delta CONS = f(\Delta RER, \Delta GI, \Delta OP, \Delta DA, GI_{t-1}, OP_{t-1},$$
$$DA_{t-1}, RER_{t-1,} CONS_{t-1}) \dots \dots \tag{5.6}$$

The following notations have been used in these above equations.

Dependent variables:

AVA   =   agricultural value added
MVA   =   manufacturing value added
MIN   =   mineral sector value added
NT   =   nontradable sector value added
CONS   =   construction sector value added

Independent variables:

RER   =   RER for export sector
GEX   =   government expenditure
OP   =   trade restriction substituted by the openness of an economy (proxied by X+M/Y)
DA   =   domestic absorption net of government expenditure

All variables are measured at 1990 prices and are in natural logarithms.

Using annual data, the model is estimated over the sample period 1970-94. The economy has been decomposed into major traded sectors of agriculture, manufacturing and minerals; and nontraded sectors comprising services, construction and utilities for analytical purposes. This division enables separate examination of the effects of the RER on the growth of the nontradable construction sector, in order to verify the 'construction boom' theory in the context of the PNG economy. Regarding the most important determinants of sectoral growth, the most direct measure of the real exchange rate (RER2) from Chapter 4 has been used, since the real exchange rate for the export sector most closely indicates competitiveness of an economy.[2] Government investment (government expenditure minus government consumption) has used separately to examine the effect of government investment on the construction sector. Other explanatory and dependent variables have been taken from a variety of sources, including The World Bank, *World Tables*, IMF, *International Financial Statistics*, Bank of PNG, *Quarterly Economic Bulletins* and from the National Centre for Development Studies International Economic Data Bank.

The estimation procedure was begun by testing the order of integration of time series data. The order of integration for every variable used in the model has been tested by the Dickey-Fuller and Augmented Dickey-Fuller tests. The results are reported in Appendix Table A5.1. It was found that a number of the key variables are non-stationary. Therefore, the general to specific Hendry-type error correction model building methodology was employed as in the previous chapter, to guard against estimating spurious regression relationship while retaining long term information.

The above equations have been "tested down" using OLS by dropping statistically insignificant differenced and lagged terms. The testing procedure continued until a parsimonious error correction representation was obtained which retained the *a priori* theoretical model as its long term solution. The selection of final equations was made after careful diagnostic check tests on the OLS error process.

5.4   Results

The parsimonious estimates of the model together with the most common diagnostic tests are reported in Tables 5.1 and 5.2. The long-term elasticities, with respect to key explanatory variables and their t-ratios are given in Table 5.3. In general, the results are statistically acceptable. All equations pass the F-test for overall fit. The adjusted R^2s range from 43 per cent to 78 per cent suggests the models have fairly good fit. The coefficient of the error correction term in each equation is negative and statistically significant and provides powerful support for the existence of lag adjustment. The Jarque-Bera test statistics for residual normality for equations are less than the critical value for a chi-square distribution with 2 degrees of freedom, indicating normality of residuals of the models. A residual correlogram up to six years indicates no significant serial correlation in the error terms. The Lagrange multiplier $LM-\chi^2$ test for residual serial correlation also indicates the calculated χ^2 values are much smaller than the tabulated value $LM-\chi^2=16.81$, at a 1-per-cent significance level, indicating no serial correlation in residuals. $ARCH-\chi^2$ test for error variance shows that computed values of $ARCH-\chi^2(1)$ are smaller in all models than the tabulated value $ARCH-\chi^2(1) = 6.63$ at a 1-per-cent significance level. Thus, the computed statistics suggest that error variances are not correlated in the equations. Ramsey's RESET test for specification error indicates that calculated F values are much smaller than critical value at 1-per-cent significance level. Hence computed RESET-F values for the equations are not significant, indicating the equations are not mis-specified.

The RER has the anticipated sign in the equations for each of these five major (agriculture, manufacture, minerals, nontradables and construction) sectoral groupings. The empirical results of sectoral growth for each sector will be discussed separately.

Agricultural sector

Equation (5.7) suggests that depreciation of the RER has a significant positive impact, both in the short and long term, on the agricultural sector. Over the study period, a 1-per-cent depreciation of the RER improves the agricultural output by 0.21 per cent in the short term and by 0.20 per cent in the long term.

Increased government expenditure has a significant contractionary impact on the agricultural traded sector as it increased demand and price of nontradables relative to tradables, as predicted by the theoretical propositions. A 1-per-cent increase in government expenditure reduced the output of the agricultural sector by 0.38 per cent in the long term, as an increased share of government expenditure is generally spent on the nontradable sector.

Greater openness increases profitability of domestic tradables at given world prices induced by greater export supply. Increased openness in the external trade regime significantly improved the output of the agricultural sector in PNG. It seems to reflect the combined favourable impact of reduced costs of imported inputs and improved international competitiveness. In the long term, openness in the trade regime increases the output of the agricultural sector by about 0.21 per cent.

Table 5.1
Determinants of sectoral output: traded sector

Agriculture sector (Equation 5.7)

$$\Delta AV = 13.62 + 0.21\ \Delta RER - 0.23\ GEX_{t-1} + 0.13\ OP_{t-1} + 0.12\ RER_{t-1} - 0.60\ AV_{t-1}$$
$$\qquad\quad (3.55) \qquad\quad (3.80) \qquad (2.25) \qquad (2.40) \qquad (4.28)$$

Adjusted R^2 = 0.60 F(5,16) = 4.59 JBN–χ^2(2) = 0.13 LM–χ^2(6) = 4.47

ARCH–χ^2(1) = 2.73 RESET(2)–F(1,13) = 1.86 CHOW–F(9,13) = 0.92

Manufacturing sector (Equation 5.8)

$$\Delta MVA = -4.66 + 0.67\ \Delta DA + 0.54\ DA_{t-1} + 0.28\ OP_{t-1} + 0.34\ RER_{t-1} - 0.71\ MVA_{t-1}$$
$$\qquad\qquad\quad (3.40) \qquad (1.93) \qquad (2.01) \qquad\quad (3.99) \qquad\quad (5.27)$$

Adjusted R^2 = 0.72 F(5,16) = 9.77 JBN–χ^2(2) = 0.08 LM–χ^2(6) = 5.84

ARCH–χ^2(1) = 0.01 RESET(2)–F(1,14) = 0.22 CHOW–F(9,13) = 3.06

Minerals sector (Equation 5.9)

$$\Delta MIN = 14.10 + 1.11\ \Delta RER2 + 0.38\ RER2_{t-1} - 0.49\ MIN_{t-1}$$
$$\qquad\qquad\quad (1.97) \qquad\quad (3.15) \qquad\quad (6.78)$$

Adjusted R^2 = 0.78 F(3,18) = 25.15 JBN–χ^2(2) = 0.99 LM–χ^2(6) = 2.96

ARCH–χ^2(1) = 0.29 RESET(2)–F(1,17) = 0.60 CHOW–F(9,13) = 1.31

The following notations have been used:
AVA = agricultural value added, MVA = manufacturing value added, MIN = mineral sector vale added, RER = RER for export sector, GEX = total government expenditure, OP = openness in trade regime, DA = domestic absorption.
Notes:
1. Figures in parentheses are t-statistics.
2. The F statistic is against the null that all coefficients = 0. The Durbin Watson for first order serial correlation is not reported for these models since it is not strictly valid in these models with lagged dependent variables. The lagged error correction terms are statistically significant at the 5 per cent level and have the expected negative signs.
3. LM is the Lagrange multiplier general test for residual serial correlation. ARCH is the test for Autoregressive Heteroscedasticity, RESET is the Ramsey's RESET test for functional mis-specification, residual normality test for skewness and excess kurtosis is given by Jarque Bera Normality test.

Table 5.2
Determinants of sectoral output: nontradable sector

Nontradable sector (Equation 5.10)

$$\Delta NT = 11.71 + 0.43\ \Delta DA + 0.22\ DA_{t-1} - 0.13\ RER_{t-1} - 0.75\ NT_{t-1}$$
$$\qquad\quad (2.60)\qquad (1.28)\qquad (2.61)\qquad\quad (3.63)$$

Adjusted $R^2 = 0.43$ F(4,17) = 4.41 JBN–χ^2(2) = 1.16 LM–χ^2(6) = 3.23

ARCH–χ^2(1) = 0.13 RESET(2)–F(1,16) = 1.30 CHOW–F(6,16) = 2.19

Construction sector (Equation 5.11)

$$\Delta CONS = 16.49 - 0.87\ \Delta RER2 + 0.09\ GI_{t-1} + 0.13\ DA_{t-1} - 0.14\ RER2_{t-1} - 0.97\ CONS_{t-1}$$
$$\qquad\qquad (3.44)\qquad (3.22)\qquad\quad (2.05)\qquad\quad (0.99)\qquad\quad (4.98)$$

Adjusted $R^2 = 0.74$ F(6,15) = 8.42 JBN–χ^2(2) = 0.08 LM–χ^2(6) = 6.25

ARCH–χ^2(1) = 0.01 RESET(2)–F(1,14) = 0.13 CHOW–F(9,13) = 1.75

The following notations have been used:

NT = nontradable sector value added, CONS = construction sector value added, RER = RER for export sector, GEX = total government expenditure, OP = openness in trade regime, DA = domestic absorption, GI= government investment expenditure.

Notes:

1. Figures in parentheses are t-statistics.
2. The F statistic is against the null that all coefficients = 0. The Durbin Watson for first order serial correlation is not reported for these models since it is not strictly valid in these models with lagged dependent variables. The lagged error correction terms are statistically significant at the 5 per cent level and have the expected negative signs.
3. LM is the Lagrange multiplier general test for residual serial correlation. ARCH is the test for Autoregressive Heteroscedasticity, RESET is the Ramsey's RESET test for functional mis-specification, residual normality test for skewness and excess kurtosis is given by Jarque Bera Normality test.

Manufacturing sector

A 1-per-cent depreciation of the RER led to a significant expansion of manufacturing output by 0.45 per cent in the long term, as real depreciation made the sector more competitive by raising the relative price of tradables to nontradables. Increased openness also increased output of the manufacturing sector significantly in the long term. As predicted by the theoretical model, a 1-per-cent increase in openness increases manufacturing output by 0.32 per cent in the long term.

Table 5.3
Estimates of long-term elasticities of sectoral growth, 1970–94

Independent variables	Agri-culture	Manu-facturing	Mining	NT	Con-struction
GEX	−0.38** (2.25)				
OP	0.21** (2.82)	0.32 (1.96) *			
GI					1.02** (5.07)
DA		1.48** (2.65)		0.29* (1.83)	0.16** (3.42)
RER2	0.20** (2.64)	0.45** (2.19)	0.65** (2.79)	−0.18** (4.21)	−0.30 (1.32)

Note: Figures in parentheses are t-statistics. ** denotes significant at 1% , * denotes significant at 5 %.

Source: Computed from the long run steady state solutions to the estimated models reported in Table 5.1 and 5.2. All equations passed the Chow tests for parameter stability as the computed F-values of Chow-test are insignificant.

Domestic absorption, net of government expenditure, significantly increased manufacturing output in the short term and it also has a significant positive effect on long term output growth of the manufacturing sector, due to an expansion of aggregate demand. A 1-per-cent increase in domestic absorption increased manufacturing output by 0.67 per cent in the short term and 1.48 per cent in the long term.

Mineral sector
The impact of the RER on the mineral sector was positive and significant in the short term, as well as in the long term (Table 5.3). Increased export prices relative to the domestic price level raise profitability and output of the sector. A 1-per-cent depreciation of the RER increases output of the mineral sector by 1.11 per cent in the short term and 0.65 per cent in the long term.

Nontradable sector
The effects of a resources boom on PNG's nontradable sector supports the theoretical proposition that a depreciation of the real exchange rate significantly

reduces profitability and output of the nontradable sector. A 1-per-cent depreciation of the real exchange rate reduced output of the nontradable sector by 0.18 per cent in the long term. But an increase in domestic absorption raised demand and prices for domestic nontradable goods and services as well as significantly raised output of the sector, in the short term by 0.43 per cent and by 0.29 per cent in the long term.

Construction sector
In an attempt to extend the analysis of the consequences of the RER on the nontradable capital market, an ECM was estimated on the nontradable construction sector. The econometric results support the prediction of the theoretical model since a depreciation of the RER significantly lowered the output of the construction sector by 0.87 per cent in the short term. But the impact of the RER becomes insignificant in the long term. As predicted by the 'construction boom' theory, over the study period increased domestic absorption stimulated the construction sector of PNG significantly as increased demand for domestically produced goods raised the level of construction activities. A 1-per-cent increase in domestic absorption increased construction output by 0.16 per cent in the long term. Finally the results indicate increased government investment significantly increased the output of the construction sector in the long term by more than a one-to-one basis. A 1-per-cent increase in government investment increased construction output by 1.02 per cent in the long term. This result reflects the occurrences of construction booms associated with government investment in the PNG economy over the past two and a half decades.

5.5   Investment and Saving Behaviour in Papua New Guinea

This section examines the determinants of domestic savings behaviour in the PNG economy. The possible repercussion of various macroeconomic policies on long-term growth reflecting changes in savings behaviour of the PNG economy over the past two and a half decades are discussed. The econometric results of the savings functions are evaluated in Chapter 6 while discussing the savings and investment performance of the economy in response to resources booms in detail.

5.5.1   Determinants of Savings: Theory and Hypothesis

The traditional analysis of the relationship between growth and savings stems from the analysis of the impact of domestic savings on investment, which subsequently transforms into higher growth. Although investment levels determine short-run growth, the effect of investment on long-term growth is controversial. Orthodox (neoclassical) economists believe that there is no correlation between investment and long-term growth. Long-term growth of a country may be influenced by various determinants, which are totally independent of public policy choices with respect to investment. The most important determinants of long-term growth of a nation are stated to be education, a skilled labour force, research and training, population growth and an exogenously given rate of technological progress. Thus, increased public spending on health, education and research and development enhances human capital formation, which can greatly influence a country's output growth.

There is a growing body of literature based on endogenous growth theory (Romer, 1986; Lucas, 1988) which attributes long-term growth to changes in the savings rate – contrasting with the neoclassical model where long-term growth is driven by the exogenous rate of technological change and changes in the savings rate have only a level effect in the long term. However, attempts have been made to develop theoretical foundations and empirical support for the view that higher levels of savings and the related quality of investment are also critical determinants of long-term growth.

There is a sizeable body of theoretical and empirical literature on the determinants of savings behaviour. Different authors have dealt with specific aspects of savings including the effects of interest rates, inflation and financial retardation, on the one hand, to the contribution of social security and political stability, on the other. Because of the vast theoretical complexity and different policy objectives, no one single model has been able to deal with the entire spectrum of the effects of savings behaviour on a country (Edwards, 1996).

Private sector savings behaviour is essentially an intertemporal choice, that is, current consumption vs. future consumption (savings). There is ample theoretical work, which has captured the intertemporal optimisation of the savings function. In the rest of the section, some major determining factors and policy issues such as real interest rate, growth rate of GDP, changes in TOT, inflation, development in the financial system and foreign savings affecting the savings behaviour of PNG over the past two and a half decades will be discussed.

Real Interest Rate: The role of interest rates on savings is possibly the most controversial and broadly discussed topic on economic policy reforms in both developed and developing countries. In Keynesian monetary theory, income is considered to be the prime mover of savings. But the substitution and income effects of a given change in interest rates may work in opposite directions. The increased interest rate has 'secondary and relatively unimportant' effects on consumption postulated by early Keynesian theory (Keynes, 1936, p. 94). On the other hand, the Keynesian accelerator effect shows a positive impact from changes in income on capital accumulation. In a recent discussion on the subject Gylfason (1993) showed that the savings response to increased interest rates primarily depends on the strengths of substitution and wealth effects. The neoclassical model of investment assumes the cost of capital affects the desired capital stock in the same way expected output does, so that an artificially low interest rate can generate profit and promote investment. Until the 1970s, interest rate policies in developing countries were primarily guided by the neoclassical view that the interest rate should be kept low in order to accelerate capital accumulation.

In the early 1970s, McKinnon (1973) and Shaw (1973) forcefully attacked the low interest rate policy in developing countries. They argued that in the absence of a developed market in stocks and bonds, a low interest rate policy to stimulate investment is not consistent in typical developing countries where self-financing and bank loans are the major sources of investible funds. Since portfolio choices are limited in these developing economies, savings behaviour tends to be highly money intensive, and a low interest rate policy impacts adversely on aggregate savings and investment by increasing current consumption. The McKinnon-Shaw proposition indicates that financial repression retards economic growth by reducing capital accumulation in the economy, which is subsequently emphasised by their financial liberalisation hypothesis. A number of recent empirical studies on rapidly growing East Asian economies suggest a positive impact from financial institutional development and high interest elasticity of savings (Fry 1980, 1988; Fry and Mason 1981).

Many have challenged the views of McKinnon-Shaw on financial repression on savings. The neo-structuralist development economists (Taylor 1983, 1988; van Wijnbergen 1982) criticised the McKinnon-Shaw proposition, arguing that high interest rates on bank deposits may generate a 'financial crowding out' by shifting the portfolio away from other assets in the household asset portfolio towards bank deposits with higher interest rates which may reduce the net increase in total savings (Athukorala, 1998). A large number of empirical studies on both developed and developing countries have failed to find any significant positive effect on domestic savings due to interest rate changes. Giovannini (1983) cast serious doubt on the view that the interest elasticity of savings is significantly positive for developing countries, finding that there was no significant positive impact of higher interest rates on domestic savings for seven Asian countries. Interestingly, other studies suggest a relaxation in borrowing constraints, due to financial reform programmes, reduces savings rates. Using cross-country data for some developed economies, Jappelli and Pagano (1994) found support for this view. Schmidt-Hebbel et al. (1992) also found that household savings behaviour is negatively related to the relaxation of borrowing constraints for a group of developing countries. McKinnon (1991, p. 22) also acknowledges that aggregate savings does not respond strongly to a higher interest rate. Thus, the effect of an increased interest rate on savings behaviour is still clouded with mists of ambiguity and controversy, which prompted both analysts and policy makers to consider alternative policy mechanisms for encouraging savings.

Income Growth: The growth rate of GDP positively influences savings behaviour by increasing overall income of a country. In a life-cycle setting, Modigliani (1970) argued that income growth has a positive impact on private savings. Using detailed household level data, Carroll and Weil (1993) also found support for the positive effect of income growth on private savings. Recent higher savings performance by East Asian countries provides the evidence of the positive influence of income growth on savings behaviour bringing subsequent higher growth in these countries. The expected positive influence of GDP growth on savings behaviour also indicates consumption smoothing behaviour. Ogaki et al. (1994) argue that the degree of intertemporal substitution is a function of per capita income, which is supported to a large extent by their empirical results.

Terms of Trade: Change in a country's TOT can also affect savings behaviour, through real income losses or gains brought about by changes in the price of foreign goods in terms of domestic goods. Theoretically, TOT changes are part of real GDP. However, price deflators generally do not capture price structural effects on the level and growth of real income due to changes in the TOT. Thus changes in the TOT can be expected to have an additional effect to that of changes in GDP on savings (Ady, 1976). In general, an improvement in TOT has a positive impact on private savings, which reflects intertemporal consumption smoothing by the private sector in response to a temporary TOT shock. However, the effect of TOT can go in the opposite direction, depending on whether the changes in TOT are perceived to be temporary or permanent. An improvement in TOT perceived to be temporary, may lead to an increase in savings so as to keep real expenditure constant. By the same reasoning, households reduce savings when faced with a permanent improvement in TOT.

Inflation: Inflation, as a measure of macroeconomic stability, can also exert an important influence on the savings behaviour of an economy. Increased inflation, representing economic instability, tends to have a negative impact on the savings rate. Another view of the adverse impact of high inflation finds support in the theoretical work of McKinnon and Shaw's 'financial repression'. During a period of high inflation, where government pegs nominal interest ceilings, a large withdrawal of funds from the banking sector occurs due to the lower real interest rates. This reduces household savings and increases consumption. Thus, financial repression, and lower real interest rates, results in an inefficient allocation of funds for productive investment in the absence of market price rationing (Giovannini, 1983). However, if consumers attempt to maintain a target rate of consumption to wealth, or liquid asset to income, the anticipated inflation may increase household savings.

Foreign Savings: The open economy model incorporates two perspectives to savings analysis. First, in an open economy, agents can use foreign savings (borrowing) to smooth consumption through time. Secondly, domestic and foreign interest rate differentials induce capital inflow. Foreign savings, induced either by a higher domestic interest rate relative to foreign interest rates or through borrowing, can act as a substitute for domestic savings and increases both private and public consumption. Thus, the coefficient on the foreign saving variable in the private saving function measures the degree of substitutability between foreign savings (or current account deficit) and the national private and/or total domestic savings (Edwards, 1996). The estimated coefficient of this variable would be negative if foreign savings crowd out private savings.

5.5.2 The Model

In an attempt to capture the key hypotheses, two savings functions have been estimated separately for a total domestic savings function and a private savings function for PNG. A separate private savings function was estimated to show the contrast with a total savings function where public savings is a significant element in total savings. Edwards (1996) showed that the process of determination of public and private savings could be significantly different, especially when the political stability of a country is in question.

The behavioural relationships of the savings functions are specified as follows:

$$\Delta PS = f(\Delta GY, \Delta IR, \Delta TOT, \Delta INF, \Delta FS, \Delta FD, DS, GY_{t-1},$$
$$IR_{t-1}, TOT_{t-1}, INF_{t-1}, FS_{t-1}, FD_{t-1}, PS_{t-1}) \dots \dots \dots \quad (5.12)$$

$$\Delta TDS = f(\Delta GY, \Delta IR, \Delta TOT, \Delta INF, \Delta FS, \Delta FD, DS, GY_{t-1},$$
$$IR_{t-1}, TOT_{t-1}, INF_{t-1}, FS_{t-1}, FD_{t-1}, TDS_{t-1}) \dots \dots \dots \quad (5.13)$$

The following notations have been used in the above equations (with expected signs of the regression coefficient in parentheses):

Dependent Variables:
- TDS = total gross domestic savings
- PS = domestic private savings

Independent Variables:
- GY (+) = growth rate of GDP;
- IR (+ or −) = real interest rate on time deposit;
- TOT (+ or −) = terms of trade;
- INF (−) = expected rate of inflation proxies by the rate of inflation with one year lag used as a measure of macroeconomic stability;
- FS (+ or −) = foreign savings in billion kina;
- FD (+) = financial institutional development, measured as the ratio of broad money to GDP; and
- DS = a dummy variable which takes value of 1 for boom years (1972–74, 1976–77, 1991–94) and 0 for other years. The dummy variable (DS) is included to capture the effects of broad policy responses during the boom years of the PNG economy.

The model was estimated over the sample period 1970–94 using annual data. Data on total gross domestic savings were taken from The World Bank, *World Tables* 1994 and deflated by the GDP deflator (1990=100). Private savings were estimated by subtracting the government savings from the total domestic savings. Government savings is the difference between government revenue and operating expenditure.

Foreign savings are defined as equivalent to the current account deficit (sign revised) to GDP. Due to unavailability of data on depreciation allowances, gross rather that net saving is used. All variables are measured at 1990 prices. Except for foreign savings, the real interest rate and the expected rate of inflation, all variables are measured in natural logarithms.

In line with standard practice in modern time series econometrics, testing the time series properties of the data series began the estimation process. The order of integration for every variable used in the model has been tested by the Dickey-Fuller and Augmented Dickey-Fuller tests, with results reported in the Appendix Table A5.1. Since a number of key variables are non-stationary, the general to specific Hendry-type Error Correction Model building methodology was employed as in the previous chapter to guard against estimating spurious regression relationship whilst retaining long-term information.

The above equations were 'tested down' using OLS by dropping statistically insignificant differenced and lagged terms. The testing procedure continued until a parsimonious error correction representation was obtained which retains the *a priori* theoretical model as its long-term solution. The selection of final equations was made after careful diagnostic check tests on the OLS error process.

5.5.3   Results

The estimated savings equations are presented in Table 5.4. The long-term elasticities of explanatory variables, which are computed from the steady state solutions from estimated equations in Table 5.4, are presented in Table 5.5.

The results are generally statistically satisfactory and consistent with the theory. Both equations pass the F-test for overall fit at a 1-per-cent significance level. The adjusted R^2 for each equation suggests the model has a good fit. A residual correlogram up to six years indicates no significant serial correlation in the error terms. The Lagrange multiplier LM–χ^2 test for residual serial correlation also indicated no serial correlation in residuals. The ARCH–χ^2 test for error variance shows that in all models the computed values of ARCH–$\chi^2(1)$ are smaller than the tabulated value at a 1-per-cent significance level. Thus, the computed statistics suggest error variances are not correlated in the equations. Ramsey's RESET test for specification error indicates the equations are not mis-specified. Some of the variables, such as financial development and dummy variable for policy measures during the boom years were found to be consistently statistically insignificant for both private and total savings in the experimental runs and dropped from the final equations.

A common practice in the literature on the determination of savings has been to impose an income homogeneity assumption on coefficient estimates. That is, other things being equal, savings are proportional to income. In reality, income and savings may not always move in the same direction and also may not change by the same proportion. Hence, an income homogeneity assumption may distort coefficient estimates (Athukorala, 1998). As the coefficient of income in the restricted model

Table 5.4
Determinants of savings in Papua New Guinea, 1970–94

Private savings (Equation 5.12)

$$\Delta PS = -14.4 + 1.86\ \Delta GY - 0.75\ \Delta FS + 0.94\ \Delta TOT + 1.54\ GY_{t-1} - 0.11\ IR_{t-1}$$
$$\qquad\qquad (4.27)\qquad (3.22)\qquad (2.97)\qquad (4.70)\qquad\ (4.98)$$

$$-1.09\ INF_{t-1} - 0.12\ FS_{t-1} - 0.90\ PS_{t-1}$$
$$\ \ (2.52)\qquad (2.89)\qquad\ (4.36)$$

Adjusted $R^2 = 0.86$ F(9,13) = 12.1 JBN–$\chi^2(2) = 1.59$ LM–$\chi^2(6) = 1.08$

ARCH–$\chi^2(1) = 0.001$ RESET(2)–F(1,12) = 0.01 CHOW–F(11,11) = 0.65

Total domestic savings (Equation 5.13)

$$\Delta TDS = -22.93 + 1.47\ \Delta GY - 0.84\ \Delta FS + 1.22\ \Delta TOT + 1.94\ GY_{t-1} - 0.14\ IR_{t-1}$$
$$\qquad\qquad (2.30)\qquad (2.47)\qquad (2.56)\qquad (3.62)\qquad\ (3.67)$$

$$-1.93\ INF_{t-1} - 0.14\ FS_{t-1} - 0.90\ TDS_{t-1}$$
$$\ \ (1.85)\qquad (2.38)\qquad\ (3.67)$$

Adjusted $R^2 = 0.74$ F(9,13) = 8.4 JBN–$\chi^2(2) = 2.52$ LM–$\chi^2(6) = 7.13$

ARCH–$\chi^2(1) = 0.03$ RESET(2)–F(1,12) = 0.08 CHOW–F(11,11) = 1.61

Notes:
1. Figures in parentheses are t-statistics.
2. The F statistic is against the null that all coefficients = 0. The Durbin Watson for first order serial correlation is not reported for these models since it is not strictly valid in these models with lagged dependent variables. The lagged error correction terms are statistically significant at the 5-per-cent level and have the expected negative signs.
3. LM is the Lagrange multiplier general test for residual serial correlation. ARCH is the test for Autoregressive Heteroscedasticity, RESET is the Ramsey's RESET test for functional mis-specification, residual normality test for skewness and excess kurtosis is given by Jarque Bera Normality test.

The following notations have been used in the private and total domestic savings equations: PS = private savings, TDS = total domestic savings, FS = foreign savings, GY = growth of real GDP, IR= real interest rate, INF = expected rate of inflation.

Table 5.5
Estimates of long-term elasticities of savings functions

	Explanatory variables			
	GY	INF	IR	FS
PS	1.72*	−1.22*	−0.13**	−1.34**
	(5.17)	(2.36)	(4.92)	(5.57)
TDS	2.16**	−2.15**	−0.15**	−1.54**
	(4.73)	(2.16)	(4.68)	(4.27)

Notes: Figures in parentheses are t-statistics. ** denotes significant at 1% and * denotes significant at 5%.

Source: Computed from the long-term steady state solutions to the estimated models reported in Table 5.4.

of savings functions with income homogeneity assumption is not statistically significant for PNG, the equations are estimated without imposing any restrictions on the parameters.

Growth in real GDP shows a very strong positive effect on savings behaviour, both in short as well as in long-term savings behaviour. A 1-per-cent increase in real GDP in PNG increased private and total domestic savings more than 1 per cent in short term, and increased private savings by 1.7 per cent and total savings by 2.2 per cent in the long term.

The coefficient of foreign savings is significantly negative for both private and aggregate domestic savings, indicating that both in the short term and in the long term, foreign savings crowd out PNG's private as well as total domestic savings. As foreign savings fell, indicated by a rise in the current account balance to GDP, private savings increased by 0.75 per cent in the short term and 1.34 per cent in the long term.

Increased foreign savings also substituted the total domestic savings of PNG by 0.8 per cent in the short term and 1.5 per cent in the long term.

The coefficient of TOT suggests a positive short-term impact for improvement in TOT on PNG's savings behaviour. A 1-per-cent increase in TOT induced a 0.9-per-cent increase in private savings and a 1.22-per-cent increase in total domestic savings in the short term. However, there is no statistically significant long-term TOT impact on the savings behaviour of PNG. This result is consistent with the hypothesis of consumption smoothing behaviour.

An increase in the real interest rate significantly lowered both private and total savings in PNG. It seems that the negative income effect overweighted the positive substitution effect of increased interest rates (Dornbusch and Reynoso, 1989). As indicated by Giovannini (1985), in a life cycle hypothesis setting, the 'consumption profile' of an individual does not change with change in the real interest rate. The interest elasticity of savings tends to be negative in the steady state for a developing country like PNG. In the long term a 1-per-cent increase in the real interest rate is associated with a 0.13-per-cent reduction in private savings and 0.15 per cent for total savings.

Increased inflation erodes the real value of wealth, and has a negative impact on household savings, given a constant consumption level. It has been found in many studies that inflation induces the withdrawal of deposits from the banking system, increasing current consumption and reducing savings. PNG's private savings are also found to have been negatively affected by higher inflation over the study period. The inflation rate, used as the measure of macroeconomic stability, is found to have a significant negative impact on private and total savings behaviour in PNG in the short term. In the long term, a 1-per-cent increase in inflation significantly reduced private savings by 1.2 per cent and total savings by about 2.1 per cent.

5.6　Summary and Conclusion

This chapter examines both the impact of RER movements on sectoral transformation of the PNG economy over the past two and half decades, and the macroeconomic policy responses on long-term growth, by estimating the total (private and public) and private savings function of the economy.

As predicted by theory, a depreciation of the RER is found to be positive for tradable sectors and negative for the nontradable sectors. A real depreciation stimulates the output of the tradable sector whereas increased government consumption on nontradables reduces the output of agricultural sector by increasing the demand and price for domestic nontradables. It is also found that government expenditure in the form of investment increases the output of the nontradable construction sector. The econometric results indicate that increased domestic absorption raises the output of agriculture, manufacturing and nontradable sectors whereas it adversely affects the output of the mineral sector in this study. Increases in domestic absorption and government investment demand have expansionary effects on the nontradable construction sector whereas a depreciation of the RER reduces the size of the sector.

The econometric results relate into TOT variable support the theoretical proposition of intertemporal consumption smoothing behaviour of the country. The findings also suggest that while an increase in the interest rate and inflation lowers private savings and total domestic savings, foreign savings substitute for both private and total savings in the short as well as in the long term.

Notes

1   A negative sign of real exchange rate in relation to other variables indicates a real appreciation, whereas a positive sign for the real exchange rate in relation to other variables means a real depreciation.
2   The results are, however, robust to the use of the other two real exchange rate measures (RER1, RER3).

6

Impact of Major Resources Booms
in Papua New Guinea

6.1   Introduction

This chapter examines the nature and impact of major resources booms and internal policy responses in relation to growth and the sectoral composition of output, and savings behaviour of the PNG economy. Only major positive shocks in the form of resources booms and their consequences on the PNG economy are analysed over the study period of 1970–94. The objective of this discussion is to analyse whether the available empirical evidence of resources booms in PNG substantiates the theoretical predictions of the framework of the study postulated in Chapter 2. This chapter also examines the PNG government's responses to these resources booms, in the short as well as the long term. Sections 2–9 identify the major resources booms in PNG during the 1970s and the first half of the 1990s, together with overall policy responses, and their sectoral impact on the economic performance of the PNG economy over the past two and a half decades; Section 10 discusses the long-term policy impact on savings and investment behaviour; and Section 11 provides a summary.

6.2   The Major Resources Booms: 1971–77

PNG experienced three major resources booms in the 1970s. The first was an upsurge in investment associated with the construction of the Bougainville Copper Mine, and can be termed as an 'investment boom' during the financial years[1] 1971 and 1972. The Bougainville Copper Mine belongs to Bougainville Copper Ltd. (BCL), a Papua New Guinean mining company, which is 53 per cent owned by Rio Tinto, a company dual-listed in the United Kingdom and Australia. The second boom was a sharp increase in minerals production and exports by the BCL mine which coincided with increasing world copper prices and generated a massive foreign revenue income for the economy during 1973–74. The third boom originated from increased supply from the agricultural and non-mineral exportable sectors induced by higher prices for agricultural commodities during 1976–77.

6.2.1   BCL Investment Boom 1971–72

Construction of the Bougainville Copper Mine brought the first major investment boom to the PNG economy. PNG experienced major foreign capital investment flow in the early 1970s from the Bougainville Copper Project amounting to approximately A$400 million. During the construction period of the Panguna mine of BCL, a massive capital inflow of K223 million in 1971 and K212 million in 1972 was recorded. During these two financial years, BCL accounted for nearly 72 per cent of all fixed capital formation in the country. Thus, 1971 marked the beginning of the *'BCL investment boom'* as investment in the construction sector grew at the rate of 62 per cent from the previous year's level.

During the height of BCL construction, the growth rate of gross domestic investment was striking, increasing from 35 per cent of GDP in 1970 to about 47 per cent of GDP in 1971. Total (private and government) consumption increased from K410.0 million in 1968 to K614.5 million in 1972. Export value also increased at a rate of above 26 per cent of GDP in 1971. Imports increased substantially from the previous years and capital goods constituted the major share of imports.

Adjustment towards new economic activities in 1972 was influenced by a number of internal and external factors. Among them, a sharp increase in the world price for major export commodities and a substantial revenue flow from overseas sales of mineral ore by BCL, were the major factors altering the sectoral composition of the PNG economy during this period.

6.2.2   Mineral Boom: 1973–74

The growth rate of approximately 28 per cent in the monetised sector between 1972 and 1973 was wholly contributed by the increased production of mineral (copper and gold) ore from BCL. The mine came into full production at a time when the world prices for copper and gold were rising. The Bougainville mine contributed about 20 per cent of the monetised sector's GDP in 1972, 28 per cent in 1973 and 32 per cent in 1974 (Table 6.1). The increase in the export price index during 1973 outweighed the increase in the import price index and brought an average annual change in the TOT index of 25.6 per cent and 30.2 per cent in 1973 and 1974, respectively, and contributed significantly to export revenue earnings. Thus, 1973 can be marked as the first *'mineral boom'* in PNG.

The share of exports to GDP increased significantly after the mine went into production in April 1972. The growth in total export revenue was four-fold over the first four financial years of the 1970s, increasing from K101.7 million in 1971 to K363.5 million in 1974. The BCL mine alone contributed about 50 per cent of total export revenue in 1973. The export value of minerals accounted for 63 per cent of total merchandise export receipts in 1973. The import share of consumer goods, fuels and petroleum also increased rapidly during 1973.

Table 6.1
Bougainville Copper Mine's impact on monetised sector GDP, 1968–74
(kina million at 1968 constant prices)

Year	1968	1969	1970	1971	1972	1973	1974
Gross fixed investment	85	91	172	251	204	99	75
BCL	na	20	90	180	130	20	20
Percentage of total	na	22	52	72	64	22	27
Export of goods and NFS	77	87	97	111	151	308	363
BCL	na	na	na	na	20	150	174
Percentage of total	na	na	na	na	13	49	48
Imports of goods and NFS	165	184	262	328	309	237	226
BCL	na	10	77	146	85	25	20
Percentage of total	na	5	29	45	28	11	9
GDP in Monetised sector	309	326	376	431	441	555	568
BCL	na	5	39	70	90	155	183
Percentage of total	na	2	10	16	20	28	32

Note: na = not applicable
Source: World Bank (1976) Report No. 1150-PNG, Table 2.6, p. 24.

6.2.3   Commodity Boom: 1976–77

Another major boom in PNG economy that began after the national independence, in September 1975 and monetary independence in January 1976, can be marked as the 'agricultural commodity boom'. This boom originated from the increased supply of agricultural and other non-mineral exportable sectors which was supported by favourable world market prices for PNG's primary commodities. The nature and impact of this boom was substantially different from the other major booms as the effects of this boom demonstrate dissimilar changes in relative prices, sectoral growth and income distribution patterns in PNG.

The pattern of income distribution between PNG nationals and expatriates changed during this boom. Papua New Guineans were the major beneficiaries of this boom as they became the direct recipients of an increasing share of income from cash crops exports. As the majority of the PNG population was involved with the agricultural sector for subsistence, most of cash crops which had been dominated by expatriates before independence were now produced under the ownership of local people. The amount of GDP directly accruing to PNG nationals grew at about 10 per cent per annum, in real terms, between 1973/74 and 1981 (Garnaut and Baxter, 1984, p. 66).

Excluding copper concentrate, the export price index for all commodities greatly increased between late 1976 and early 1978. Table 6.2 indicates that the TOT improved significantly by 20.6 per cent in 1976 and 22.2 per cent in 1977, from a negative 54.7 per cent in 1975. From the September quarter of 1976 the value of PNG's exports grew strongly, largely attributable to buoyant prices for cash crops, particularly coffee and cocoa. The value of PNG's exports continued to rise, mainly due to higher volume of coffee exports, together with increases in the volume of copper ore and concentrates and other agricultural export commodities.

During 1976, the export value of coffee increased dramatically to K132.62 million, almost a four-fold increase compared to K33.55 million in 1975. The large export receipts contributed by coffee exports were influenced by the high world market price (the export price index of coffee rose by 189 per cent during 1976) and the higher volume (about 35-per-cent increase from the 1975 level) of coffee exported during this year.

6.3   Policy Response

Since PNG did not achieve national independence until 1975, it could not pursue independent policy fully to counteract any revenue and price instability in the economy brought about by BCL investment and mineral booms between 1971 and 1974. During the first half of the 1970s, PNG relied heavily on budgetary support from Australia to cover the major part of government expenditure since it was part of the Australian monetary system.

The second half of the 1970s will be remembered as the legacy of prudent and successful macroeconomic policy implementation by a PNG government. The

Table 6.2
Trade indices of Papua New Guinea, 1972–79
(1977=100)

	1972	1973	1974	1975	1976	1977	1978	1979
Export price index	51.0	64.9	98.0	61.4	75.3	100.0	88.4	119.7
Import price index/a	55.8	56.5	65.4	90.5	92.1	100.0	118.3	135.5
Terms of trade index	91.6	115.0	149.8	67.8	81.8	100.0	74.7	88.3
% change in TOT index	7.5	25.5	30.3	–54.7	20.6	22.2	–25.3	18.2

Source: World Bank (1981) Report No. 3544a-PNG.

following measures considerably reduced the impact of fluctuating world prices and other uncertainties on producers and the budget.

6.3.1 Fiscal Policy

The fiscal response to the *'investment'* and *'mineral'* booms in the early 1970s was expansionary. As seen from Table 6.3, government expenditure grew substantially. From 1971 to 1975, current expenditure to GDP increased by 30.3 per cent, dominated by wages and salaries (45 to 50 per cent of total) and purchase of goods and services (35 to 40 per cent of total). Capital expenditure shows a declining trend over the same period.

Total revenue increased from 74.2 million in 1971 to 136.7 in 1974 with a 49-per-cent increase in tax revenue and 235-per-cent increase in non-tax revenue (Appendix Table A6.1). The large increase in government revenue over these four years was contributed mainly by the big boost in income and profit, dividends, and royalties from the operation of the BCL mine. The contribution of personal income tax accounted for 30 per cent, while import duties accounted for 28 per cent of total revenue collection.

As predicted by the booming sector literature, government spending increased sharply during the boom years. The phenomenal increase in government expenditure increased the demand and price for nontradables and reduced the price of tradables relative to nontradables bringing a real appreciation in PNG's exchange rate.

To deal with the downturn in the PNG mineral sector in 1973–74, the government established the Mineral Resources Stabilisation Fund (MRSF) in 1974 to smooth out the impact of large export revenue flows on the budget and the domestic price level.

Table 6.3
Central government revenues and expenditures, 1971–77
(percentage share of GDP)

Share of GDP (%)	1971	1972	1973	1974	1975	1976	1977
Total revenue	11.9	13.2	11.8	13.1	17.9	20.6	17.9
Tax revenue	9.9	11.1	9.4	9.1	13.4	16.7	12.1
Non-tax revenue	2.0	2.1	2.4	4.0	4.5	3.9	3.0
Total expenditure	32.9	36.2	31.7	29.5	37.3	38.8	32.7
Current expenditure	26.1	30.0	27.1	26.6	34.0	34.6	29.0
Capital expenditure	6.8	6.2	4.6	2.9	3.3	4.3	3.7

Source: Constructed from World Bank(1976) Report No. 1150-PNG Table 4.2 and 4.4, and World Bank (1981) Report No. 3544a-PNG Table 5.2 and 5.6.

Payments into the MRSF come only from large scale mining projects (until then, only BCL) revenues, with funds subsequently transferred into consolidated revenue to produce a steady flow into each year's budget.

Between 1975/76 and 1980, the MRSF built up reserves in years of exceptionally large mining revenues (1974 and 1980) and ran them down again in years of exceptionally low revenues (1976 and 1978). In 1978, when mineral related receipts dropped by 60 per cent, the flow of funds out of the MRSF fell by less than half yet still contributed 12 per cent of domestic revenue. The MRSF, as a major policy tool of the PNG government, worked successfully to reduce the instability of the internal economic balance until the late 1980s.

Commodity Price Stabilisation Funds (CPSF) operated by the commodity board for three major export crops (copra, coffee and cocoa) also stabilised the prices along a moving long-term average price trend. At the end of 1980, these funds held K160 million and were preparing to pay bounties to producers to compensate for falling commodity prices.

During the agricultural boom, PNG pursued pragmatic economic policies. During 1976–77, the government implemented reductions in real expenditure. Central government expenditure fell 14 per cent as a share of GDP in 1977, from its 1975 level, as financial management focused on the requirements of stability and a deliberate reduction in Australian aid and budgetary grants. In 1977, capital expenditures rose about 41 per cent from the 1975 level, whereas current expenditures grew only 6 per cent between 1975 and 1977 (Appendix Table A6.1).

Over the 1975–77 period, real public consumption expenditure fell by more than 22 per cent and the total real public expenditure fell by slightly less than 9 per cent. A National Public Expenditure Plan (NPEP) was introduced in 1978 to facilitate careful allocation of increases in government expenditure in the light of national priorities. A target of a 3-per-cent increase in real expenditure for goods and services was implemented successfully during 1978–79. The NPEP was also successful in raising the share of capital expenditure in the budget to about 20 per cent before 1980. The Government's fiscal revenue effort also increased significantly during the second half of the 1970s. Since independence, every budget had included new sources of revenues and steadily reduced the reliance on Australian budgetary support.

Another noticeable influence on economic stability was the steady reduction of Australian aid since 1976. In 1976, the two governments reached an agreement on a five-year aid package in which Australia undertook a policy to provide a minimum annual grant of A$180 million, with annual supplements to be determined on a year to year basis. This arrangement was a great improvement over the previous system which had sometimes resulted in serious disparities between expected and actual assistance. Between 1975 and 1977 Australian aid fell 17 per cent per annum in US dollar terms (Appendix Table A3.7). The 1976 agreement also opened the way for the development of the NPEP based on a steady growth of government spending. Since the level of aid was specified in Australian dollars, devaluation of the Australian dollar, and several revaluations by PNG, further reduced the value of aid to PNG over the period until 1980.

Overall, real government spending up to 1979 reflected macroeconomic prudence. The econometric investigation of RER determinants in Chapter 4 confirms that a reduction in foreign aid and government expenditure improves the competitiveness of an economy. It is clear that, during 1976–77, tight government budgets and reduced reliance on foreign aid helped maintain a stable domestic price level and prevented RER appreciation.

6.3.2   Monetary Policy

Policy instruments for maintaining a stable monetary system have been strengthened since independence, as the monetised sector expanded and the financial system became more developed.

Under the influence of a large balance of payments surplus, the money supply grew 49 per cent in 1976 and 54 per cent in 1977 from K186 million in 1975 to K428 million in 1977, contributed by increased income in the stabilisation funds for coffee, cocoa and copra growers. This large increase in the money supply in 1976 and 1977 also indicated the growing reliance in monetary policy.

The CPSF, which were set up to stabilise prices to producers, also helped dampen the effects of commodity price cycles on the domestic money supply, since the majority of their assets was held in the Central Bank. The CPSF reduced monetary instability as they developed substantial reserves between 1976 and 1979 when export prices were exceptionally high. About 60 per cent of these reserves were deposited in the Central Bank. The remaining 40 per cent deposited in the trading banks was available to support increased bank lending and thereby increased the money supply. The disbursements from the deposits held with the BPNG had reduced the monetary contraction associated with low export prices.

During 1976 to 1979, the stance of monetary policy was more or less passive. Domestic interest rates remained steady and were generally below international levels. From the early 1980s, there was a shift towards a more active and interventionist monetary policy.

6.3.3   Trade Policy

In the early years after Independence, PNG maintained a very open trade policy regime with primary reliance on market forces to promote industrialisation. During the 1970s, established firms experienced very little government interference in the form of quantitative trade restriction. Until the early 1980s, taxes on international transactions were low and generally comprised of a low and uniform import tax. No import bans or quotas were imposed although some interventions were made on an ad hoc basis to protect certain infant industries such as flour, poultry and animal feed (World Bank, 1981). Capital goods and raw materials were exempted from tariffs. Duties on manufacturing goods ranged between 10–18 per cent. A basic levy of 2.5 per cent was imposed on most imported goods, except for medicine and basic foods, and a tariff of up to 50 per cent was imposed on luxury goods. Given the lack of clear policy objectives, the impact of these ad hoc trade policy measures is not clear (World Bank, 1981).

Export taxes on primary products were set at 2.5 per cent. An export incentive scheme and tariff draw back system was also available during the 1970s for manufactured export industries. As a result of improved agricultural export prices, a 2.5-per-cent export tax for copra, tea and rubber was reintroduced from 1 January 1977. PNG also enjoyed duty free access for most of its primary exports to Australia, New Zealand and the EEC countries under the Lome Convention.

6.3.4   Exchange Rate Policy

In a period of rapid international inflation, the PNG government followed an exchange rate policy designed to help control imported inflation and achieved high level success in this regard as PNG's rate of inflation has been one of the lowest in the world in 1975 (Goodman et al., 1985). Because of the very high import content of most consumer goods and intermediate goods. In the absence of trade restrictions in PNG, the relative prices of goods and services within the domestic economy were determined to a large extent by the corresponding relative prices set in international markets. Allowing these relative prices to determine an efficient allocation of resources, the government used the exchange rate to influence the absolute level of domestic prices. As shown in Table 6.4, there have been a number of exchange rate changes since monetary independence. The exchange rate of the kina appreciated against most currencies except the German Mark and the Japanese Yen. Currency appreciations relative to its major trading partners, combined with measures to

Table 6.4
The foreign exchange value of kina, 1975–80
(1K = units of foreign currency)

End of period	$A	$US	YEN	DM	$NZ
1975	1.00	1.26	361	3.29	1.27
1976	1.13	1.23	317	2.90	1.30
1977	1.16	1.32	281	2.77	1.30
1978	1.26	1.45	348	2.65	1.37
1979	1.31	1.45	315	2.50	1.48
1980	1.32	1.55	315	3.50	1.63

Source: Garnaut and Baxter (1984) Table 2.1, p. 13.

prevent a real increase in wages, resulted in a rate of inflation lower than that experienced by PNG's major trading partners during the second half of the 1970s.

6.4 Effects of Resources Booms: 1972–78

It is difficult to trace the exact effects of each boom over a short period of time as prices and product markets react slowly to sudden unanticipated changes. Thus, an analysis of the effects of these three different booms, the BCL investment boom (1971–72), the mineral boom (1973–74) and the agricultural boom (1976–77) has been taken together. This gives us a much clearer picture of the consequences of these booms. The impact of these booms has been analysed in the light of the theoretical framework postulated in Chapter 2, on (1) key macroeconomic variables, (2) relative prices and (3) wages and employment.

6.4.1 Effects on Key Macroeconomic Variables

The effects of a resources boom on the key macroeconomic variables are examined by analysing the changes on the aggregate demand side of the economy. Both private and government consumption increased during 1972–74 but export growth was much larger than the growth in consumption. The fall in private consumption by expatriates in 1972 was compensated by increased consumption by locals, with final private consumption remaining at around K357 million over 1971–72 (Table 6.5). Government consumption was about 0.9 per cent higher in 1973 than the 1970 level.

Private foreign investment in the construction sector increased from A$96.9 million (K107 million) to A$414.8 million (K454 million) in 1972 at current prices. Investment spending on the BCL mine fell to A$20 million in 1972 from an average of A$100 million in the previous years (World Bank, 1976). Other private investment was much the same in money terms as in previous years. The large volume of copper production and exports by the BCL mine, contributed to a large surplus in PNG's balance of payments (BOP) in 1973.

In 1973, the trade account exhibited a surplus of K15.5 million from a deficit of K160 million in 1972. Most of this improvement was offset by the distribution of income and dividends payable to overseas shareholders plus the payment of interest and debt repayments. Nevertheless, the balance of payments on the current account improved from a deficit of K140 million in 1972 to a surplus of K42.5 million in 1973. The current and capital account surplus over 1973–74 brought a balance of payments surplus of K29.2 million in 1973 and K153.2 million 1974. The non-market primary and subsistence sector, which then accounted for 40 per cent of the economy, grew by more than 4 per cent with an output of K132 million in 1973 from K126.5 million in 1971.

Data on consumption expenditure show a declining trend in the real growth of

Table 6.5
Gross domestic expenditure, 1968–74
(at constant 1969 prices, kina million)

Key economic variables	1968	1969	1970	1971	1972	1973	1974
GDP	430.8	453.3	503.9	557.2	572.5	687.4	695.8
Market	308.9	326.1	375.6	430.7	439.7	488.3	568.4
Non-market	121.8	127.3	128.3	126.5	131.4	132.3	127.4
Consumption	425.9	453.9	488.4	508.4	519.9	494.9	483.5
Government	144.9	150.7	155.0	151.8	162.3	156.4	155.4
Private	280.8	303.2	333.4	356.6	357.6	338.5	328.1
Market	160.2	176.1	207.4	227.5	227.5	209.2	201.3
Non-market	120.6	127.1	126.0	130.1	130.1	129.3	126.8
Gross fixed capital formation	86.1	91.4	174.0	250.9	204.9	102.1	75.0
Market	84.9	91.3	171.6	250.8	203.6	99.1	74.4
Non-market	1.2	0.1	2.3	0.1	1.3	3.0	0.6
Increase in stock	7.0	6.7	5.4	14.6	8.4	9.6	0.3
Exports (goods and NFS)	77.4	86.8	96.6	110.7	149.9	252.8	363.5
Imports (goods and NFS)	164.7	184.2	261.6	328.0	309.3	237.3	226.5
Statistical discrepancy	–0.9	–1.2	1.1	0.5	–2.8	–1.8	–11.4

Note: Continued on Table 6.6.

Source: World Bank (1976) Report No. 1150-PNG.

both private and public consumption spending over the period of 1976–77 (Table 6.6). Real private consumption increased moderately but public consumption fell 22 per cent in 1977. Most private consumption expenditures were on food, beverages, cigarettes, beer and motor vehicles. During 1976/77, gross fixed capital formation grew by 23 per cent in real terms, to K113.0 million in 1977 compared with K87.5 million in 1975, mostly contributed by the private sector.

Gross domestic investment increased by 26 per cent in 1977 from its previous year's level and contributed 13 per cent to total GDP. Private investment also showed an increasing trend over the same period. Expenditure on plant, equipment and buildings increased with a very significant increase indicated for plant and equipment in the Highlands in 1976, during the December quarter. Inventory investment for raw materials and intermediate inputs and stock of finished goods also showed an increasing trend in this quarter.

Table 6.6
Gross domestic expenditure, 1975–78[a]
(at constant 1969 prices, kina million)

Key economic variables	1975	1976	1977	July–Dec 1977	1978
GDP	642.9	570.2	628.0	348.0	701.7
Market	553.9	475.3	530.4	295.5	593.9
Non-market	109.0	94.9	97.6	52.5	107.8
Consumption	543.6	511.8	494.2	277.2	492.2
Government	210.1	196.1	171.8	85.2	182.1
Private	333.5	315.7	322.4	186.0	392.1
Market	225.6	221.9	225.9	134.1	285.6
Non-market	107.9	93.8	96.5	51.9	106.5
Gross fixed capital formation	119.4	87.2	113.0	65.0	136.4
Market	118.5	86.2	111.9	64.4	135.1
Non-market	0.9	1.0	1.1	0.6	1.1
Increase in stock	22.7	16.0	16.9	7.5	22.3
Exports (goods and NFS)	274.1	213.8	270.0	170.0	294.3
Imports (goods and NFS)	287.1	251.4	263.0	161.9	318.7
Statistical discrepancy	–5.9	–6.9	–3.1	–3.9	–4.3

Note: a. Beginning in 1978, the fiscal year was changed to coincide with the calendar year.

Source: World Bank (1981) Report No. 3544a-PNG.

By industry classification, investment in primary production, building and construction, motor vehicle and machinery distribution reported strong growth. Both gross domestic savings and investment increased substantially with gross domestic investment increased from 15 per cent in 1973 to more than 22 per cent in 1978 which indicates that the boom was perceived by households as a temporary one. As a result, the agricultural boom in 1976–77 induced a subsequent construction boom, indicated by increased production in the construction and building sector, and reduced inflationary pressure on the nontradable goods market. Between 1975/76 and in 1980, the public sector's real investment doubled which was very conducive to long-term steady growth. This outcome is predicted by the theoretical propositions of a construction boom where the private sector correctly perceived the nature of a resources boom and increases investment in nontradable capitals due to imperfection in the under-developed capital market. This outcome is also verified by the econometric results of Chapter 5.

In 1977, the total value of exports increased relative to the total value of imports and brought a large current account surplus. The strong current and capital account balance during 1976–77 brought an overall balance of payments surplus of K34.6 million in 1976 followed by a huge K110.3 million in 1977. This substantially reduced PNG's net foreign indebtedness over the first four years of monetary independence.

6.4.2   Relative Price Effect

The indices of most important price series have been shown in Tables 6.7 and 6.8, indicating the relative price movements over 1970–80. The CPI shows a sharp increase in 1973. The CPI rose 5.6 per cent in 1971 followed by 3.5 per cent in 1972.

But the index rose by 31 per cent during 1973, with food components (including alcohol, tobacco and betel nuts) dominating the index. Following the sharp increase during 1973, the rate of price level increase slackened markedly from the first quarter of 1974 and the inflation rate stood at 7.5 per cent over the year. Imported inflation

Table 6.7
Changes in key price indices, 1970–80
(1970=100)

Year	CPI	PT	NEER	RER1	% change CPI	% change PT	% change NEER	% change RER1
1970	100.0	100.0	100.0	100.0	na	na	na	na
1971	105.6	102.1	99.9	96.7	5.60	2.13	−0.12	−3.28
1972	109.3	104.7	99.7	95.8	3.50	2.48	−0.22	−0.99
1973	143.3	113.0	96.3	78.9	31.11	7.97	−3.40	−17.65
1974	154.1	136.6	95.1	88.6	7.54	20.86	−1.23	12.39
1975	167.3	152.4	98.6	91.1	8.57	11.55	3.72	2.75
1976	173.6	151.3	91.7	87.1	3.77	−0.74	−7.04	−4.34
1977	174.3	159.4	91.8	91.4	0.40	5.38	0.15	4.96
1978	184.0	156.4	87.7	85.0	5.55	−1.91	−4.44	−7.07
1979	193.6	164.3	83.8	84.8	5.26	5.09	−4.46	−0.16
1980	219.5	186.3	82.9	84.9	13.38	13.40	−1.11	0.02

Notes: CPI = consumer price index, PT = price of tradables, NEER = nominal effective exchange rate, RER1= trade-weighted real exchange rate; na = not applicable.

Source: Constructed from Table 4.1.

Table 6.8
Changes in key price indices of export and import-competing industries, 1970–80 (1970=100)

Year	% change EPI	% change IPI	% change PNT	RER2	RER3	% change RER2	% change RER3
1970	na	na	na	100.0	100.0	na	na
1971	–6.75	10.55	2.3	91.2	108.1	–8.8	8.1
1972	10.46	3.95	2.83	97.9	109.2	7.4	1.1
1973	63.35	25.95	8.75	147.1	126.5	50.2	15.8
1974	23.77	46.48	15.3	157.9	160.7	7.4	27
1975	–8.52	1.72	14.86	125.7	142.3	–20.4	–11.4
1976	17.98	–1.52	6.07	139.9	132.2	11.2	–7.2
1977	25.14	5.82	1.99	171.6	137.1	22.7	3.8
1978	–6.84	16.5	7.8	148.3	148.2	–13.6	8.1
1979	15.94	19.58	7.61	159.8	164.7	7.7	11.1
1980	–1.15	18.93	10.0	143.6	178.1	–10.1	8.1

Notes: NEER = nominal effective exchange rate, RER1= trade-weighted real exchange rate, CPI = consumer price index, PT = price of tradables; na = not applicable.

Source: Constructed from Table 4.2.

impacted on PNG's inflation rate during 1975. Table 6.7 also indicates an increasing trend for the prices of tradables. The average trade-weighted nominal exchange rate (RER1) appreciated 1.2 per cent against major trading partners' currencies over 1971–74. The increase in domestic CPI was much higher than the increase in the price of tradables, bringing a significant reduction in the relative price of tradables to the domestic CPI during 1973. While the trade-weighted real exchange rate (RER1) appreciated 18 per cent in 1973 from the previous year's level, the real exchange rate for exports and the import-competing sector depreciated by 50 and 16 per cent, respectively, in 1973, due to increases in world price for PNG's export commodities (Table 6.8).

Table 6.8 indicates that the real exchange rate for export- and import-competing industries depreciated as the export and import price indices rose more rapidly than the domestic price of nontradables (weighted average of nontradable components of CPI) over the 1972–74 period. It can therefore be concluded from the empirical analysis and the econometric investigation that the appreciation of the trade-weighted real exchange rate in 1973 might have been overestimated due to a sharp increase in the CPI which itself contains a considerable amount of tradable items.

During the commodity boom of 1976–77, the kina value price of tradables continued to rise, while domestic inflation began to decline in 1976. Increased tradable prices, and an inflation rate of 0.4 per cent in 1977, increased the prices of tradables relative to the domestic CPI (Table 6.7). This change in relative prices brought about a 5-per-cent depreciation of the trade-weighted real exchange rate which was a significant improvement over a 4-per-cent appreciation of the real exchange rate in the previous year.

Real exchange rates for the export and import competing sectors also indicate a substantial depreciation. In 1977, the export price index increased by 25 per cent and the import price index increased about 6 per cent compared with a 2-per-cent increase in the domestic price of nontradables (Table 6.8). It is interesting to note the real exchange rates depreciated significantly in terms of all alternative measures at the height of the agricultural boom in 1977, which can be attributable to prudent policy choices during the 1976–77 period.

Figure 6.1 indicates that the actual real appreciation of the trade-weighted exchange rate was greater than estimated real appreciation due to the very high inflation induced by the dramatic increase in nominal wages and government spending in the nontradable sector during the mineral booms of 1973. But during the 1976–77 commodity boom, the actual real depreciation was much higher than

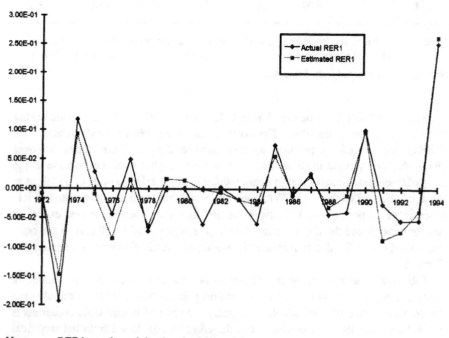

Note: RER1= trade-weighted real exchange rate

Source: Equation 4.1

Figure 6.1   Actual and estimated real exchange rates in PNG, 1972–94

what is predicted by the estimated model. It seems to reflect the impact of income and wage restraint policies, as well as reduced aid and grants flow from Australia. The proposition that the open trade regime of the 1970s also reduced appreciation of the real exchange rate over the period, is supported by the econometric results in Chapter 4.

6.4.3   Effects on Employment and Wages

This section attempts to analyse the changes in employment and real wages in PNG during the resources booms of the 1970s. As discussed in the theoretical framework, a resources boom shifts labour from the non-booming traded sector to the nontradable sector as the price of traded goods falls relative to nontradables. This shift of labour is likely to have enormous ramifications for wages and overall distribution of income.

Available data on employment in monetised activities suggest there was an increase in total formal employment during the boom years. Total formal employment increased from the 1968 level by about 11 per cent in 1973 with a substantial increase in public and mining sector employment, although private non-mining employment shows a declining trend (Appendix Table A3.6). This outcome confirms the booming sector theoretical proposition that labour shifts from the non-booming private sector to the more profitable booming mining and nontradable public sectors. Available limited data on wage rates in Table 6.9 indicate that both real and nominal wage increased rapidly during the early 1970s, with employment in the non-mining sector failing to keep pace with the wage rise.

The declining trend for private non-mining employment growth appears to have been closely related to the increase in real wages. The rise in domestic CPI was 13 per cent on average whereas the nominal weekly wage rose 56 per cent for urban workers and 13 per cent for rural workers over the 1972–75 period.

As a result, rural and urban real wages increased on average by 0.5 per cent and 30 per cent, respectively (Table 6.9). The higher cost of labour due to this substantial increase in money wages and salaries added upward pressure to domestic prices, exacerbated inequality between rural and urban incomes, and adversely affected employment. It is evident from the wage and price data that the increase in real wages during the high inflationary period was clearly influenced by the deliberate implementation of a wage policy which raised the urban nominal wage faster than domestic price level changes.

It is noticeable that during the BCL investment and mineral boom in 1971–74, a large share of the wages bill went to pay skilled expatriate labourers. As a result, the enclave nature of these booms did not have much spill-over effect on the vast non-mining sector's employment and spending behaviour. The mobility of labour across national boundaries reduced the spending effects of the resources boom which might have helped to keep the domestic price level relatively stable, as discussed in the extension of 'Dutch disease' theory under the openness of the labour market in Chapter 2.

Table 6.9
Changes in real and nominal weekly wages, 1967–85

Year	Rural nominal	Urban nominal	Real rural (1977 prices)	Real urban (1977 prices)	% change rural nominal	% change urban nominal	% change real rural	% change real urban
1967–71*	4.7	6.9	8.6	12.7	na	na	na	na
1972	5.9	8	9.6	13.0	25.5	15.94	11.6	2.36
1975	8.9	25.8	9.8	28.5	16.9	74.2	0.7	39.7
1978	11.5	28.5	10.8	26.9	9.7	3.5	3.4	−1.9
1979	11.9	30.8	10.7	27.5	3.48	8.07	−0.93	2.23
1980	12.4	33.2	9.9	26.5	4.20	7.79	−7.48	−3.64
1981	13.7	36.8	9.9	26.6	10.48	10.84	0.00	0.38
1982	14.5	38.8	9.8	26.2	5.84	5.43	−1.01	−1.50
1983	15.5	41.5	9.6	25.8	6.90	6.96	−2.04	−1.53
1984	16.3	43.6	9.7	26.0	5.16	5.06	1.04	0.78
1985	17.0	45.5	9.7	26.0	4.30	4.40	0.0	0.0

Note: * period average; na = not applicable.
Source: World Bank (1991) Table 4.2, p. 75 and AusAID (1995) Table A22.

It has been the policy of the PNG government, since independence, to maintain a steady trend in real wages. The wage structure that was determined between 1972 and 1975 posed a number of problems. The wages study by Garnaut and Baxter (1984, p. 99) suggested that employment growth was very slow when urban minimum wages were rising 50 per cent during 1972–76, and indicated that the high level of wages was one of the major factors responsible for depressing the level of employment and the pace of employment generation in PNG.

Except for the mining sector, urban wage employment growth was relatively stronger from 1976 because of the direct spending effects of the agricultural boom. The growth in rural wages shows this effect. The growth in urban wages is also quite significant, given that they were already artificially high as a result of the MWB ruling in 1972/73. The government's institution of a temporary wage freeze in 1976, was successful as an initiative to reduce the inflationary wage spiral. After that, until 1992 wages were indexed at, or slightly below, the growth rate of the urban based consumer price index. Minimum Wage Boards had accepted the argument that wage determination should be restrained to encourage the growth of income earning opportunities and to allow the government to increase the share of new development spending in the budget. Although rural wages rose slightly, the result was a reduction of 2 to 6 per cent in the real value of urban minimum wages for unskilled labourers between 1976 and 1980.

Over the period 1977–79, total wage employment increased by 1.7 per cent annually, with an increase of 2 per cent in private sector employment, while employment in the mining and public sector remained steady (Appendix Table A3.6). Rural nominal wages increased on average by 9.7 per cent, but urban wages rose by only 3.5 per cent in 1978, from the 1975 level. Costs and prices increased due to continued increases in the cost of materials and supplies, but labour costs increased only marginally. In 1978, real rural wages rose by 3.4 per cent, but real urban wages fell by 1.9 per cent as a result of temporary wage freeze in 1976.

6.5   Changes in Sectoral Composition

It is clearly evident that the onset of full operation of the BCL project, and the subsequent mineral boom and agricultural commodity boom in the second half of the 1970s, together with government policy responses, had significant identifiable effects on both the relative prices of tradables to nontradables and wages and employment. This section examines sectoral composition changes over 1971–78, and investigates the overall effects of the resources booms and the policy implications on the sectoral composition of the PNG economy over the decade of the 1970s.

Table 6.10 shows the sectoral composition of GDP, from late 1968 to 1977. The data indicate a declining trend in agricultural share to GDP between 1971–74, although the value of agricultural output increased from K216 million in 1971 to K273 million in 1974. The share of the agricultural sector to total output in 1971 accounted for 35 per cent before declining sharply to 26 per cent of GDP in 1974. By contrast, the sectoral share of mining increased dramatically, from a very low 0.2 per cent in 1971 to 25 per cent of GDP in 1974.

The share of mining exports also grew dramatically, from a low of 0.1 per cent in 1971 to 17 per cent of total GDP in 1973. But the agricultural export share of GDP fell from 6 per cent in 1972 to 5 per cent of GDP in 1973. In the manufacturing sector, general business activities seemed to increase but the share of this sector to GDP shows slow growth, from 6 per cent in 1971 to 7 per cent GDP in 1974.

The share of the services sector to GDP declined from 38 per cent of GDP in 1971 to 32 per cent in 1973 and increased again to 38 per cent in 1974. The building and construction sector also slowed, due to declining investment in the BCL project, and cut-backs in government capital spending. The contribution of non-market products fell from 28 per cent in 1968 to 18 per cent, although more than half the population survived on subsistence agriculture in 1974.

Towards the end of 1974 world commodity prices slumped and the prices for most of PNG's major tree crops declined. In 1974, the real value of GDP fell a massive 18 per cent, indicating an economy wide recession in that year. PNG's

Table 6.10
Gross domestic product by industrial origin, 1968–77
(percentage share of GDP)

	1968	1969	1970	1971	1972	1973	1974	1975	1976	1977
Agriculture, hunting, forestry and fishing	43	44	40	35	34	31	26	30	30	36
Mining and Quarrying	0.4	0.1	0.1	0.2	3	17	25	13	11	9
Manufacturing	5	5	5	6	6	5	7	8	9	9
Construction	13	12	13	18	14	8	8	8	6	6
Electricity, gas, water and sanitary services	0	0.5	0.6	1	0.8	1	0.7	0.7	1	1
Wholesale and retail trade	8	8	8	7	7	6	6	9	7	8
Transport, storage and communications	5	5	6	5.6	6	5.5	5	7	5	5
Financing, insurance and real estate	4	4	4	4	5	6	5	4	6	6
Less imputed bank service charge	0.4	0.6	0.7	0.8	0.8	0.9	0.7	0.5	1	1
Community, social and personal services	11	11	11	10	10	9	8	9	13	11
Public authority, n.e.i. and defence	9	9	10	10	11	10	8	10	10	8
GDP excluding import duties	98	98	97	96	96	98	98	97	97	97
Import duties	2	2	3	4	4	2	2	3	3	3

Source: Computed from World Bank (1976) Report No. 1150-PNG, and World Bank Report (1981) No. 3544a-PNG.

export revenue declined by 24 per cent in 1975 from 1974, reflecting both lower world prices for PNG's exports and lower export volumes. On completion of the Bougainville construction the share of construction sector to GDP fell from 18 to 14 per cent. This sector accounted for only 8 per cent of GDP as the government responded to the 1974's downturn by cutting capital expenditure, with a subsequent contractionary effect on building and construction sector.

In 1974, following the large increase in the urban wage, private investment became sluggish, while private consumption was buoyant. Copper prices fell sharply which reduced the share of the BCL mine in total export value — although it accounted for almost 50 per cent of total exports in 1974. Imports fell from their previous level because of the lack of new investment projects. However, overall, the economic environment and prospects appeared more stable at the end of 1974.

Benefits from the commodity boom in the second half of the 1970s were more evenly distributed in the economy. Because of the nature and origin of this boom, the price impact was more moderate than the booms in the early 1970s. In 1977, the real growth rate of GDP was 10 per cent, compared with –12.0 per cent in 1976. The share of the agricultural sector to GDP improved significantly from 26 per cent in 1974 to 36 per cent in 1977, and remained stable until 1979. The mining sector contributed an average 10 per cent to GDP and its share increased to 15 per cent of GDP in 1979 due to the continued escalation of world gold prices together with the maintenance of high prices for copper.

The boom had important growth effects on manufacturing output, fixed capital formation and a wide range of private sector services. Increased domestic production increased the supply of goods and services. The share of the manufacturing sector to GDP increased from 8 per cent of GDP in 1975 to 9 per cent in 1977. The contribution of the services sector to GDP rose from 33 per cent in 1976 to 38 per cent in 1977. Since independence, the building and construction sector has experienced increasing growth. In 1977, the construction sector experienced strong growth associated with investment in general office buildings and hotel accommodation. The expansion of the construction sector associated with the commodity boom in PNG confirms the propositions of the construction boom theory.

During 1978, economic activities slowed down, due to falling world market prices for PNG's agricultural export commodities. The share of agricultural exports fell to 15 per cent of total exports in 1978 from 22 per cent in the previous year. The share of mining exports grew moderately, private and government consumption was modest, with government expenditure only slightly above budget projections and total revenue collection for the year close to expectations. Gross domestic investment as a percentage of GDP increased moderately by one percentage point in 1978 from 1977. In 1978, current account balance was only K4.3 million, with an almost 50 per cent reduction compared with 1977, and an overall balance of payments deficit of K1.8 million. The TOT fell by 25.3 per cent, as the import price index rose to 118.3 in 1978, compared with an export price index of 88.4. The weak balance of payments associated with the lower commodity prices in 1978 caused monetary expansion to fall. The growth of real GDP fell to 1.8 per cent due to decline in mining sector output, the result of decline in the ore content of the copper concentrate produced by the BCL mine.

PNG economy experienced an appreciable pick-up in economic activities since the mid-1980 following an extended period of slow growth during the first half of the decade. Investment in the mining sector peaked at nearly 15 per cent of GDP in the early 1980s at the height of investment in the Ok Tedi mine.[2] Real GDP grew by 3.7 per cent per annum between 1985 and 1988. Gross domestic investment increased from 22 per cent of GDP in 1985 to 25 per cent in 1990 (Table 3.2). But public investment was on a declining trend throughout most of the 1980s, falling steadily from nearly 9 per cent of GDP in 1981 to around 5 per cent by 1987. Private non-mining sector also exhibited a similar trend, declining from more than 13 per cent of GDP in 1981 to just over 8 per cent in 1987 (World Bank, 1991). In the final two years of the decade there was an encouraging recovery, but it was mainly confined to the construction sector as a result of increased demand for residential and office accommodation.

During the second half of the 1980s, PNG established a sound overall fiscal management. Following several years of large fiscal deficits in the early 1980s, the government increased its revenue efforts and tightened control over expenditures. As a consequence, the overall fiscal deficit fell to 2 per cent of GDP in 1985 and just over 1 per cent between 1987–89 (World Bank, 1991). The government placed considerably more emphasis on public investment and by 1989 public investment had risen to 4.5 per cent of GDP. Another notable aspect of PNG's fiscal performance in the 1980s was the extent to which the country increased its self reliance in revenue generation and financing. Budgetary grants from Australia which represented almost one third of current revenues in 1981, had fallen in relative importance to less than one fifth by the end of the decade. After having an extended period of balance of payments deficits during 1981–83, PNG's balance of payments improved significantly from the mid-1980s owing primarily to the production Ok Tedi mine and higher world prices for copper and gold. Official reserve peaked at the end of 1987 at just over K564 million, equivalent to more than 6 months of non-mineral imports. Government also adopted a prudent approach to external borrowing from the middle of the 1980s and a contractionary monetary policy was followed from 1989. There was a substantial decline in total formal sector employment during the first half of the 1980s followed by a moderate recovery during the second half of the decade. Domestic price level became more stable at around 3.2 per cent per annum between 1985–88 from a double digit inflation rate in the early 1980s (Appendix Table A3.2).

6.6   Resources Boom in the Early 1990s

PNG experienced another resources boom in its mineral sector over the 1991–93 period, due to the new discovery of petroleum as well as buoyant gold prices in the world market. The strength of this boom was determined by the world market prices of gold, copper and petroleum, as well as domestic and foreign investment conditions. Real GDP grew from a low –3.0 per cent in 1990 to 9.5 per cent in 1991, 11.8 per cent in 1992 and 16.6 per cent in 1993. This spectacular performance resulted in a significant increase in levels of real per capita income, rising from K665 in 1991 to K828 in 1993.

Background

After achieving admirable economic growth in the second half of the 1980s, PNG faced enormous setbacks in May 1989. The abrupt cessation of BCL operations brought the economy to a sudden halt; unrest in the North Solomons resulted in a sharp downturn in tree-crop exports; as virtually all the prices of the country's leading tree crop exports fell, in some cases, quite drastically. As a result, real GDP fell by 1.5 per cent in 1989.

The impact of these shocks was severe. Between 1989 and 1991, the adverse average annual impact on national income and fiscal revenue was at 10.9 and 3.7 per cent respectively. The average annual impact on the balance of payments was at about US$375 million, or, about one-quarter of total exports in 1988. Roughly half of these losses were attributable to the BCL mine closure and the other half to the fall in TOT and loss of non-mineral output from North Solomons province. During 1989 and 1990, private consumption and gross domestic investment declined from the 1988 level.

However, the government committed itself to implementing widespread reform (Elek, 1991). The PNG authorities undertook large cuts in government expenditure and significant revenue-raising efforts, which held the fiscal deficit at about 3 per cent of GDP in 1990. Since 1989, monetary policy was kept tight, by means of ceilings on domestic credit to the private sector. Growth in the broad money supply fell from 10.7 per cent in 1988 to 6.5 per cent in 1989 and 5 per cent in 1990. Inflation was on a declining trend from 1989 to 1992.

The burden of the adjustment was reasonable and broad throughout the economy. Output in the agricultural sector declined by 4.9 per cent in 1989. Real GDP fell to –3.0 per cent in 1990. Contribution of the services sector to GDP dropped to –12 per cent from the previous year, owing to the impact of restraint in government spending, and weakness in both wholesale and retail trade. Among the other major sectors, construction and utilities recorded a sharp decline of 8 per cent in output growth, reflecting a drop-off from the high rates of building activity and mine construction in 1989. Output in manufacturing continued to grow at a modest rate which was typical of the previous years, except for the big dip in 1990.

6.6.1   Resources Boom: 1992–93

The rapid economic growth in the early years of the 1990s came largely from growth in minerals and petroleum production along with spin off activities in other non-mining sectors. Oil production from the Kutubu oil project accounted for 10 per cent of GDP in 1992. Oil exports earned K301 million in 1992 increasing up to an estimated K848 million in 1993. Production of petroleum from the Kutubu project alone provided 37 per cent of total exports in 1993 from nothing in 1991. The combined share of the minerals and petroleum sector in GDP improved from 15 per cent in 1990 to about 30 per cent in 1993, and provided 30 per cent of government revenue. Non-mining GDP also increased by 5 per cent in 1991 but then came down to 1.1 per cent in 1993.

Between 1991 and 1994, the value of total exports increased enormously. Mineral exports increased from K758 million, or 32 per cent of GDP, in 1990 to K1768, or 53 per cent of GDP, in 1993. From K205 million in 1990, agricultural exports increased to K270 million in 1993 and K375 million in 1994. Revenues from log exports increased more than six fold from K80 million in 1990 to K494 million in 1994.

6.7   Policy Response

Since independence until 1989, PNG maintained confidence in the financial system by exercising successful expenditure restraint policy, and a 'hard kina' policy that kept domestic inflation at a low level. But from 1990 the country failed to maintain this reliable policy package, due to a series of budget deficits caused largely by the closure of BCL mine and subsequent fiscal indiscipline.

6.7.1   Fiscal Policy

The PNG government's undisciplined fiscal policy was a major issue of concern during 1990–94. The fiscal deficit widened in 1990 with the closure of the Panguna mine at Bougainville. Government internal revenue and grants fell from K1014 million in 1989 to K998 million in 1990 while total government spending increased from K1049 million in 1989 to K1089 million in 1990. In 1991, government revenue recovered to 1989 levels and grew rapidly over 1992 to 1994, owing to increased revenue flows from the boom in the minerals and petroleum sector.

In 1991 central government expenditure increased by K99 million with large increases on education, defence, transport, public debt servicing and transfers to local and provincial governments.

The economy absorbed the mineral windfalls through current consumption as the boom was perceived as lasting a longer period. This is evident from the sharp rise in government expenditure over the years 1991 and 1993, which contributed to a fiscal deficit of 5.6 per cent in 1992 and 5.9 per cent in 1993.

The 1994 budget was expansionary at the beginning of the year but later changed to a more restrictive policy stance owing to the sharp increase in the fiscal deficit. By early 1994, the price support programme announced in 1992 was creating significant pressure on government expenditure, and the budget deficit had grown to 11 per cent of GDP by the middle of the year. The government announced another mini budget to reduce the deteriorating fiscal situation largely due to an unexpected but sharp decline in oil prices. As prices rose in mid-1994, the subsidy for coffee became redundant. By the end of the year, the adoption of an expenditure restraint policy

Table 6.11
Key economic indicators, 1989–94

	1989	1990	1991	1992	1993	1994
Real economic growth (annual %)						
Real GDP	−1.5	−3.0	9.5	11.8	16.6	3.1
Per capita GDP (kina 1983 prices)	656	622	665	727	828	834
Sectoral growth						
Agriculture, forestry and fishing	−4.9	3.9	−1.8	6.2	25.8	10.6
Mining and quarrying	−40.6	23.1	26.7	4.1	−6.9	11.0
Petroleum	na	na	na	na	166.7	−19.4
Manufacturing	17.5	−21.4	16.9	10.1	1.3	−1.6
Services	10.2	−11.7	15.1	5.6	0.6	5.3
Construction	24.3	−7.6	35.0	−8.4	−13.2	9.8
Growth in prices and wages (annual %)						
Consumer Price Index (1990=100)	5.2	6.0	5.0	4.0	6.7	4.4
Implicit GDP deflator	−2.1	4.0	6.0	2.0	2.3	6.6
Urban real minimum wage (1977 prices)	0.7	−4.0	−0.8	0.4	−63.4	−2.8
GDP by expenditure component (million kina in current prices)						
Consumption	2707	2580	2974	3326	3550	4051
Private consumption	1962	1816	2166	2396	2532	2969
Government consumption	745	764	808	930	1018	1082
Domestic investment	707	752	988	984	943	884
Exports	1238	1250	1524	1870	2516	2456
Minerals and petroleum	676	758	1005	1372	1768	1783
Agriculture and marine	278	213	215	233	278	386
Forestry (log and other)	96	80	90	148	410	494
Imports	1607	1506	1881	2040	1993	1980

Source: Constructed from various Tables, AusAID (1996).

had reduced total government expenditure to K1570 million. Higher than expected mining revenues, as well as cuts in crop price support and transport costs, increased total revenue and grants of K1446 million, reducing the budget deficit to 2.3 per cent (AusAID, 1996).

A positive balance in the MRSF over this period gave a misleading conception of the government as a net saver. Over this period, continuous fiscal deficits simply indicated that the government effectively borrowed from the private sector to augment the MRSF. Between 1990 and 1994, public sector debt increased to K2.9 billion, or 48 per cent of GDP, and the debt servicing requirement increased to K86 million. To finance these continuous budget deficits, foreign debt rose to US$4.2 billion with debt servicing costs rocketing to over 30 per cent of export earnings (AusAID, 1995).

6.7.2   Monetary Policy

In mid-1991, the BPNG changed monetary policy from a liquid asset requirement to a base money management approach, adopting open market operations as the principal policy instrument. This monetary approach was reasonably successful in keeping liquidity growth under control. As fiscal deficits grew, and interest rates remained above those in Australia the BPNG faced enormous pressure to keep interest rates under control. However, at the end of 1992 and in mid-1993, lending rates were lowered, narrowing the spread somewhat (Table 3.9).

During 1992 and 1993, private sector credit growth was above 4 per cent but liquidity had fallen due to a substantial decline in foreign assets. Total money showed an increasing trend over the period. The growth rate of money supply increased from 4.2 per cent in 1990 to 17.7 per cent in 1991 and then eased back to 12.5 per cent in 1992 whereas real GDP grew at a slower rate than money supply by 9.5 per cent in 1991 and 11.8 per cent in 1992.

In 1993, money supply of about 27 per cent was much higher than 16.6 per cent growth of real GDP (Table 3.9, Table 6.11 and Table 6.12). The econometric results in Chapter 4 indicate an excessive growth rate of money supply (growth of money exceeds GDP growth) had an adverse impact on the real exchange rate of PNG. The RER appreciated by 5 per cent in 1993 (Table 6.15).

Although the growth rate of money supply fell dramatically to 2.3 per cent in 1994, the burden on the banking system of financing the entire budget deficit domestically, resulted in tighter credit conditions in the private sector and foreign assets, putting further upward pressure on interest rates.

The introduction of a floating exchange rate system in October 1994 impacted substantially on how monetary policy was conducted. Since the BPNG has no obligation under the floating system to sell or buy foreign currencies at a particular exchange rate, it could set the level of the money supply independently, and the weighted average of commercial bank lending rates increased substantially from 10 per cent in December 1994 to 15.4 per cent by December 1995. Private sector demand for credit was affected by adverse fiscal and monetary conditions in 1994, the subsequent high interest rates in 1995 and the uncertain investment climate.

Table 6.12
Major economic indicators before and during the 1991–93 boom

	1989	1990	1991	1992	1993	1994
GDP (million kina, current prices)	3046	3076	3606	4140	5016	5411
Central government fiscal operation						
Central government revenue and grants	1014	998	1026	1126	1309	1446
Expenditure and net lending	1049	1089	1188	1358	1605	1570
Budget deficit/surplus as % of GDP	–1.2	–3.0	–4.5	–5.6	–5.9	–2.3
Monetary conditions (kina million)						
Narrow money (M1)	352	353	458	509	528	571
Broad money	1035	1080	1271	1431	1811	1854
Total money supply	1038	1082	1273	1432	1813	1854
Sectoral share of GDP (%)						
Agriculture, forestry and fishing	28.1	29.0	26.0	24.7	26.6	28.6
Mining and quarrying	11.6	14.7	17.0	15.8	12.7	13.6
Petroleum	0.0	0.0	0.0	6.5	14.9	11.6
Manufacturing	11.1	9.0	9.6	9.4	8.2	7.8
Services	43.9	52.3	40.8	38.6	33.8	34.2
Construction	5.3	5.0	6.6	5.1	3.8	4.2
Balance of payments (kina million)						
Trade balance	–20	86	75	607	1437	1346
Balance on current account	–312	–88	–144	94	632	576
Balance on capital account	211	207	60	–146	–701	–605
Overall balance	–52	9	–81	–68	–96	–26
Terms of trade and exchange rates						
Terms of trade (1990=100)	114.9	100.0	102.6	100.9	103.3	105.4
Nominal effective exchange rate	88.4	100.0	101.1	99.1	100.2	134.3
Real effective exchange rate (trade-weighted)	90.5	100.0	97.4	92.2	87.3	112.1

Source: Constructed from various tables, AusAID (1996). Real and nominal effective exchange rate indices series are constructed by the author.

6.7.3   Trade Policy

Until the early 1980s, PNG followed an open trade regime, with taxes on imports and exports quite low and relatively uniform. From the mid-1980s, an increasing number of trade interventions were introduced to achieve an assortment of revenue, protection and distributional objectives. Tariff policy has been seen as an instrument of industry policy to promote the interest of a particular sector or industry. The protective policy introduced in PNG produced widely differing rates of effective protection and served the interest of producers focussed on the domestic market. Import bans and very high duties on selected products created an incentive structure with high levels of effective protection for a limited range of activities and a strong bias against exports and the agricultural sector. Table 6.13 shows that currently 68 per cent of 5,366 total tariff items are taxed at rates of 11 per cent or below. The remaining 31 per cent items are protected at rates of 40 per cent or higher. In the early 1980s, the tariff rate for a smaller number of import competing industries was 10 per cent which was increased to 17.5 per cent in the mid-1980s, and sharply increased in the early 1990s to 30 per cent for all goods where there was domestic production (Fallon et al., 1995). The rise in import protection has been accompanied by bans on certain food items, import quotas, and special privileges given to cement, canned meat and sugar industries.

As shown in Table 6.13, currently 2 per cent of imports are duty-free. Basic food items such as rice as well as medical supply and equipment, books and kerosene are exempted from duty, while a 5 per cent tariff is imposed on 22 per cent of tariff items classified as basic inputs to production.

The basic tariff rate of 11 per cent is imposed on the largest category which

Table 6.13
Tariff regime in Papua New Guinea as in mid-1990s

Existing tariff regime	Tariff rate	Number of tariff items	
Free	0%	127	(2%)
Input rate	5%	1178	(22%)
Basic rate	11%	2377	(44%)
Protective rate	40%	1051	(20%)
Restrictive/luxury rate	55%	504	(9%)
Prohibitive rate	Specific rates or *ad valorem* (75% – 175%)	129	(2%)
Total		5366	(99%)

Source: Internal Revenue Commission of Papua New Guinea (1997), Table 2.

includes many foodstuff items, textiles, production inputs and raw materials. The current rate of 40 per cent is on the category of goods that are produced or potentially can be produced in PNG. A 55-per-cent restrictive tariff is imposed on 504 tariff items, including fish, some toiletries, photographic flim, wood boards, carpets, pearls and precious stones, steel netting and fencing, double cab vehicles and motor cycles, arms and ammunition and furniture. Another 2 per cent of importable items are subject to a prohibitive tariff rate of 75 to 175 per cent. The specific import duty rates are imposed K3.50 per kg of poultry and K0.05 per box of matches. When these special rates are converted into *ad valorem* form, they provide very high levels of protection. The *ad valorem* rates include many vegetables and fruits (75%), vehicles (75%), sugar (85%), tinned mackerel (99%), beer (125%), cigarette and cigars (125%), veneer and plywood (100%), and door frames (100%).

Table 6.14 indicates currently in PNG the average nominal tariff rate is 21.9 per cent and the trade-weighted tariff rate is 14.3. At a broader industry classification level, the highest level of nominal protection is given to fisheries (53.9%), agriculture (46.3%) and food processing (46.1%). Both the nominal and trade-weighted tariff is on manufactured articles imposed at about 30 per cent.

Table 6.14
Average sectoral tariff rates in Papua New Guinea
as in mid-1990s

Category of goods	Nominal tariff rate (average)	Trade-weighted tariff rate (average)
All goods	21.9	14.3
Agriculture (excluding fish)	46.3	10.9
Fish and fish products	53.9	48.9
Food processing	46.1	39.4
Wood, pulp, paper and furniture	35.7	19.3
Textiles and clothing	23.3	25.9
Leather, rubber and footwear	27.8	37.2
Metals	12.9	11.4
Chemical and photographic supplies	10.8	13.8
Plastics	20.4	15.7
Transport equipment	19.6	16.7
Non-electric machinery	6.6	5.9
Electric machinery	12.7	13.4
Mineral products, precious stones and metals	21.0	7.5
Other manufactured articles	29.6	30.4

Note: The average trade-weighted tariff rate is the nominal tariff rate weighted against trade data. Tariff schedule as of January 1997.

Source: Internal Revenue Commission of Papua New Guinea (1997), Table 3.

Although PNG's nominal rate of tariff is not exceptionally high, some of the tariff barriers, especially on fish and fish products, food processing, leather, rubber and footwear and other manufactured articles have been imposing significant costs on the most efficient import-competing and export-oriented sectors as well as on consumers.

The limitations of this trade policy have been recognised by successive governments, and several unsuccessful attempts have been made in recent years to reform the system.

In the 1990s, promotion of export oriented manufacturing was regarded as a longer term goal. Under this programme the PNG government decided to remove all import bans and introduce tariffs where protection was required to continue. The result was high tariffs on several items, such as poultry, but a decision to remove the remaining bans was postponed (AIDAB, 1993, p. 19). In 1992, the PNG government took further initiatives to reform trade policy by replacing quantitative restrictions with more uniform and simple import duties (at around 10 per cent). This reform was also directed at removing export taxes, except for logs and unprocessed shells (AusAID, 1995, p. 142). Tariffs on a number of commercial inputs, including fuels, spare parts and transport equipment were subsequently reduced in the 1993 budget, but the general import levy was also increased, from 8 per cent to 10 per cent, and again to 11 per cent in 1994 with its coverage extended to a range of goods including some agricultural and manufacturing inputs that had previously been exempted.

The 1993 budget also proposed highly restrictive tariff protection on some chosen goods and individual manufacturers and projects and continued a ban on sugar imports which was overtly inconsistent with underlying trade reform principles. This budget increased further restrictive protection for the Lea Mackerel Cannery and the Halla Cement Factory. From September 1993, a nominal monopoly was given to the sole domestic producer of cement, where users could import cement only with a special licence. As a result, the prices of cement increased more than 50 per cent. The 1994 budget again imposed a protective rate of duty of another 11 per cent on basic consumer goods used by the low income consumer while reducing duties on luxury items. The Supply Bill of November 1994 raised the protective rate of duty to 40 per cent.

6.7.4   Exchange Rate Policy

Since monetary independence, under the influence of the 'hard kina' policy, PNG maintained a convertible currency and until 1980 was successful in maintaining low inflation, relative to world inflation. Domestic inflation increased sharply in 1981–82 and remained relatively high up until 1984 (Appendix Table A3.2). From June 1978 to October 1994 the kina was pegged to a basket of currencies of its major trading partners. The kina was devalued by 10 per cent in early 1990 and in 1993 appreciated by 1.7 per cent against the Australian dollar, 0.9 per cent against the US dollar, and 10.3 per cent against the German Deutschemark but depreciated by 9.4 per cent against the Japanese yen. On 12 September 1994, the kina was devalued by

12 per cent against the US dollar. The PNG government decided to float the kina in the face of a worsening foreign exchange crisis on 4 October 1994. By mid-1995 the kina had declined by more than 40 per cent in nominal terms from the level 12 months earlier.

6.8   Effects of Resources Boom: 1991–94

In this section the effects of the resources boom of 1991–93 on the key macroeconomic variables are analysed by examining the expenditure side of the national income accounts.

6.8.1   Effects on Key Macroeconomic Variables

During 1991–93, both private and public consumption growth were moderate. The share of private consumption to GDP fell from 60 per cent in 1991 to 51 per cent in 1993. Overall government demand remained at about 28 per cent of total GDP with a public consumption demand of 20 per cent of total GDP in 1993 compared with 22 per cent in 1991. Total private demand (consumption and investment) declined significantly from around 88 per cent of GDP in the early 1980s to around 68 per cent of GDP in 1993 (AIDAB, 1994). This relative decline in private spending reflected diminished optimism in private consumption and private investment. The construction of the Porgera and Kutubu projects contributed to a sharp increase in private fixed investment which accounted for more than 23 per cent of GDP in 1991. Gross domestic investment increased to 27.4 per cent of GDP in 1991 and then declined to 20.3 per cent of GDP in 1993.

The value of merchandise imports grew by 26.5 per cent from 1990 to 1991 due to K250 million in capital imports associated with the construction of the Kutubu oil project. General imports also increased by 25 per cent indicating a general recovery in the economy. However, a continuous rise in export revenue and a substantial reduction in capital imports more than offset the increased imports of consumer goods between 1992 and 1994. The value of merchandise imports declined by 4.6 per cent in 1992 as a result of reductions in mining, petroleum and general imports. A further decline of 14.9 per cent in merchandise imports in 1993 was due to a lower level of imports by the mining and petroleum sectors. As a result, the trade surplus grew rapidly to K1437 million in 1993 from K75 million in 1991. The balance on the current account changed from a deficit of K144 million in 1991 to a surplus of K632 million in 1993 despite a large increase in services payments and net transfers associated with the mining sector.

Despite a large current account surplus, and a 10-per-cent devaluation of the kina in 1990, the overall balance of payments continued to weaken over the period 1991–93 with an overall deficit of K68 million in 1992 and K96 million in 1993. This large deficit in 1993 was mainly brought about by the large capital account deficit of K701 million. The capital account deficit was mainly attributed to substantial increases in the private capital outflow, reflecting deterioration in private sectors' confidence in a volatile investment climate. The outflows were also facilitated by the liberalisation of foreign exchange controls in 1992. As a consequence, international reserves fell to K112 million in 1993 from K309 million in 1991. In 1994, the value of merchandise imports increased by 16.9 per cent due to increased capital imports by the Porgera mine. However, the surplus in the trade account increased to K1346 million and the deficit in the capital account was K605 million. The overall balance of payments situation improved substantially in this year. The lower balance of payments deficit of K26 million was the result of higher merchandise exports, lower service payments and lower outflows of private capital.

6.8.2   Relative Price Effect

The inflation rate was 6 per cent in 1990 and 5 per cent in 1991 easing back to 4 per cent in 1992. This relative decline in the price level was mainly influenced by lower inflation in Australia, the major source of PNG's imports, as well as by the appreciation of the kina against the Australian dollar. The CPI index rose to 7.2 per cent in 1993 but slowed down to a lower rate of 4.6 per cent during 1994. The kina value of tradables increased more than 17 per cent in 1990 which brought a 10.5-per-cent depreciation of the trade-weighted real exchange rate.

Over 1991–93 period, price of tradables increased less than one per cent (0.76 per cent) on average whereas domestic CPI rose by 5.6 per cent. The increase in the domestic price level relative to PNG's major trading partners resulted from increased government spending, which appreciated the trade-weighted real exchange rate by 4.4 per cent. As the price of tradables increased substantially with a fall in the domestic price level to 4.5 per cent and a depreciation of the nominal exchange rate by 34 per cent, the trade-weighted real exchange rate depreciated more than 28 per cent in 1994 (Table 6.15).

Until 1992, the growth in the export price index was slower than the domestic price of nontradables but the index increased sharply during 1993–94 due to improved world market prices for PNG's mineral and agricultural products. Real exchange rate for export sector depreciated by 8.5 per cent in 1993 and 15.4 per cent in 1994. In both years this was the outcome of greater increase in export prices compared to an increase in domestic price of nontradables.

The real exchange rate for import competing industries appreciated over 1991–93 before depreciating slightly at about 0.6 per cent in 1994 (Table 6.16). The movement of real exchange rates suggests that the relative price of tradables to nontradables declined over the 1991–93 period.

Appreciation of the real exchange rate was driven by a rapid fall in the inflation rates of PNG's major trading partners. Increased domestic inflation was also aggravated by persistent expansionary fiscal policy and an increasingly restrictive trade regime. From the late 1980s until 1993, the increase in the domestic price level was higher than the price of tradables, which greatly reduced competitiveness of the economy and appreciated the real exchange rate substantially. This outcome

Table 6.15
Changes in relative price indices, 1988–94
(1990=100)

Year	NEER	RER1	PT	CPI	% change NEER	% change PT	% change CPI	% change RER1
1988	91.03	94.23	84.15	89.30	−0.06	4.36	9.08	−4.33
1989	88.37	90.51	85.09	94.02	−2.92	1.13	5.28	−3.94
1990	100.00	100.00	100.00	100.00	13.47	17.03	6.36	10.48
1991	101.07	97.36	102.64	105.42	0.79	2.08	5.42	−2.64
1992	99.09	92.16	101.29	109.91	−1.96	−1.31	4.26	−5.35
1993	100.22	87.28	102.83	117.82	1.14	1.52	7.20	−5.29
1994	134.27	112.01	138.00	123.20	33.98	34.20	4.57	28.34

Notes: NEER = nominal effective exchange rate, RER1= trade-weighted real exchange rate, CPI = consumer price index, PT = price of tradables.

Source: Computed from Table 4.1.

Table 6.16
Changes in relative price indices of export and
import-competing sectors, 1990–94 (1990=100)

Year	% change EPI	% change IPI	% change PNT	% change RER2	% change RER3
1990	4.5	6.4	6.3	−1.68	0.09
1991	−0.9	−1.0	5.4	−6.0	−6.4
1992	1.8	2.7	3.8	−1.9	−1.1
1993	11.8	−3.4	3.3	8.5	−6.7
1994	16.6	1.8	1.2	15.4	0.6

Notes: EPI= export price index, IPI=import price index, PNT= price of nontradable, RER2= real exchange rate for export industry, RER3= real exchange rate for import industry.

Source: Computed from Table 4.2.

is supported by the econometric results in Chapter 4, which indicates increased government spending significantly appreciates the real exchange rate, at least on a year to year basis. From 1994, PNG began to regain some competitiveness for its export commodities.

6.8.3   Effects on Employment and Wages

In 1990–91 employment in the private non-mining sector declined by about 4 per cent on average. Mining sector employment was also in a declining trend because of this sector's capital intensive nature. The employment situation recovered in 1992 due to increased spin off activities in the non-mining sector, especially in agriculture. Employment in the formal sector declined by 3 per cent in 1993. The BPNG's 1994 employment survey recorded a 10-per-cent decline in private formal sector employment. Both rural and urban nominal wages rose about 11 per cent in 1992 from 1990 levels whereas the real wage remained constant at about K25 weekly for urban and K9.4 weekly for rural workers over the 1990–92 period at 1977 prices (Table 6.17).

Introducing a land mark wage policy in 1992, the Minimum Wages Board Determination (MWBD) lowered urban minimum wages for new entrants and abolished wage indexation. Since 1992, private sector wages have been determined by market forces, subject to a national minimum wage set by the MWBD. The MWBD decision changed the focus of wage negotiation from an income based approach to a productivity based approach. It unified the dual system of urban and rural minimum wages at the much lower rural wage level and introduced a new national youth wage set at 75 per cent of the new national minimum. This

Table 6.17
Real and nominal weekly wages, 1988–93

Year	Rural nominal	Urban nominal	Real rural (1977 prices)	Real urban (1977 prices)	% change rural nominal	% change urban nominal	% change real rural	% change real urban
1988	19.1	51.3	9.7	26.0	2.7	3.0	–2.0	–2.3
1989	20.1	54.0	9.8	26.2	5.4	5.3	1.0	0.8
1990	20.8	55.7	9.4	25.2	3.3	3.2	–4.1	–3.8
1991	22.0	59.1	9.3	25.0	5.8	6.1	–1.1	–0.8
1992	23.0	61.8	9.4	25.1	4.6	4.6	1.1	0.4
1993	23.8	23.8	9.2	9.2	3.5	–61.5	–2.1	–63.4

Source: Constructed from AusAID (1995) Table A22.

policy opened the way for achieving a reduction in the real exchange rate through a nominal exchange rate devaluation. A decline of 61 per cent in the nominal urban wage in 1993 brought a 63 per cent reduction in real urban wages compared with the 1992 level. A 3.5-per-cent growth in the nominal wage in 1994 resulted in a less than expected 2.1-per-cent decline in the minimum real wages.[3]

6.9   Changes in Sectoral Composition

Between 1991 and 1993, the contribution of the agricultural sector to GDP remained stable at around 26 per cent. Within the agricultural sector, logging showed the greatest expansion and provided more than half of the sector's exports. The agricultural sector grew at the rate of 11 per cent in real terms and the share of agricultural output to GDP expanded to 29 per cent in 1994. Improvement in world prices for PNG's agricultural cash crops in 1993 and devaluation of the kina improved the competitiveness of this sector. In the second half of 1994, export prices for coffee, copra and palm oil all moved above their respective support prices and contributed about 14 per cent of total export revenue.

The share of the manufacturing sector declined from 10 per cent of GDP in 1991 to 8 per cent in 1993, due to a substantial reduction in both private and public consumption growth. This outcome is consistent with the econometric results in Chapter 5 suggesting a positive relationship between domestic absorption and output of this sector.

The services sector also indicated a declining trend over the period, from a share of 40 per cent of GDP in 1991 to 34 per cent of GDP in 1993. Benefit from the opening of major new projects, the construction sector had real growth of 35 per cent in 1991. The growth of this sector declined to 13 per cent in 1993, attributed to a lack of new investment and the completion of a number of large construction projects. After the sharp decline in 1993, this sector's growth rate picked up in 1994 and was at around 10 per cent in real terms as a result of major building projects such as the Lamana Hotel and the Royal Papua Yacht Club Marina. The econometric results of sectoral growth in Chapter 5 indicate that appreciation of the real exchange rate, an increase in domestic absorption, and increased government investment, expand the output of the construction sector.

The real growth rate in the mining and quarrying sector was 11 per cent, but the growth in petroleum sector declined to 19.4 per cent in 1994 from 167 per cent in 1993, as petroleum output fell substantially from the Kutubu oil field. This sector's contribution to export revenue fell to 26 per cent in 1994 and is expected to continue to decline as reserves are depleted.

As major projects were completed, a slowdown in mining activities, low prices for PNG's petroleum and a tightening in government expenditure, led to a slowdown of the growth rate to 3.1 per cent during 1994. A decline in mineral revenues, employment bottlenecks, a slowdown in construction activity and loss of investor confidence are also responsible for this fall in economic growth.

From the above discussion on sectoral transformation in response to resources boom and policy management, it is clear the share of the mining sector to GDP rose unambiguously, whereas the contribution of the agricultural traded sector remained constant due to improved world prices for PNG's export commodities. The cumulative effects of an increasing domestic price level adversely affected output of the manufacturing traded sector. Large fiscal deficits and an inward-looking trade regime over 1991–93 kept the domestic price level relatively higher than PNG's major trading partners. The real exchange rate of PNG would have depreciated to a great extent with a more open trade regime and more disciplined fiscal policy. This impact on sectoral growth is also verified by the analytical framework and econometric results in Chapter 5.

6.10   Investment and Savings

This section discusses the effects of broad policy incentives laid out by the government in response to the resources booms on the long-term savings behaviour of PNG. The main policy focus for the mining and petroleum sectors in recent years was to promote foreign investment and a fair distribution of resource rents among the stakeholders. By clearly stating the rights of resource owners, making a fair return on investment and also taking into account the rights of state, landowners and local communities to share in the resulting benefit, the PNG government has been attempting to attract foreign as well as domestic investment to this sector. Another feature of this policy is that the government is taking out its equity share in all new mining projects and selling-off existing equity to nationals as investment matures. This, in turn, would transfer significant equity holdings to the national private sector (AusAID, 1995).

Over the first half of 1990s, the government showed strong support and encouragement for investment in the non-mining sectors. Establishment of industry corporations allowed the transfer of research and development to non-mining sectors. Other supporting policies include a progressive reduction in the existing tariff rate (set at around 40 per cent) and replacing import bans and quotas with tariffs. Exemption of import duty for selected inputs used by the non-mining exporters, the replacement of quantitative restrictions with tariffs for selected agricultural products, such as fruits, vegetables, beef, sugar and some small goods, had a positive impact on investment in the manufacturing sector. The next section discusses PNG's public and private sector savings and investment performance over the last two and a half decades.

6.10.1   Contribution of Savings and Investment

Given the constraints on the mobilisation of foreign direct investment and other kinds of foreign resources, a sustainable rate of investment can only be achieved by a raising of the domestic savings rate. Investment is therefore crucially dependent on the overall economic condition that is conducive to mobilising both private and public savings and the ability to attract foreign savings and direct foreign investment.

From the late 1960s, investment policies of the PNG government have addressed these two key issues, as well as providing incentives to influence investment in specific key sectors. Private sector contribution to gross domestic savings and investment played a crucial role in the development of the economy as it had a positive and direct influence on the long-term growth of PNG.

During the 1970s, PNG's investment and savings performances were high enough to build a foundation for long-term growth. Between 1970 to 1972, the contribution of gross domestic investment to GDP was 40 per cent, funded mainly by foreign savings and direct foreign investment. During 1973–76, the contribution of gross domestic investment to GDP declined sharply with the completion of the BCL mine and the lack of new foreign investment projects.

The share of gross domestic savings to GDP began to rise from 1972 and accounted for 28 per cent of GDP on average over 1973–76. Gross national savings

Table 6.18
Investment and savings, 1970–94
(percentage share of GDP)

	1970– 72	1973– 76	1977– 80	1981– 85	1986– 90	1991– 94
Gross domestic investment	40	18	23	27	23	22
Resource balance[a]	–21	10	4	–13	0	5
Gross national savings[b]	5	19	20	13	17	32
Gross domestic savings[c]	19	28	27	14	23	27
Foreign savings[d]	14	9	7	1	6	–5

Notes: a. Calculated as gross domestic savings less domestic investment
b. Calculated as gross domestic savings less foreign savings
c. Calculated as gross national savings plus foreign savings
d. Calculated as equivalent to the balance of payments deficit on the current account

Source: World Bank (1981, 1991) and AusAID (1996), Constructed from various Tables from Report No. 3544a-PNG (1981), Report No. 9396-PNG (1991) and AusAID 1996 Report.

also rose to 19 per cent of GDP on average over this period and resulted in a positive resources gap which accounted for 10 per cent of GDP (Table 6.18).

Between 1977–80, the share of investment to GDP increased compared with the previous period and both national and domestic savings remained at comfortably high levels.

These figures indicate the PNG government was wise to utilise its windfall gain from the first two major resources booms of the 1970s and to save a large portion of its windfall, facilitating economic development in later years. During the 1980s, PNG's share of investment to GDP was comparable with other lower middle income countries of the world. Between 1981–85, gross domestic investment averaged around 27 per cent of GDP and a large share of this was in the form of direct foreign investment. Over the first half of the 1980s, both domestic and national savings declined due to unfavourable economic conditions but regained a satisfactory level during the second half of the 1980s.

In 1991, gross domestic investment reached a peak of 28 per cent of GDP and declined over the next three years due to a reduction in mining investment. Among other factors, instability in government policy relating to resource development was the major factor in explaining this declining trend of gross domestic investment over the period.

During 1991–94, private sector investment averaged about 17 per cent of GDP, but public sector investment fell to about 5 per cent over the period (Table 6.19). Until 1992, domestic investment was funded mainly by private and foreign savings. From 1992, major investment projects were solely funded by domestic private savings as foreign and public savings continued to decline. The share of private savings to GDP declined substantially in 1993, as the private sector was called on to finance

Table 6.19
Gross domestic investment and gross national savings, 1991–94
(percentage share of GDP)

	1991	1992	1993	1994
Gross domestic investment	28.0	23.8	18.8	16.3
Private investment	23.3	18.6	12.5	13.2
Mining	15.9	11.1	4.6	5.0
Non-mining	7.4	7.5	7.9	8.2
Public investment	4.7	5.2	6.3	3.1
Gross national savings	23.4	26.0	31.4	27.0

Source: AusAID (1996), constructed from various Tables.

large budget deficits and to make up the shortfall in foreign financing of government transactions. Despite the large capital flight during 1992–93, and significant public and foreign dis-saving since 1992 as a result of large debt repayments by the government and diminished confidence by investors in the mining sector, private saving's contribution averaged 30 per cent of GDP over 1991–93. Thus, private sector savings have played an important role in building up the necessary capital stock conducive to the long-term growth of the country.

Private sector savings behaviour clearly indicates the consumption smoothing behaviour which supports the central theme of the theory of 'construction boom' by the private sector. The econometric results in Chapter 5 confirmed that there is a significant positive effect of real GDP growth (contributed mainly by the increased windfall income) on the private and total savings of the nation. These empirical and econometric findings indicate the farsightedness of private sector savings decisions.

6.11 Summary and Conclusion

This chapter has examined the policy responses by the government to resources booms during the 1970s (the BCL investment boom in 1971–72, the copper boom in 1973–74 and the agricultural boom in 1976–77) and the 1990s (the mineral boom during 1992–93) and their effect on the long-term growth of the country. These booms have impacted significantly upon the sectoral composition of output. The overall policy response to these shocks were admirably positive in insulating the economy during the 1970s, as indicated by the average depreciation of real exchange rate and a more even distribution of income. The share of the agricultural and manufacturing sectors to GDP increased significantly during the second half of the 1970s, indicating that, although the economy was moderately affected by the 'Dutch disease' type of phenomenon in the early 1970s, prudent macroeconomic policies in the second half of the 1970s moderated these adverse resources boom effects.

On the other hand, an undisciplined fiscal stance in the early 1990s brought about considerable economic problems for PNG, as the real exchange rate appreciated significantly and reduced external competitiveness in the 1991–93 period. Following an improvement in world market prices for PNG agricultural commodities, the implementation of radical wage reform in 1992, and flotation of the kina in 1994, PNG has managed to regain its external competitiveness to a great extent.

Long-term policy effects indicate that, despite some adverse economic events and large public sector dis-saving in the early years of the 1990s, the contribution of domestic private savings to gross domestic investment was encouraging. The increased savings during the boom years also indicated consumption smoothing behaviour by the private sector, confirming the theoretical propositions of construction booms in PNG.

Notes

1   Until 1977, PNG had a July-June fiscal year. Beginning in 1978, the fiscal year was changed to coincide with the calendar year.

2   As mentioned earlier the discussion of the investment and mineral boom from the early 1980s associated with the Ok Tedi mine establishment follows a similar analytical interpretation to that of investment and mineral booms in the early 1970s associated with the BCL mine.

3   The figures reported here need to be taken cautiously because they referred to minimum wages and the lowered minimum wages generally applied only to new entrants.

A Comparative Study
of Resources Booms in Papua New
Guinea, Indonesia and Nigeria

7.1   Introduction

From time to time, between the early 1970s and the early 1980s, high price levels prevailed for several minerals and primary commodities bringing price instability and sectoral transformation to the economies of some primary commodity-exporting countries. Like PNG, many other agricultural-based small open economies experienced large fluctuations in their external trade as well as in their internal economic environment. Indonesia and Nigeria are two other agricultural-based, primary commodity-exporting countries which experienced a large transfers of wealth, brought about by two major oil booms over 1972–82 (1973–74 and 1979–81). PNG experienced major booms in the same period (construction and mineral boom in 1971–74, and an agricultural commodity boom in 1976–77 which continued in another mineral boom during the 1978–79 period).

This chapter examines whether the divergent economic performance of these countries was the result of unequal magnitude of the resources booms, or the different policy measures adopted and implemented by the respective governments.

Although these countries are quite heterogeneous in terms of size, population, and stages of development, they possess many similar economic characteristics, resembling each other in their agricultural base and abundance of mineral resources. They are also comparable in terms of significant agricultural and primary sectors, which, in each case, provide the chief source of non-mineral exports. The main differences over the study period lie in their macroeconomic policies and the impact of these policies on real exchange rates, sectoral transformation and long-term savings and investment behaviour.

The organisation of this chapter is as follows: Section 7.2 briefly discusses the nature and magnitude of the oil booms in Indonesia and Nigeria during 1972–82. Section 7.3 provides a description of policy responses by the Indonesian and Nigerian governments. Section 7.4 presents a comparative study of the oil booms in Indonesia and Nigeria with that of the resources booms in PNG, and attempts to compare the magnitude of the booms and the different policy measures adopted in response. This section also analyses the effects of these booms on domestic inflation, real exchange rates and employment and wages movements and provides a brief discussion on the sectoral transformation of these economies over the boom years. Section 7.5 summarises the findings of the comparative study and draws conclusions.

7.2   Mineral and Oil Booms in PNG, Indonesia and Nigeria: 1972–82

PNG, Indonesia and Nigeria all experienced several short-lived booms over the period 1970–82, of which two major booms are particularly notable in terms of their enormous impact on sectoral changes within these economies. During the period, 1973–74, the dramatic rise in the world price of oil and minerals brought resources boom in PNG, Indonesia and Nigeria. The first oil boom was experienced by Indonesia and Nigeria in early 1974 after the world real oil price began to rise in 1973. The world real price of oil quadrupled in 1974 from its 1971/72 level and remained relatively constant over the next five years.

Nigeria experienced a large quantitative rise in the production of oil from 1970. Gelb (1988) estimated the windfall (counting both quantity and prices as windfall) at about 23 per cent of non-mining GDP for Nigeria and 16 per cent for Indonesia between 1974 and 1978.

As has been discussed in Chapter 6, PNG also experienced a major mineral boom during 1973–74. In 1974 the export unit value index of copper concentrates increased by 89 per cent from its 1972 level and the export value of copper concentrates accounted for 68 per cent of PNG's total merchandise export receipts. PNG's mineral export earning rose from 3 per cent of GDP in the financial year 1972/73 to 30 per cent in 1974. It is worth noting that the share of mineral production rose dramatically in PNG, compared with Indonesia and Nigeria.

A second boom resulted when the real price of oil increased by a further 50 per cent in 1979 with another 50-per-cent increase in 1980, before peaking in 1981 at more than six hundred per cent higher than the 1971/72 levels.[1] The volume of Nigeria's oil exports increased by 50 per cent and the value of oil exports accounted for 97 per cent of total export value in 1981.[2] Indonesian oil production increased 10 per cent between 1979 and 1981 in volume terms and the export value of oil accounted for 65 per cent of total exports in 1981. Indonesian petroleum output rose by 490 per cent in US dollar terms and the unit value of petroleum rose by 350 per cent in real terms over the period 1972–82. The importance of oil in Indonesia and Nigeria and minerals (copper, silver and gold) in PNG is shown in Table 7.1.

During 1976–77, PNG also experienced an agricultural boom as discussed in detail in Chapter 6. PNG's export of non-fuel primary commodities contributed 90 per cent of export earnings in 1977 due to an increase in export volumes of agricultural cash crops (coffee, cocoa, copra, tea, etc) brought about by favourable world market prices. PNG's export unit value indices for coffee, cocoa and copra increased by 320, 160, and 62 per cent from 1975 to 1977.

All these three countries experienced a positive terms of trade shock over the decade. The TOT increased by 139 per cent for Indonesia and 245 per cent for

Table 7.1
Minerals and oil production, exports, and the current account balances in PNG, Nigeria and Indonesia, 1970–83

Year	Minerals and oil production as % of GDP			Minerals and oil exports as % of total exports			Current account balance as % of GDP		
	PNG	Niger-ia	Indon-esia	PNG	Niger-ia	Indon-esia	PNG	Niger-ia	Indon-esia
1970	0.1	8.1	5.2	na	57.5	40.3	−32.5	−3.8	−3.4
1971	0.2	11.1	8.0	na	74.5	45.8	−26.9	−3.3	−4.0
1972	3.0	13.4	10.8	24.0	81.9	51.4	−21.7	−2.4	−3.0
1973	17.0	16.6	12.3	62.6	85.0	50.1	6.6	−0.1	−2.9
1974	30.0	31.9	22.2	68.0	92.9	70.2	20.3	16.9	2.3
1975	13.0	20.4	19.7	58.8	93.2	74.8	−0.7	0.1	−3.6
1976	11.0	22.9	18.9	60.3	93.3	70.2	−2.8	−0.8	−2.4
1977	9.0	22.6	18.9	35.6	93.4	67.2	8.3	−2.1	−0.1
1978	16.7	22.6	19.2	44.8	90.5	63.9	0.6	−7.2	−2.7
1979	22.2	26.3	21.8	51.2	93.4	56.9	−3.4	2.5	1.9
1980	18.6	19.4	25.7	51.7	96.1	58.7	−18.4	5.8	4.0
1981	18.0	22.2	24.0	55.7	96.9	64.6	−31.1	−6.7	−0.7
1982	23.4	19.1	19.6	52.9	98.6	66.7	−27.5	−8.6	−5.9
1983	10.5	15.2	18.5	53.1	96.3	63.7	−19.0	−5.0	−7.8

Note: na = not applicable

Source: Constructed from World Bank (1981), (1991) and Pinto (1987), Table 1.

Nigeria between 1972 and 1974. Export price indices also rose, by 309 per cent and 429 per cent for Indonesia and Nigeria respectively over the period. This sharp increase in the export price index and terms of trade brought about impressive increases in national income for both countries. Gross domestic product was 70 per cent higher in Indonesia and 55 per cent higher in Nigeria in 1974 than it was in 1970. Indonesia's TOT increased a further 58 per cent in 1981 over its 1978 level with a 121-per-cent increase in the export price index over the period and Nigeria's TOT increased by 89 per cent and the export price index by 145 per cent. PNG's TOT increased by 16 per cent and its export price index by 80 per cent between 1971 and 1973. During PNG's agricultural boom in 1977, TOT increased by 18 per cent with a 48-per-cent increase in the export price index compared with the 1975 levels.

Table 7.2
Terms of trade and export price indices
in PNG, Indonesia and Nigeria (1978=100)

Year	Indonesia		Nigeria		PNG	
	TOT	EPI	TOT	EPI	TOT	EPI
1971	51.2	22.2	34.3	15.5	84.4	35.6
1972	43.2	20.8	32.6	16.0	90.1	39.3
1973	49.4	30.6	38.5	22.8	98.1	64.2
1974	103.2	85.1	112.3	84.4	88.3	79.5
1975	92.2	78.6	100.0	81.2	105.8	72.7
1976	105.5	88.1	109.0	87.9	105.8	85.8
1977	113.9	99.0	111.3	97.9	125.2	107.3
1978	100.0	100.0	100.0	100.0	100.0	100.0
1979	123.8	143.1	123.3	139.9	97.0	115.9
1980	149.5	207.1	172.5	146.0	80.7	114.6
1981	158.1	220.3	189.1	244.9	69.8	101.0
1982	152.3	201.7	174.9	221.5	74.3	100.3
1983	144.1	184.0	169.4	204.3	77.6	100.9
1984	145.6	181.6	171.2	201.2	84.1	105.9

Source: Constructed from World Bank (1993).

PNG experienced another boom in the petroleum and mineral sector over 1992 and 1993 which attributed for the largest contribution by this sector to the country's export revenue and GDP growth. In 1993, the petroleum and mineral sector accounted for 30 per cent of GDP and contributed 70 per cent to total exports. A detailed discussion of this boom appears in Chapter 6.

7.3   Policy Responses: Indonesia and Nigeria

In this section various macroeconomic policy measures adopted by the governments of Indonesia and Nigeria, are analysed, such as fiscal, exchange rate and trade policies, together with their crucial role in determining structural change within these two economies.

7.3.1   Indonesia

Fiscal policy

The composition and timing of government spending are very important as windfall revenue from a resources boom accrues to the government through direct sales, royalties and taxes. As a result of the oil boom, government revenue in Indonesia increased from 11 per cent of GDP in 1970 to 32 per cent in 1974. Government revenue accounted for 24.4 per cent of GDP in 1981 and then fell to 21 per cent of GDP in 1982. Oil and gas was responsible for nearly 33 per cent of total government revenue in 1973–74, over 50 per cent in 1979–80 and 62 per cent at its peak in 1981–82. Government expenditure increased by 29 per cent in 1974 from its 1973 level and by a further 63 per cent in 1981 from its 1978 level. The budget deficit increased 10 times between 1970 and 1982 in absolute terms, but the budget deficit to GDP declined from 2.0 per cent in 1972 to 1.9 per cent in 1982.

Development expenditure

During the boom years the share of development expenditure (capital expenditure spent mostly on investment to support the private sector) to total expenditure increased from 48 per cent in 1973–74 to around 50 per cent in 1981–82 (Table 7.3). Though the share of development expenditure in the agricultural sector declined moderately in 1982 from its 1972 level, absolute government spending on agriculture increased from 16 per cent in 1972 to 22 per cent of total expenditure in 1982. After it was forced to import a large quantity of rice in 1973 at a time of high world prices the Indonesian government was committed to rapid development of the rice sector and the achievement of rice self-sufficiency. Through rapid increases in rice yield, rice production grew by 4.2 per cent per year from 1968 to 1978, and by 6.7 per cent from 1978 to 1984.

The commodity board, BULOG, adopted a pricing policy for agriculture to stabilise the price of rice and ensure the prices for agricultural exports moved in line with international price trends. The main policy emphasis of BULOG was to increase rice production together with increased investment in irrigation, research and extension, credit programme and subsidisation of major inputs and fertiliser (Pinto, 1987). As a result, the agricultural sector gained self-sufficiency in rice and was also able to increase its production of cash crops, like rubber, coffee, tea and spices, over the oil boom period. Even though the effective rate of manufacturing protection penalised the agricultural export sector by 11 per cent, the production of agricultural output increased substantially in absolute terms, and the agricultural price level was moving slightly higher than the general price level over the 1970s (Scherr, 1989).

In an attempt to strengthen the infrastructure of the economy and diversify exports from oil to non-oil commodities, the Indonesian government substantially increased development expenditure on education and training, roads and construction and health and family planning – from 63 per cent of total expenditure in 1969–70 to 74 per cent in 1982–83.

Table 7.3
Real government revenue and expenditure of Indonesia
(at constant 1980 prices, billion Rupiah)

Year	Government revenue			Government expenditure			
	Develop-ment[1]	Routine[2]	Total	Oil and gas	Develop-ment[3]	Routine[4]	Total
1973/74	632.91	3003.75	3636.66	1186.35	1422.57	2214.09	3636.66
1974/75	535.99	4051.56	4587.54	2211.41	2240.06	2451.45	4691.51
1975/76	949.34	4329.38	5278.72	2410.04	2705.31	2573.41	5278.72
1976/77	1298.18	4813.10	6111.28	2708.49	3411.90	2699.38	6111.28
1977/78	1160.72	5305.93	6466.66	2924.61	3241.58	3225.07	6466.66
1978/79	1459.26	6011.91	7471.16	3253.48	3604.66	3866.50	7471.16
1979/80	1520.53	7372.90	8893.44	4689.64	4421.56	4471.88	8893.44
1980/81	1406.36	9627.70	11034.05	6608.25	5573.84	5460.12	11033.96
1981/82	1488.68	10638.15	12126.83	7515.33	6048.78	6078.05	12126.83
1982/83	1540.91	9863.38	11404.29	6489.59	5847.50	5557.03	11404.53
1983/84	2753.48	10235.96	12989.43	6752.91	7023.62	5965.82	12989.43

Notes: 1. Government Foreign Borrowing and Loans to support the private sector.
　　　　　2. Domestic revenue including oil and gas.
　　　　　3. Mostly spent on investment to support private sector.
　　　　　4. Mostly for consumption expenditure.

Source: Nota Keuangan Dan Rancangan Anggaran Pendapatan Negara Republik Indonesia
　　　　　(Income Statement), various issues.

7.3.2   Trade Policy

During the early 1960s, there were extensive barriers to international trade in Indonesia. Apart from establishing a unified exchange rate, Soeharto's 'New Order' regime moved decisively towards more open trade policies between 1967 and 1971. From then until the mid-1980s, Indonesia's trade regime again became increasingly inward-oriented as the government taxed or banned some traditional exports, pursued its goal of self-sufficiency in rice and invested a large share of oil revenue to set up import-substituting manufacturing industries. The primary instrument of trade protection was a high and disparate tariff structure. Import tariffs became the major form of protection from the early 1970s and over the 1976–78 period the average tariff rate on manufactured imported items was about 66 per cent. The import competing manufacturing sector also received substantial trade protection in the form of import quotas and direct input subsidies. Import bans reappeared from the early 1970s, especially in the automobile and textiles industries.

In 1970, export taxes and import duties constituted about 37 per cent of non-oil domestic revenue (Hill, 1996). Table 7.4 summarises protection estimates by several authors. It is apparent that the effective rate of protection for importables increased over 1971–84 whereas all studies found negative protection for exportables over the period. The trade regime became more restrictive during 1982–85. After the second oil boom, as a result of steady decline in Indonesia's commodity exports and the adverse effects of the world recession on the Indonesian economy.

Tariff protection was supplemented by a proliferation of non-tariff barrier (NTBs) in the form of restrictive licences. In addition, export restrictions in the form of bans; taxes and quotas were implemented for unprocessed agricultural commodities. During 1980, bans on log exports were introduced in stages and all log exports were banned after 1985. Little et al. (1993) found that during the tight trade regime of 1983–84 Indonesian imports fell by 11 per cent and trade tax revenue by 7 per cent.

Table 7.4
Estimates of effective rates of protection of Indonesia (per cent)

	Pitt 1971	World Bank 1975	Parker 1984
All tradables	33	30	133
Exportables	–11	–2	–4
Importables:	66	58	224
import competing	na	61	na
non-import competing	15	9	na
Sub-sectors:			
cigarettes	556	4	na
sugar refining	154	–9	141
weaving	NVA	192	589
motor vehicles	526	718	2948

Notes: These series are generally not directly comparable except where the same author or methodology is involved. NVA indicates negative value added at international prices, na indicates there were no estimates presented for this category.

Source: Hill (1996), Table 6.8, p. 112.

7.3.3   Exchange Rate Policy

The aim of the exchange rate policy was to maintain the Indonesia's external competitiveness, and this was achieved by a series of nominal devaluations in a situation of rising domestic inflation. The most noticeable macroeconomic policy undertaken by the Indonesian government was two massive currency devaluations in 1978 and 1983.

Over 1971–78, Indonesia's nominal exchange rate was pegged to the American dollar. As the government spent most of its windfall revenue domestically, the money supply increased by 30 per cent in 1974. This led to high domestic inflation and a subsequent appreciation of the real exchange rate. In November 1978, to reverse the erosion of competitiveness in its non-oil sector Indonesia devalued its currency by 50 per cent and changed the exchange rate system from a fixed to a flexible regime.

As a result, the real exchange rate depreciated significantly. As pointed out by Warr (1986), following the devaluation, the index of tradables to nontradables price ratio reached a peak (real depreciation) after 3 to 5 months, indicating a substantial rise in the tradable sector's competitiveness. There was a sharp increase in non-oil exports in 1977. But the second oil shock during 1979–81 led to monetary expansion, and increased inflation. Thus, the effects of the devaluation were eroded by domestic inflation and then wiped out by late 1982 (Arndt and Sundrum, 1984). In March 1983, Indonesia devalued its currency again by 38 per cent in an attempt to stimulate non-mining exports, and combat high inflation and low TOT.

7.3.4   Nigeria

Fiscal policy

During the two oil booms, government revenue in Nigeria increased substantially from only 11 per cent of non-mining GDP in 1970, to 41 per cent in 1974 and 37 per cent in 1981. Both current and capital expenditure also showed an increasing trend over the period 1974–82. Capital expenditure accelerated rapidly from only 3.6 per cent of non-mining GDP in 1970 to 18 per cent in 1974 and 43 per cent by 1982. Current expenditure accounted for 11.6 per cent of non-mining GDP in 1974 and 21.1 per cent in 1981 (Table 7.5). As a result Nigeria's budget surplus of 6 per cent of GDP in 1974 turned into a budget deficit of 8 per cent in 1982.

Development expenditure

Spending on agriculture and rural development rose from 3–5 per cent of GDP in 1970 to 9–10 per cent in 1982 (World Bank, 1985). Import subsidies for agriculture were quite generous, at around 50 per cent for tractors and 85 per cent for fertilisers. But the share of government real expenditure for tree crop production, processing and marketing declined markedly. Most of the capital intensive and large-scale projects that dominated the agricultural development programme turned out to be inefficient, drawing resources away from smallholders. Some benefited from the fertiliser subsidies, but there were no definite subsidy programmes for the dominant food crop sector provided by smallholders (Scherr, 1989).

Nigeria's public capital spending was geared towards the nontradable sector and the transport and communications sector received a large rise in public funding allocation. Other public spending on infrastructure was also directed to the urban population. Capital spending on education increased sharply, from 3.9 per cent of total spending in 1973/74 to 18.2 per cent in 1975/76. Increased investment in buildings, and roads, as well as schools, led to another boom in the construction sector.

The services and construction sectors' value added increased from the 1974 level by about 30 per cent in 1976 and 48 per cent in 1982. Public investment spending on heavy manufacturing increased rapidly after the decision to build a steel industry in the late 1970s.

7.3.5   Trade Policy

Trade policy in Nigeria has traditionally protected local manufacturing industries by imposing relatively high tariffs and import duties. Domestic manufacturing received

Table 7.5
Federal budget of Nigeria, 1970–82
(percentage of non-mining GDP)

Year	Total revenue	Non-oil revenue	Oil revenue	Current expenditure	Capital expenditure
1970	10.7	7.9	2.8	8.5	3.6
1971	16.0	8.2	7.8	8.6	4.9
1972	16.2	7.7	8.5	9.6	5.7
1973	24.0	7.5	16.5	10.9	7.5
1974	40.6	7.7	32.9	11.6	17.8
1975	34.3	7.2	27.1	15.9	27.5
1976	33.9	7.5	26.4	13.2	29.5
1977	33.0	8.6	24.4	14.7	28.0
1978	24.9	8.1	16.8	13.3	20.3
1979	42.2	7.7	34.5	18.1	26.7
1980	47.2	8.7	38.5	21.1	26.5
1981	37.2	8.7	28.5	21.1	29.6
1982	29.7	7.0	22.7	42.7	42.7

Source: Constructed from Gelb (1988), Table 13-2, p. 240.

high levels of protection and artificially expanded production assisted by prohibitive tariffs and other quantitative import restrictions, price controls and subsidies which acted as incentives to the sector. Overall, these policies made the manufacturing sector behave as a nontradable sector at the margin. At the end of the first oil boom, particularly when oil exports tended to fall, Nigerian authorities decided to tighten import restrictions via increasing tariffs and quantitative restrictions on imports.

Gelb (1988) shows the net effective rate of protection for consumer goods rose from 55.8 to 124.9 per cent between 1977 and 1980. The share of manufacturing in GDP increased by more than 9 per cent in 1981–83. But after the collapse of the oil price, together with reductions in tariffs and dismantling of quantitative restrictions in 1986, the share of the manufacturing sector in GDP fell substantially.

Trade protection for agriculture has been highly erratic and inconsistent, and mainly in response to foreign exchange availability, rather than a systematic policy of protection. The government tried to increase agricultural production by giving producers higher price incentives. Between 1974–81, producers' prices doubled for many agricultural commodities but agricultural production did not increase as was expected. In spite of an increase in agricultural protection in the early 1980s, agricultural crops generally received less protection than the manufacturing sector, and, within the agricultural sector, export crops received less protection than food crops (Table 7.6). As a result, the agricultural sector as a whole contracted sharply.

Table 7.6
Effective rates of protection for selected agricultural crops in Nigeria (per cent)

Commodity	1970–76	1979	1980	1981	1982
Maize	13	61	95	189	247
Rice	35	1	–4	13	59
Sorghum	13	86	67	190	197
Millet	13	8	9	5	3
Yams	na	1	1	1	0
Cassava	na	1	1	0	1
Cowpeas	na	4	4	2	2
Groundnuts	–53	–1	–11	18	na
Palm oil	–29	na	na	na	na
Cocoa	–42	–31	22	138	114
Rubber	na	–1	–23	34	na
Cotton	–43	–21	–16	18	20

Note: 'na' means not available. Effective rates of protection are computed taking into account purchased inputs subject to import duties and sales taxes.

Source: Oyejide (1986), Table 7, p. 31.

The more pervasive effects of protection impacted upon the real exchange rate. Given industrial protection, the real exchange that maintains external balance was lower than the equilibrium real rate that would have prevailed otherwise. In the absence of import restrictions, food grains are considered to be potentially tradable. Collier (1988) pointed out the production of food grains declined during the oil boom but food prices rose relative to the price of nontradables. He termed this phenomenon the 'Nigerian disease', since the standard theory of 'Dutch disease' could not explain the decline of the food grain sector at a time of high prices for them. The spending effects of the oil boom raised the demand for food grains, but the production of food grains declined relative to the labour force. This paradoxical outcome is explained by Collier (1988) as the result of a massive rural labour migration to the cities induced by higher public sector demand for labour, which contracted food production and increased its relative price.

7.3.6   Exchange Rate Policy

Nigeria's exchange rate policy appears to have focused on maintaining a relatively stable nominal exchange rate over the period from the 1970s to the mid-1980s. In 1973, an ad hoc devaluation of the Naira brought a small adjustment to the exchange rate. However, during 1974–78, the Central Bank of Nigeria adopted a strategy of gradual nominal appreciation of the Naira against the US dollar and British pound sterling, primarily with the aim of maintaining the country's balance of payments situation. Nigeria also discounted the important contribution of the agricultural sector. Nigeria did not devalue its currency until the mid-1980s, on the premise that cheap imports were essential to political stability and that the expected economic benefits of higher agricultural exports were insignificant (Oyejide, 1986).

7.4   Comparative Studies of Resources Booms

For the purpose of a comparative study the key economic indicators for Indonesia, Nigeria and PNG are summarised in Table 7.7.

7.4.1   The Magnitude of Booms

To begin with the mineral sectors' contribution to GDP – PNG's mineral sector's share to GDP increased dramatically, from only 0.8 per cent in 1970 to 30 per cent in 1974 (Table 7.7), whereas the contribution of the Indonesian mineral and petroleum sector increased from 12.3 in 1973 to 22.2 per cent to GDP in 1974.

PNGI, PNGII and PNGIII refer to the resources booms in PNG in 1974, 1977 and 1992–93 respectively. INDOI, INDOII and NIGI, NIGII refer to two oil booms in 1974 and 1981–82.

The contribution of Nigeria's oil production also increased to 32 per cent of GDP

Table 7.7
Comparative economic indicators in PNG, Indonesia and Nigeria

	PNG I	PNG II	PNG III	INDO I	INDO II	NIG I	NIG II
	1974	1977	1993	1974	1982	1974	1982
Share of mineral and petroleum/GDP	30	11	30	22	14	32	30
Share of mineral and petroleum/total export	68	36	70	70	75	93	99
Per capita GNP (US dollar)	460	550	1130	150	610	360	1120
Population (million)	2.6	2.9	4.1	130	155	73	91
Average annual growth rate of population (%) 1970–82	1.9	na	2.3*	2.3	na	2.5	na
Per capita average growth rate of GDP 1970–82	5.7ª	na	5.5ᵇ	7.7	na	3.8	na
Inflation (% per annum) 1975–82	7.6	na	5.0ᵇ	14.2	na	17.7	na
Central government expenditure/GDP (as %)	30	30	32	14.3	27.3	13.6	23.3
Current account balance/total merchandise export (as %)	42	18	25	8.2	–3.3	50.5	–37.6
External Public debt/ GDP (as %)	18	32	26	33.5	21.5	7.0	8.5

Notes:　a. The entry provides the average for 1970–80.
　　　　　b. The entry provides the average for 1991–94.
　　　　　* provides the average for 1980–93.
　　　　　na = not available.

Source:　World Bank (1981), (1983–84), (1984), (1993), (1995) and IMF, *International Financial Statistics*, various issues.

in 1974 compared with 17 per cent in 1973. The swing in PNG's current account balance was also dramatic in 1974. PNG's current account surplus accounted for more than 20 per cent of GDP in 1974 compared to 17 per cent for Nigeria and 2.3 per cent for Indonesia. In 1982, while the mineral export share accounted for 75 per cent for Indonesia and 99 per cent for Nigeria, PNG's mineral sector to GDP and share of mineral export to total export declined substantially.

Indonesian real GDP grew at 8 per cent in 1974 and 8.3 per cent in 1981. The annual average growth rate of per capita GDP was 7.7 per cent between 1970 and 1982. The average annual real GDP growth rate for Nigeria was more than 7 per cent during 1970–80 compared with 4 per cent during the 1950s and 1960s. Nigeria's real per capita income increased by almost 60 per cent between 1972 and 1974, and by more than 200 per cent between 1972–80. The growth rate of PNG's real GDP was at around 7 per cent in 1973 and 10 per cent in 1977. PNG achieved reasonably high average annual per capita GDP growth of 5.7 per cent over 1970–80 and 5.5 per cent over 1991–94.

These figures show the order of magnitudes of the resources booms in the three economies, indicating that the magnitude was similar in terms of their impact on exports and overall output of the economy. The next section discusses the different policy measures adopted by the respective governments in response to these booms.

7.4.2   Policy Measures

Since the early 1970s, PNG, Indonesia and Nigeria have all gone through a wide range of policy experiments in the wake of resources booms. This section attempts to compare the various macroeconomic policies adopted by the respective governments and their crucial role in determining structural change and seeks to identify relevant factors that can explain the divergent performances of these three economies.

Fiscal policy

This section compares and contrasts the PNG government's fiscal policy and domestic demand responses over the boom years with those of Indonesia and Nigeria during the 1970s and early 1980s. As discussed in Chapter 6, after national independence, the main aim of the PNG government was to increase government revenue whilst holding real government spending at a low level to reduce reliance on Australian aid. These policy objectives succeeded to a remarkable degree over the second half of the 1970s.

Government consumption and domestic absorption increased sharply over the decade of the 1970s, both in Indonesia and Nigeria, while PNG maintained relatively more stable levels as indicated by Figure 7.1. Over the period 1970–82, the average annual real growth rate of Indonesian public consumption (11.9 per cent) and public investment (13.7 per cent) were much higher than in PNG and Nigeria. Government consumption increased three fold in PNG, compared with almost 26 times in Indonesia and 10 times in Nigeria (Table Appendix A7.1).

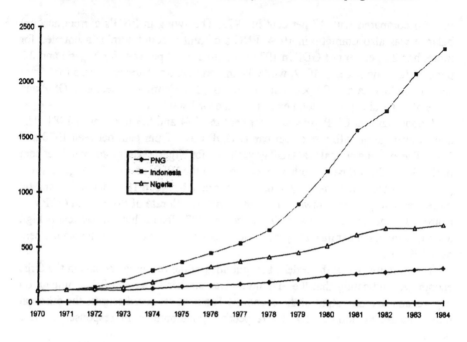

Source: Table Appendix A7.1.

Figure 7.1   Index of real domestic absorption in PNG, Indonesia and Nigeria, 1970–82 (1970=100)

General consumption by the PNG government increased by 73 per cent in 1974 compared to the 1970 level, whereas the Nigerian government increased consumption by 117 per cent, and Indonesia by 187 per cent. The PNG government was successful in reducing consumption levels during the second half of the 1970s by implementing income and wage restraint and by reducing dependency on Australian budgetary support.

Between 1977 and 1982 government consumption increased by 39 per cent in PNG. By contrast, government consumption rose by 262 per cent in Indonesia and 75 per cent in Nigeria from 1977 to 1982.

Real domestic absorption[3] increased significantly higher in Indonesia and Nigeria over the period (Figure 7.1). From the 1970 level, the index of domestic absorption increased by 22, 80, and 188 per cent in PNG, Nigeria and Indonesia, respectively, in 1974. In 1977, PNG's domestic absorption increased by only 38 per cent whereas Indonesia increased domestic absorption by 85 per cent and Nigeria by 106 per cent from the 1974 level. By 1982, domestic absorption had increased a further 226 per cent in Indonesia, and 81 per cent in Nigeria, compared with 65 per cent in PNG.

PNG's public debt as a ratio of GNP was moderate compared to Indonesia in 1973, but increased sharply in 1982. This increase, caused by a down grading of ore grades at the major copper mines, pushed PNG to borrow in order to cover its current account deficit. PNG's foreign debt increased by 67 per cent from early 1977 to 1982, while exports revenue increased by only 58 per cent in US dollar terms (Harvey, 1987). While Indonesia's public debt to GNP fell substantially in 1982 from its 1973 level, the ratio for Nigeria increased moderately over the period, as seen in Table 7.7. In 1982, debt service ratios to total exports were also lower for Indonesia and Nigeria compared with PNG.

However, the PNG government failed to maintain fiscal discipline during the 1990s, and increased agricultural price support schemes and increased defence expenditure for the Bougainville rebellion caused fiscal deficits to explode during the first few years of the 1990s. PNG's fiscal deficit increased significantly from 1 per cent in 1988 to 5.9 per cent in 1993, with government consumption at K1018 million in 1993. None of the stabilisation funds (MRSF and CPSF) actively restrained government spending. Domestic absorption also increased from K2568 million in 1990 to K4493 million in 1993. Since the budget deficits were financed domestically, the demand for goods and services was satisfied by rising imports, eroding the international reserves of the Central Bank, until a foreign currency crisis emerged in September 1994 when international reserves were almost exhausted (AusAID, 1996). Contractionary policy measures were then successfully implemented by the PNG government, which reduced the budget deficit to 2.3 per cent of GDP in 1994. Radical labour market reform undertaken in 1992 also helped regain price stability and competitiveness to a large extent by the end of 1994.

Exchange rate and trade policy

After monetary independence in 1976, the PNG government undertook a series of revaluations of the nominal exchange rate during the second half of 1970s as discussed in Chapter 6. PNG revalued its exchange rate by 6.5 per cent in 1978, Indonesia and Nigeria devalued their nominal exchange rates in 1973. In 1978 while Indonesia undertook a large devaluation to restore export competitiveness eroded by increased domestic inflation induced by the first oil boom, Nigeria also devalued its currency by 10 per cent (Table 7.8).

Between 1970 and the mid-1980s, there were virtually no trade restriction in PNG and the country was literally a 'free-trade country' which helped to keep the domestic price level lower than its major trading partners and prevented erosion of the competitiveness of the export sector. By contrast, both Indonesia and Nigeria followed increasingly restrictive trade policies. Indonesia adopted more protectionist trade policies from the mid-1970s to the mid-1980s and increased protection rates even further after the second oil boom in 1983–84. Nigeria pursued relatively open trade strategies during the 1973–74 period but after the second oil boom reverted towards a more restrictive trade regime during 1980–85.

As a result of the oil price decline in 1982–83, Nigeria faced a large balance of payments crisis, as did Indonesia. In 1983, in the face of this crisis, Indonesia devalued its currency but increased trade restrictions. Nigeria held on to its fixed exchange rate policy and did not devalue its currency until the mid-1980s, when it

Table 7.8
Import-weighted real exchange rates in
PNG, Indonesia and Nigeria (1980=100)

| Year | Inflation (%) | | | Nominal exchange rate | | | Real exchange rate | | |
	PNG	Indon-esia	Niger-ia	PNG	Indon-esia	Niger-ia	PNG	Indon-esia	Niger-ia
1970	3.0	12.4	13.6	127.2	43.4	99.8	114.6	91.8	156.0
1971	5.6	4.4	16.1	127.0	47.2	102.0	111.3	100.5	146.1
1972	3.5	6.4	2.8	126.4	54.1	100.6	110.5	113.2	148.5
1973	31.1	31.0	5.5	123.0	59.5	108.6	91.6	105.8	164.6
1974	7.5	40.6	12.5	122.0	58.1	100.5	102.7	87.6	154.5
1975	8.6	19.1	33.8	124.9	57.8	100.0	106.3	82.6	131.0
1976	3.8	19.8	24.2	113.5	56.7	92.8	100.3	74.2	108.7
1977	0.4	11.0	19.5	112.2	59.1	97.6	105.3	75.1	112.8
1978	5.6	8.1	18.6	104.9	70.1	107.9	97.4	86.2	109.0
1979	5.3	20.6	11.1	100.4	101.0	108.0	99.0	109.1	106.1
1980	13.4	18.5	11.4	100.0	100.0	100.0	100.0	100.0	100.0
1981	11.9	12.2	20.9	101.0	98.7	96.8	96.7	94.3	87.8
1982	3.4	9.5	7.7	98.3	96.0	94.2	96.6	87.5	85.4
1983	14.1	11.8	18.9	107.2	128.9	93.7	96.0	107.9	72.4
1984	9.3	10.5	39.6	107.8	145.2	90.1	90.5	112.8	52.2

Note: Inflation = changes in domestic CPI; Nominal exchange rate = trade-weighted nominal effective exchange rate and Real exchange rate = import-weighted real exchange rate.

Source: Pinto (1987), Table 3, p.427. PNG's exchange rate indices are constructed by the author.

also severely tightened import restriction by a series of quantitative trade restrictions (Little et al., 1993). As a result, resources were diverted from the tradable to nontradable and import-competing sectors, put upward pressure on the domestic price level and rapidly appreciated the real exchange rates of these two countries.

From the mid-1980s, the trade regime of PNG also became more restrictive driven primarily by revenue collection motives. The rise in trade protection was accompanied by higher levels of tariffs, bans on certain food items, import quotas and special privileges for certain industries. This impacted severely on the cost structure of the rest of the economy and had a negative impact on domestic price level and competitiveness of the economy in the world market. This outcome is confirmed by the econometric results in Chapter 4, indicating that the introduction of a restrictive trade regime from the mid-1980s appreciated the real exchange rate of PNG and significantly reduced the competitiveness of both export and import-competing sectors.

The nature of trade policy regimes plays a very important role in determining the outcome of a resources boom and the overall economic performance of a country. The difference in exchange rate and trade policies in these three countries had severe economic ramifications in later years. The next section attempts to analyse the impact of policy measures on the domestic price level and the relative price of tradables to nontradables for these economies.

7.4.3   Comparison of the Effects of Booms

This section compares how external shocks and government policy measures in these three economies impacted upon domestic price levels, real exchange rates, employment and wages.

Domestic price level

Compared with Indonesia and Nigeria, the impact of the booms on the domestic price level was relatively moderate in PNG. Throughout the period 1970–82, Indonesia's domestic price level remained higher than its major trading partners, with an average annual rate of inflation at about 16 per cent between 1975–82. In 1978, the GDP deflator had doubled from its 1971 level. The performance of the Nigerian economy was even worse in terms of inflation. The oil booms increased the inflation rate sharply in the mid-1970s as public spending rose dramatically, and the average annual rate of inflation was around 18 per cent between 1975–82 (Table 7.7). The high levels of industrial protection for domestic manufacturing were a major contributor to this rate. PNG's incomes and wage restraint policies, coupled with a 'hard kina' exchange rate policy and a very open trade regime contributed to low inflation over the same period.

A 10-per-cent devaluation of the kina in 1983, coupled with a more inward-looking trade regime was one of the major factors in causing higher domestic inflation from the mid-1980s. Another devaluation in 1990, large fiscal deficits during the first few years of the 1990s, and higher levels of trade protection for selected industries and goods, were mostly responsible for PNG having a higher inflation rate than its trading partners in the first half of the 1990s.

Real exchange rates

The movement of the real exchange rate gives some indication of the competitiveness of the tradable sector and the overall competitiveness of an economy compared with its major trading partners. This section attempts to trace how the various policy responses to the resources booms of the 1970s and early 1980s influenced real exchange rates in PNG, Indonesia and Nigeria.

Table 7.8 compares the import-weighted real exchange rate, nominal exchange rate and domestic price level for these three economies. There is very little difference between import-weighted and trade-weighted real exchange rate indices that were used for the discussion in Chapter 4. Therefore, import-weighted real exchange rate has been used for this comparative study as it excludes the major booming commodities (for example, oil, copper or other primary booming commodities) from the computation and focuses on the non-booming sectors.

The largest real exchange rate erosion was experienced by Nigeria whose real exchange rate doubled by the end of the second oil boom. The real exchange rate for Indonesia also started to appreciate in the wake of the first oil boom. Indonesia's real exchange rate appreciated by more than 17 per cent in 1974. A large devaluation of the nominal exchange rate in 1978 temporarily helped restore competitiveness of the export sector for the next few years. The real exchange rate again started to appreciate with the second oil boom during 1980–81 and continued to appreciate until another devaluation was undertaken in 1983.

PNG provides an interesting contrast to these two oil-exporting countries. On average PNG's real exchange rate showed a mild appreciation over the period of 1970–82. The real exchange rate started to appreciate in 1971, reflecting the impact of large foreign capital inflow and subsequent construction boom, due to establishment of the BCL mine (Table 7.8). High TOT over this period seems to have had a significant income effect on PNG's real exchange rate behaviour. The real exchange appreciation in 1973 might also have been partially influenced by the 'Dutch disease' phenomenon associated with the resources boom in mineral and construction sector with high levels of government consumption. When domestic inflation peaked at around 31 per cent in 1973, the import-weighted real exchange rate appreciated by almost 17 per cent.

Compared with Indonesia and Nigeria PNG's real exchange rate was relatively stable on average up until the end of the decade (Figure 7.2). After 1973, a very slight appreciation of the real exchange rate is noticeable in 1976 and 1978. It should be pointed out that PNG's real exchange rate depreciated substantially (about 5 per cent) in 1977 when the economy was at the height of an agricultural commodity boom. PNG's income and expenditure restraint policy, coupled with a sensible exchange rate policy and an open trade regime, at that time, can claim the full credit for this exceptional improvement of competitiveness of the tradable sector and domestic price stability. In 1981, the real exchange rate appreciated 3 per cent and remained stable until 1984 when it appreciated another 6 per cent, due to higher domestic inflation than PNG's major trading partners.

Indonesia's real exchange rate depreciated during 1971–72, mainly because domestic inflation was lower than in its major trading partners. Indonesia's real exchange rate started to appreciate in 1973 with the oil price hike and had appreciated 18 per cent in 1974. A substantial real appreciation between 1973–77 reflects 'Dutch disease' effects associated with the high level of government consumption on the domestic nontradable sector which increased the price of nontradables compared to tradables and reduced non-oil export competitiveness. A 50-per-cent depreciation of the nominal exchange rate in 1978 was mainly responsible for the real exchange rate depreciation between 1978–79. With the surge of the second oil boom, Indonesia's real exchange rate again started to appreciate in 1980, and continues to erode the competitiveness of non-oil tradable sector up until a second nominal devaluation undertaken in 1983 (Figure 7.2).

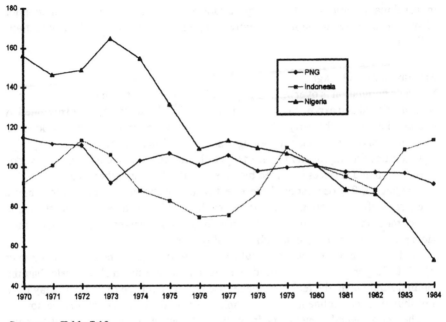

Source: Table 7.10.

Figure 7.2   Import-weighted real exchange rates in PNG, Indonesia and Nigeria (1980=100)

Nigeria's real exchange rate remained overvalued even before the resources boom in the early 1970s. However, compared with PNG and Indonesia, Nigeria's inflation rate was low, which ensured the depreciation of Nigeria's real exchange rate in 1973. As Nigeria started to have a large influx of export earnings associated with the oil boom in 1974, the real exchange rate began to appreciate, and by 1984 had appreciated more than 150 per cent whereas the nominal rate appreciated by only 12 per cent (Table 7.10 and Figure 7.2). This reflects the loss of competitiveness of Nigeria's tradable and exportable sector with a double-digit inflation rate start continued over the rest of the decade. The over valued real exchange rate substantially reduced productive incentives for Nigeria's non-oil tradable sector, particularly agriculture. Agricultural export revenue declined from over a billion dollars to less than a hundred million during the years of the oil boom (Taylor et al., 1985).

During the resources boom of the early 1990s, PNG's fiscal expansion, and a more closed trade regime, impacted adversely on the price of tradables. As the relative price of nontradables to tradables increased substantially during the 1991–93 period, PNG suffered from real exchange appreciation. However, the tradable sector was able to restore competitiveness to a large extent, due to an improvement in world market prices for PNG's agricultural exports and the government adoption of stricter measures to implement more comprehensive income and wage restraint policies.

Employment and wages

Nigeria's population is overwhelmingly rural and concentrated in the South. Over 90 per cent of food and export crop production is highly labour intensive and provided by smallholders. From the early 1970s, the major constraint on agricultural production appears to have been a labour shortage, as the rural market was distorted by high opportunities for employment in nearby petroleum activities and other public works, construction and services provided by the state, all offering higher wages.

Oyejide (1986) decomposed the effect of the oil boom on employment into a structural shift and economic growth effect. Table 7.9 indicates that total change in employment in the agricultural sector recorded a small increase. Thus, agriculture had a relative, but not absolute, fall in employment.

Table 7.10 indicates that nominal rural wage increased about five times over the 1970–75 period. As the domestic CPI increased at a much slower rate than the nominal rural wage, the real rural wage rose rapidly over the period, and may have contributed to the decline in relative employment in the rural agricultural sector.

The major overall beneficiary from the oil boom in employment terms was the services sector, which accounted for a 70 per cent rise in employment compared with little more than a 27-per-cent increase in the manufacturing sector. This empirical evidence supports the theoretical proposition of the booming sector that a resources boom shifts employment from the agricultural tradable sectors to the nontradable services sector. The increased employment in manufacturing can be explained

Table 7.9
Sectoral shifts of employment in Nigeria, 1970–82

Sector	Sectoral shift effect	Economic growth effect	Total change	Percentage change
Agriculture	−5.440	5.570	0.130	1.7
Oil and mining	0.068	0.018	0.086	1.2
Manufacturing	0.918	1.110	2.028	27.3
Services	4.454	0.732	5.186	69.8

Source: Oyejide (1986) Table 13, p. 40.

Table 7.10
Minimum wage and rural wage rate indices, 1970–82
(Naira/day, 1970=100)

Year	Rural wage Naira/day	National minimum wage Naira/day	CPI	Real rural wage	Real national minimum wage
1970	100	100	100	100	100
1971	177	100	116	153	86
1972	253	100	119	213	84
1973	330	100	127	260	79
1974	407	337	144	283	234
1975	483	337	161	300	209
1976	560	561	198	283	283
1977	637	561	231	276	243
1978	713	561	269	265	209
1979	867	645	300	289	215
1980	900	645	331	271	195
1981	934	702	400	233	176
1982	1000	702	431	232	163

Source: Oyejide (1986) Table 1, p.17.

as quantitative trade restrictions increased the demand for import-competing manufactured goods, as the sector behaved like a nontradable sector at the margin due to high protection.

Since the national minimum wage remained constant, with rising inflation, Nigeria's national real minimum wage declined significantly over 1970–73 which might have created more opportunities for urban employment. From the mid-1970s, both the national real minimum wage increased rapidly, though the rate of change in wage rates became slower from 1980.

The Indonesian situation was very different. A strong regional labour market and surplus rural labour supply minimised the adverse affects of labour migration out of agriculture. Even at the height of the oil boom, an abundant rural labour supply helped overcome the labour shortage in rice production.

There was no substantial increase in regional wage rates to attract labour from other regional rural production. Technological improvements in agriculture offset the high cost of labour in the labour shortage areas with employment rising by about 2 per cent per annum in the agricultural sector between 1971–81 (Scherr, 1989;

Sundrum, 1986). Among other non-mining sectors, the manufacturing and finance sectors accounted for the largest increase in employment both in absolute and relative terms between 1971 and 1981 (Table 7.11). Real wages also followed an increasing trend over the period except for a drop in real wages for 2–3 years following the 1978 devaluation (Warr, 1986). Real wages in manufacturing increased about 56 per cent between 1970–82. The rise in the rural real wage ranged between 3 to 39 per cent over the period (Warr, 1986).

The growth in PNG's formal employment in the agricultural sector was stagnant between 1970–80 although employment in agriculture increased in absolute terms over the period 1977–79. Since PNG's labour supply is quite elastic, the booming mining sector did not compete with other traded sectors for labour resources. It was also found that on several occasions, supply of labour to the non-mining sector was complementary rather than competitive with the mining sector's labour demand (Parsons and Vincent, 1991).

Table 7.11
Indonesian sectoral allocation of employment, 1971–81 (millions)

Sector	Employment		Annual growth	Estimated employment	
	1971	1980	(%)	1973	1981
Agricultural	24.911	28.834	1.64	15.84	29.21
Mining	.080	.387	19.14	.11	.46
Manufacturing	2.571	4.680	6.88	2.95	4.99
Utilities	0.034	.066	7.65	.04	.07
Construction	0.638	1.657	11.19	.79	1.83
Trade	4.073	6.679	5.65	4.56	7.04
Transport	0.900	1.468	5.59	1.01	1.54
Finance	0.087	.302	14.83	.12	.35
Public administration	1.379[a]	2.223[a]	5.45	1.54	2.33
Other services	2.916[a]	3.485	2.00[a]	3.05	3.54
Total	37.589	49.781	3.17	40.01	51.36

Note: a = adjusted.
Source: Sundrum (1986) Table 15, p. 59.

7.4.4   Sectoral Output Composition

Resources booms over the early 1970s to the early 1980s had an enormous impact on the key macroeconomic variables of these three economies. As discussed in the theoretical framework for this study, a resources boom affects the overall economy through a chain network of interaction among different macroeconomic variables. Increased revenue from a resources boom not only affects the allocation of factors of production, it affects demand and supply conditions in the product market. The flow of windfall revenue affects relative factor prices as well as relative product prices and the real exchange rate. Over time, a resources boom changes the sectoral composition of an economy, through changes in domestic inflation and the relative prices of traded to nontradable goods that create changes in the competitiveness of a sector.

This section compares changes in sectoral composition for these three economies that were affected by the resources booms and government policy responses during the boom years from 1970–82, when the production structure of all three economies underwent a noticeable transformation. The share of the agricultural sector to GDP declined in all three countries to varying degrees. The share of the agricultural sector to GDP declined by 18 per cent in PNG, 45 per cent in Indonesia and 55 per cent in Nigeria from 1970 to 1982.

A tight management structure for macroeconomic policy was quickly established in PNG right after national and monetary independence in 1975. These sound macroeconomic policies made it possible for PNG to reduce the price instability brought about by a large influx of windfall revenue. The share of agriculture improved significantly, from 26 per cent in 1974 to 35 per cent in 1977, before declining to 32 per cent of GDP in 1982, due to depressed world market prices for PNG's agricultural exports.

Over the period 1970–82, Indonesia was also successful in minimising the adverse effects of oil booms on the agricultural and manufacturing traded sectors. Increased government spending in the agricultural sector maintained steady growth in this sector, especially for food crops, with an average annual growth rate of 3.8 per cent, and a per capita growth rate of 1.5 per cent (Scherr, 1989). The output of rice grew an average of 3.7 per cent in 1977–82 (Gelb and Associates, 1988).

By 1982–83, Indonesia's food output per capita reached 133 per cent higher compared to 106 per cent for world per capita food output from its 1968–72 level. Though the contribution of agricultural output to GDP declined from 47 per cent in 1970 to 26 per cent in 1982, Indonesia managed to raise the supply of domestic food and agricultural products in absolute terms.

The value of agricultural exports rose compared to food imports, with a ratio of 1 to 0.68 during 1973–81, and total agricultural income also increased substantially (Scherr, 1989).

Most Indonesian manufacturing output was imperfect substitutes (partially traded) for imported goods and behaved as nontradables under quantitative trade restrictions. As a result, despite a large increase in nontradable goods and

Table 7.12

Sectoral composition of GDP in PNG, Indonesia and Nigeria, 1970 and 1982

		1970			1982	
(% of GDP)	PNG	Indon-esia	Nigeria	PNG	Indon-esia	Nigeria
Agriculture	40	47	49	33	26	22
Mining and oil	25*	12*	17*	8	14	30
Manufact-uring	0.9	10	7	10	16	6
Services	41	36	34	40	30	47

Note: * figures refer to 1973.
Source: World Bank (1993)

services during the boom years, Indonesia's manufacturing sector expanded, due to imperfect substitutability with imported goods. There was also buoyant small-scale sector linking into agricultural income growth and supported by the spread of rural infrastructure (Hill, 1996). Sundrum (1986) explained the rapid growth in manufacturing as a result of rising investment in this sector, together with a sharp rise in demand for these products. Higher levels of consumption spending also helped stimulate the growth of the manufacturing sector.

In contrast, Nigeria's agricultural performance was dismal over the 1970–82 period. Nigeria's once diversified commodity export sector declined sharply in the presence of the oil boom. Nigeria's inward-looking trade regime created several adverse effects for the agricultural traded sector. High import tariffs taxed agricultural exports, by increasing the price of imported agricultural inputs such as machinery, fertiliser and other chemical inputs. Hence, high levels of protection for industry were responsible for reducing the domestic price of agricultural tradables relative to domestic prices of industrial tradables and prices of nontradables. This change in relative prices also had an incentive effect on the labour market, with labour, and other inputs, moving out of agriculture to manufacturing and the nontradable sector over the period. This declining flow of rural labour exerted upward pressure on the rural wage rate, which tripled during 1970–75, thereby increasing the production cost for agricultural exports. A fall in relative output prices and higher relative labour input and other agricultural input prices were also responsible for the fall in profitability of agricultural tradables. Annual production declined by 65 per cent for cotton, 25 per cent for rubber, and 43 per cent for cocoa which brought an average annual 30 per cent decline for export cash crop output over the period (Scherr,

1989). Only the production of palm kernel and palm oil rose, by 30 and 23 per cent, respectively, as this sector was highly protected by the agricultural pricing policy.

Imports of food grains displaced domestic production, depressing Nigeria's agricultural share in GDP from 49 per cent in 1970 to 22 per cent in 1982. Per capita food production was stagnant and throughout the period total agricultural production declined slowly. The share of the agricultural labour force also declined by 21 per cent over the period (from 75 per cent to 59 per cent of total employment). Agricultural export production declined at an average annual rate of 5.7 per cent between 1968 and 1978 and 7.1 per cent between 1978 and 1984. After 1975, agricultural imports grew significantly, which worsened the balance of payments situation in 1975–76. From being a net exporter of agricultural goods, Nigeria became a net importer.

The mining and oil sectors of all three economies increased substantially. PNG's mining sector share to GDP increased from 0.8 per cent in 1970 to 30 per cent in 1974 and then declined to 8 per cent in 1982. In the same years, Indonesia's oil sector share occupied 14 per cent and Nigeria's 30 per cent which was much higher than the 1970 level.

From 1970 to 1982, the share of the manufacturing sector to GDP rose from 5 to 10 per cent in PNG and from 10 to 16 per cent in Indonesia. But the share of Nigeria's manufacturing sector to GDP declined from 7 per cent in 1970 to 6 per cent in 1982 (Table 7.12). The contribution of the services sector declined in both PNG and Indonesia in 1982 from the 1970 level but Nigeria's services sector grew by 38 per cent over the same period, as predicted by the theory of the 'Dutch disease' discussed in Chapter 2.

7.5   Summary and Conclusion

This chapter provides a comparative study of the movements of key macroeconomic variables, relative prices, employment and wages and sectoral transformation of PNG, Indonesia and Nigeria in response to resources booms over 1970–82 and also the early 1990s in PNG.

It is found that, although the timing and magnitude of the booms were similar, the outcome was significantly different, due, in the main, to differences in macroeconomic policy responses, particularly those in relation to trade regimes by the respective governments.

Although Indonesia managed the oil booms reasonably well, it performed worse, in terms of government spending and controlling the inflation rate, which was reflected in appreciation of the real exchange rate during the 1972–82 period. Increased spending on domestically produced goods and services, coupled with import restrictions in the form of high tariffs and subsidies, fuelled domestic inflation and exacerbated the real exchange rate appreciation. However, adopting a prudent external borrowing strategy, Indonesia was able to reduce its total debt and debt service ratio below 13 per cent by the end of the 1970s. Indonesia's development expenditures were more evenly distributed across rural and urban infrastructure, industry, education and social services than in PNG and Nigeria.

Along with the oil shocks, Nigeria also faced several policy-induced shocks Several micro and macroeconomic policies contributed to a dismal performance for the agricultural sector at a time of high overall GDP growth. Nigeria underwent dramatic sectoral transformation over the period. Supported by high government spending and various forms of trade restrictions, the country's production structure shifted in favour of the nontradable sector. The agricultural sector was particularly hard hit as this sector received less attention despite its important role in the economy. High levels of inflation compared with major trading partners reduced the competitiveness of the Nigerian tradable sector sharply which was reflected in perpetual real exchange appreciation from 1974.

Compared with Indonesia and Nigeria, PNG managed to maintain stability by the application of conservative macroeconomic policies in the context of an open trade regime. Given the lack of an indigenous capital goods sector, a low level of industrialisation and an insignificant manufacturing sector, resources booms in the 1970s did not adversely affect PNG's export oriented tradable sector. An appreciating nominal exchange rate reduced the cost of imported capital and intermediate goods over the 1970s. Overheating of the economy was avoided by sensible application of expenditure management and wage restraint policies. This is one of the major reasons PNG was able to maintain a stable price level during and after the boom years in the second half of the 1970s. Compared with Indonesia and Nigeria, PNG's trade regime was virtually open, which helped reduce pressure on the domestic price level and prevented appreciation of the real exchange rate.

It can be concluded that these three economies were all affected by 'Dutch disease' to a varying extent. Nigeria was greatly affected, and showed all the symptoms of the damaging consequences of the 'disease' over the years of the oil boom. Indonesia was also affected by 'Dutch disease', as it was not able to restrain government spending and the inflation rate at a desirable level over 1970–82. PNG's prudent macroeconomic policies, including a reduced flow of Australian aid and budgetary grants and an open trade regime, substantially offset the adverse 'spending effects' of a resources boom over these years and prevented the economy from falling prey to 'Dutch disease'.

However, PNG failed to maintain fiscal discipline during the mineral boom in the early 1990s. As well, an increasingly restrictive trade regime was introduced from the mid-1980s, and a continuous fiscal deficit from 1990 added extra pressure on the domestic price level. Domestic political instability in the late 1980s has also contributed to lower production and overall stability of the economy. As a result the real exchange rate appreciated significantly during the 1991–93 period and the economy lost international competitiveness. A radical wages policy reform, undertaken in 1992, together with stricter fiscal and monetary policies, reduced reliance on foreign aid and grants, and the adoption of a floating exchange rate regime improved competitiveness of the country from the end of 1994.

Notes

1   In nominal terms, the price of a barrel of crude oil (OPEC basket) increased from US$1.7 in 1971 to US$34.3 in 1981. By 1986, this price had fallen to US$13.6 per barrel.

2   Nigerian total exports increased from US$2.1 billion in 1972 to US$26 million in 1980. Of these total value of export, oil export revenue accounted for US$25 billion in nominal terms.

3   Private consumption, and general government consumption, plus gross domestic investment.

8

Conclusion

8.1   Introduction

The objective of this study is to investigate the impact of resources booms in Papua New Guinea (PNG) during the period 1970-94 and the effect of the government's policy response to these booms on the process of economic adjustment. The major emphasis is on how the real exchange rate responds both to the shocks and to the different policy measures undertaken by the government. The study continues to investigate the impact of resources booms on the sectoral composition of output, and savings and investment behaviour. Finally, a comparative study of policy responses to resources booms in PNG, Indonesia and Nigeria between 1973 and 1982 is undertaken to investigate the diverse outcomes of these booms and reasons underlying such differences.

The analytical framework of the study is based on the theory of booming sector economics, beginning with the core 'Dutch disease' model, where a resources boom is assumed to be of a permanent nature, and considers the consequences of a resources boom in a short-term comparative static framework. The core model is based on a number of restrictive assumptions and on the experiences of a developed country. It has been extended to make it applicable to the economy of PNG by incorporating the effects of openness in the labour market, capital market and trade regime in the context of a small open developing economy. Most resources booms are temporary with implications for the long-term growth of an economy through intertemporal choices between consumption and savings. The long-term dynamic analysis of resources booms using the theory of 'construction boom' has also been incorporated in to the study.

The study is organised into eight chapters. Chapter 1 presents the outline of the study; Chapter 2 reviews the booming sector's literature and discusses the analytical framework of the study. The core 'Dutch disease' model is extended to take into account the different types of openness in the labour market, capital market and international trade regimes in developing countries. The theory of 'construction boom' is also discussed in this chapter in an attempt to capture the long-term dynamic impact of a resources boom. Chapter 3 surveys the structure and recent development of the PNG economy to set the stage for the ensuing analysis.

Chapters 4 and 5 measure the key economic relations to provide the empirical base for the analysis. The ideal methodology is a comprehensive macroeconometric model, which captures the key relationships suggested by the theory, but given the nature of data availability, this approach was not feasible in the context of the PNG economy. Therefore, the methodology chosen is a case study approach bringing together single equation estimates of behavioural relations involving key macroeconomic variables and other relevant information, both quantitative and qualitative, in order to shed light on the key theoretical propositions. Chapter 4 provides an econometric analysis of the determinants of the real exchange rate in PNG using the General to Specific Modelling procedure. The Error Correction Modelling procedure was employed to guard against estimating spurious regression relationships while retaining long-term information. The sectoral impact of real exchange rate movements and the long-term growth of the PNG economy is also empirically evaluated in Chapter 5 by estimating private and total savings functions.

Chapter 6 identifies the major resources booms experienced by PNG, and the changes in key macroeconomic variables and their impact on the structure of the economy during 1970–94 period. The analysis of this chapter attempts to test the theoretical propositions from Chapter 2 and draws upon the results of the econometric analysis in Chapters 4 and 5. In Chapter 7, PNG's policy responses to booms are compared with those of two other resource-rich countries – Indonesia and Nigeria in order to place policy implication of the findings in perspective.

8.2   Summary of Findings

In a resources boom, the real exchange rate of a country changes. Since this indicates changes in the competitiveness of a country in the world market, the investigation began by constructing three different versions of real exchange rate indices for PNG. The results suggest that the major factors behind the real exchange rate movements in PNG included changes in government expenditure, growth of money supply over the growth of GDP, long-term capital inflow, foreign aid flow and changes in the nominal exchange rate. The findings are consistent with the theoretical propositions of the extended model of a resources boom. This empirical result also points out appreciation of the trade-weighted real exchange rate was amplified due to a sharp increase in CPI in 1973, which contains both tradable and nontradable items. A substantial price increase in tradable commodities exaggerated the rise in CPI in 1973. However, a substantial depreciation of the real exchange was achieved, through income and wage restraint policies and maintaining an open trade regime during the height of the agricultural boom in 1976–77. During 1991–93, a real appreciation of kina was induced by the mineral boom and was aggravated by continuous budget deficits.

There is also evidence in the econometric results on sectoral growth that depreciation of the real exchange rate leads to expansion of the output of the tradable sector, whereas appreciation of the real exchange rate enhances growth of the nontradable sector. Depreciation of the real exchange rate had a positive effect on the output of the agriculture, manufacturing and mineral sector, while the output of the nontradable sector as a whole, as well as the construction sector, declined. This result is consistent with the theoretical propositions of booming sector economics. There is also evidence that PNG households perceived the temporary nature of resources booms correctly and behaved rationally while dealing with the windfall gain. This is reflected in the higher savings during the boom years. PNG's less developed capital market prompted the private sector of the economy to invest in the nontradable activities, primarily in construction, during the boom years. This behaviour is consistent with the propositions of the 'construction boom' theory.

The study then discusses major resources booms and macroeconomic policy management. Since PNG did not have an independent monetary system (it came under the Australian system) during the boom years of the early 1970s, it could not pursue an independent monetary and exchange rate policy, PNG mainly followed an expansionary fiscal policy, which contained a large increase in wages and salaries and government consumption. After independence, PNG maintained a prudent macroeconomic policy stance during the agricultural boom in 1976–77. Domestic absorption was not permitted to adjust automatically to the availability of income by the setting up of various stabilisation funds (example, MRSF and CPSF). Balances were maintained in the external accounts by appropriate stabilisation measures. This sound income and wage restraint policy coupled with reduced dependence on Australian aid contributed to domestic price stability and prevented real exchange rate appreciation at the height of the agricultural boom of 1977–78. Furthermore, during the 1970s a very open trade regime contributed to a more stable real exchange rate in PNG to a great extent.

However, PNG failed to maintain fiscal discipline during the mineral boom of the early 1990s. An increasingly restrictive trade regime was introduced from the mid-1980s, and a continuous fiscal deficit from 1990 added extra pressure on the domestic price level. Domestic political instability in the late 1980s also contributed to lower production and overall stability of the economy. As a result, during 1991–93 the real exchange rate appreciated significantly and the economy lost international competitiveness. The situation improved significantly by the end of 1994 and PNG regained its competitiveness to a large extent as a result of a radical labour market reform, flotation of its currency, improved world market prices for PNG's agricultural exports and a stricter fiscal policy.

Finally, the consequences of PNG's booms and adjustment episodes are compared with those of Indonesia and Nigeria. The purpose of the comparative study was to determine the underlying causes for the variant performance of these economies in the face of resources booms. It has been found that, although the magnitudes of the booms during 1970–82 were similar, the impact on the domestic economies of PNG, Indonesia and Nigeria was distinctively different. Different policy measures were found to be the main contributors to the different outcomes for these three economies. Compared with Indonesia and Nigeria, PNG managed to maintain stability by the application of conservative macroeconomic policies in the context of an open trade regime. PNG kept a tight control over government spending, especially when revenues were rising very fast, holding down real wages and making an early response to a worsening balance of payments, rather than financing the deficit in the expectation of recovery. Over the second half of the 1970s, PNG also reduced its reliance on Australian budgetary grants and maintained a high level of reserves and unused foreign borrowing capacity and was therefore able to avoid the adverse consequences of resources booms.

One of the major reasons why PNG was able to maintain price stability during, and after, the boom years in the second half of the 1970s was that it was virtually an open trade regime when compared with Indonesia and Nigeria. An open trade regime helped keep the domestic price level largely on a par with that of its major trading partners. By contrast, Indonesia and Nigeria adopted increasingly more restrictive trade policies after the oil booms to encourage domestic production, which diverted resources from the tradable to nontradable and import-competing sectors and put upward pressure on the domestic price level, rapidly appreciating the real exchange rates.

A real devaluation was restored temporarily in Indonesia, through a substantial nominal devaluation in 1978, although this devaluation exacerbated the inflation to a double-digit figure over the next few years, which quickly took the real exchange rate back to its old levels. As the Nigerian authorities lacked farsightedness in macroeconomic policy Nigeria fell prey to the classical 'Dutch disease' syndrome. The oil booms, coupled with high government spending and various forms of trade restrictions, shifted the production structure of the country in favour of nontradables. Nigeria's once diversified commodity export sector declined, due to lack of appropriate policy management in the face of the resources booms. The country shifted from being a net exporter of grains to being a net importer.

Why was PNG unable to maintain economic stability in the early 1990s after performing relatively better in managing its resources booms during the 1970s? The findings of this study suggest three main reasons. First, PNG lost fiscal discipline in the early 1990s, and the country was experiencing continuous budget deficits which reached 6 per cent of GDP in 1993. Expansionary fiscal pressures eroded the international reserves of the Central Bank, creating a currency crisis, which forced a change to PNG's fixed exchange rate regime in October 1994. Second, a shift to an inward-looking trade regime and the centralised wage fixation policies added to the pressure on the domestic price level, eroding the international competitiveness of domestic production. By contrast, the radical wages reform policy undertaken in 1992, stricter fiscal and monetary policies, reduced reliance on foreign aid and the adoption of a floating exchange rate regime improved the competitiveness of the country from the end of 1994.

8.3   Lessons from the PNG Experience

From this detailed discussion of resources booms and macroeconomic adjustment in PNG, there are some important possible lessons for other developing countries.

It has been found that appropriate policy management has the most important bearing on the outcome of a resources boom. A conservative approach is required to maintain a stable domestic price level. Well-disciplined fiscal and monetary policy, as well as maintaining a more open trade regime, can ensure an efficient economic performance. One good example was the activity of the Mineral Resources Stabilisation Funds (MRSF) in PNG during the mid-1970s to the early 1980s when it built up the resource capacity to deal with slump periods and helped maintain stability in the domestic price level.

An economy needs to be flexible in the internal factor market. By reducing pressure on the domestic price level, flexibility in labour markets can also reduce the production cost of tradables during the boom years and maintain the competitiveness of the tradables sector by reducing the price ratio of tradables to nontradables. This will generate employment and encourage the expansion of the tradable sector, which will reap the maximum benefit from a positive trade shock.

An outward-oriented trade policy in the boom years can help develop a strong export base. By maintaining domestic prices of tradables in line with world prices, an open trade regime can also prevent rapid appreciation of the real exchange rate and improve competitiveness of exports in the world market. A nominal devaluation can help in this respect. Reduced foreign aid during the boom years can reduce the upward pressure on the domestic price level by reducing the spending effect on the nontradable sector.

Increased savings and investment on foreign assets can prevent the pressure on the domestic price level that arises from a resources boom. Investing in foreign assets would be optimal as this protects the real value of windfall gains by holding foreign assets during the boom period and repatriating them when the nontradable capital price drops after the end of the boom. Thus, the investment boom can be spread out over a longer period and building up foreign financial assets during the boom years can moderate the relative price of 'construction'. Repatriated foreign assets can also be used in the post-boom period to finance a higher level of consumption.

8.4   Qualifications and Suggestions for Further Research

This study is the first attempt to systematically undertake the theoretical and empirical analysis of a resources boom for the economy of PNG. It is therefore pertinent to comment briefly on some limitations of the analysis which should receive due consideration in assessing the policy relevance of the results. The behavioural relationship estimated in these models seem to be statistically satisfactory, both in terms of the overall explanatory power and the significance and sign of the coefficients of explanatory variables. The performance of these models as a whole is also satisfactory in terms of replicating the actual performance of the economy over the sample period. However, apart from these favourable statistical properties, first, as in any statistical analysis, the results of the study may be accepted with reservations as to the quality of the data. All the data series were taken from standard (secondary) sources with due consideration to consistency and comparability. Second, the results are essentially specific to the sample period and, therefore, care should be taken if extensions beyond the period are required. For instance, the economy was under a fixed exchange rate and central wage fixation system until 1992. Consequently, various forms of trade restrictions were introduced from mid-1980 to reconcile with the fall in export revenue in the early 1980s.

Further research is needed to provide helpful insights for policy makers to design and implement specific policy measures (for example, trade policy) to utilise a windfall gain appropriately. Two important aspects call for future research. First, the findings suggest the importance of maintaining an open trade regime to gain higher welfare from a resources boom. Since trade liberalisation can improve the output of the tradable sector and improve the competitiveness of the economy by preventing a rise in the domestic price level, further research on trade liberalisation in resource-rich economies could be a useful area for future research. The conclusion on the importance of a more open trade regime is based on limited (readily available) data and *a priori* reasoning. Unavailability of required data on trade restrictions prevented the undertaking of an extensive investigation into the outcomes of the openness of the trade regime in PNG.

Second, a study of economy-wide effects of booms using a computable general equilibrium (CGE) model could also be a very useful area of future research. This approach provides for examining the impact of a resources boom while appropriately controlling the impact of other relevant factors such as trade liberalisation, labour market conditions, the likely decline of aid and budget grants, and changes in fiscal operation. The general case study approach used in this study was largely dictated by the nature of readily available data, and the time and financial constraints on undertaking a major data generation effort.

Statistical Appendix:
Supplementary Statistical Tables, Notes and Basic Data

Appendix to Chapter 3

Table A3.1
Social development indicators

Social Development Indicator	Papua New Guinea			Lower-middle income countries	
	1971*	1992*	2000*	1992	2000
Total population (millions)	2.73	4.18	5.13	941.0	5082.0
Urban population (% of total population)	12.0	16.0	17.4	54.0	42.0
Average annual growth rate of population[1] (%)	2.4	2.3	3.1	1.7	1.5
Life expectancy at birth (years)[a]	47.0	56.5	59.0	67.0	69.0
Infant mortality [b]	90.0	67.0	56.0	65.0	33.0
Total fertility rate[c]	6.0	5.0	4.2	3.1	2.9
Food, Health and Nutrition					
Daily per capita calorie supply (cal)[d]	2090.0	2403.0	2974.0	2768.0	na
Daily per capita protein supply (cal)[d]	41.0	49.0	54.0	72.0	na
Index of food production per capita (1979/81=100)[e]	104.0	97.0	107.8	101.0	127.0
Population per physician (number)	11733.0	12874.0	na	2850.0	1.9**
Access to safe water (% of population)	30.0	37.0	42.0	78.0	92.0
Education					
Primary school enrolment [f] (%)	46.0	70.0	84.0	100.0	105.0
Secondary school enrolment (%)	10.0	12.0	21.0	56.0	na
Adult literacy rate (%)	32.0	52.0	65.0	70.0	75.0

Continued over

Table A3.1 (continued)
Social development indicators

Social Development Indicator	Papua New Guinea			Lower-middle income countries	
	1971*	1992*	2000*	1992	2000
Annual energy consumption per head (kg oil equivalent[g])	206.0	231.0	na	1102.0	1171.0

Source: World Bank (2002a),World Development Indicators CD-ROM, AusAID (1996), (1995).

Notes: *   The reference period refers to 1971 is for 1970–75, 1992 for 1980–93 and 2000 for 1994–2000.

1. The population growth rate in 1992 is for 1980–93 and in 2000 is for 1994–2000.
a. Latest year in 2001.
b. Number per thousand live births.
c. Number of children per woman, World Development Indicators 2001.
d. The most recent estimate refers to 1997.
e. The most recent estimate refers to 1996–98 with base year 1989–91=100.
f. This ratio could exceed 100 per cent because of the possibility of enrolment by persons outside the age group designated as primary or secondary school-age population.
g. Relatively high energy consumption levels are largely due to the requirements of mining projects.

na = not available
** = physicians per 1,000 people

Table A3.2
Growth rate of real GDP and inflation
in Papua New Guinea, 1970–95
1990 =100

Year	Growth rate of real GDP (1990=100)	CPI	GDP-deflator	Inflation-CPI	Inflation-GDPdeflator
1970	10.40	24.97	27.19	4.50	5.32
1971	6.30	26.37	28.12	5.60	3.41
1972	5.64	27.29	30.12	3.50	7.13
1973	6.53	35.78	36.07	31.11	17.74
1974	2.61	38.47	39.28	7.54	8.92
1975	−0.88	41.77	40.18	8.57	2.27
1976	−3.39	43.34	48.10	3.77	19.74
1977	0.83	43.52	51.68	0.40	7.44
1978	8.55	45.93	50.63	5.55	−2.03
1979	1.83	48.35	58.78	5.26	16.10
1980	−2.30	54.82	62.94	13.38	7.09
1981	0.18	61.33	61.85	11.88	−1.75
1982	0.32	63.42	64.14	3.41	3.71
1983	3.02	72.36	76.26	14.10	18.89
1984	−0.56	79.07	82.10	9.27	7.66
1985	4.34	77.55	83.16	−1.92	1.29
1986	4.92	78.35	84.10	1.03	1.14
1987	2.60	81.87	90.96	4.49	8.15
1988	2.99	89.30	98.09	9.08	7.84
1989	−1.86	94.02	96.02	5.28	−2.11
1990	−3.01	100.00	100.00	6.37	4.14
1991	10.17	105.42	106.39	5.42	6.39
1992	12.46	109.91	108.62	4.26	2.10
1993	17.54	117.82	111.14	7.20	2.32
1994	3.10	123.20	119.05	4.57	7.11
1995	−3.32	141.28	126.77	14.67	6.44

Source: Constructed from various issues, World Bank, *World Tables* and Bank of Papua New Guinea, *Quarterly Economic Bulletins*.

Table A3.3
Government revenues and expenditures, 1971–2000
(current prices, kina million)

	1970	1975	1980	1985	1990	1993	1994	2000
GDP	531.0	1004.0	1708.1	2423.9	3076.0	5016.0	5411.0	10555.0
Total revenue and grants	162.8	317.1	519.1	739.2	998.0	1309.0	1446.0	3008.7
Tax revenue	46.6	100.1	239.6	404.3	592.0	718.0	852.0	2314.9
Non-tax revenue	16.2	44.7	47.5	102.2	161.0	133.0	148.0	187.2
MRSF	na	34.7	56.6	17.2	6.0	276.0	283.0	na
Foreign grants	100.0	137.6	175.4	215.5	239.0	182.0	163.0	506.6
Total expenditure	222.1	373.9	597.3	787.3	1089.0	1605.0	1570.0	3201.0
Current expenditure	109.0	330.5	474.1	729.2	937.0	1392.0	1443	2352.2
Capital expenditure	113.1	43.4	123.2	58.1	152.0	213.0	127.0	848.8
Overall deficit	140.7	56.8	78.2	48.1	91.0	296.0	125.0	192.3

Note: na = not available

Source: Constructed from World Bank, Table 5.1, Report No. 3544a-PNG,(1981), Table
5.1 and Table 5.2, Report No. 9396-PNG, (1991), and AusAID (1996), Table A13,
Table A15, Table A17 and Table A18, Quarterly Economic Bulletin (2001), Table
8.1.

Table A3.4
Minerals and agricultural exports of PNG, 1971–2000
(current prices, US dollar million)

Year	Mining exports	Agricultural exports	Non-mining exports	Total exports*
1971	0.62	53.24	67.50	89.67
1972	19.40	43.09	58.72	106.85
1973	88.62	37.66	51.73	160.72
1974	216.32	68.66	100.53	333.75
1975	182.48	99.71	123.50	321.86
1976	159.11	82.32	101.91	287.32
1977	147.26	227.52	267.89	438.37
1978	164.65	148.18	189.36	400.16
1979	254.96	196.32	243.39	538.75
1980	216.01	154.30	214.00	471.81
1981	201.40	110.62	164.89	379.49
1982	224.29	121.58	180.12	422.84
1983	309.67	192.15	245.10	570.54
1984	290.85	338.73	420.35	731.58
1985	489.90	330.20	409.60	926.20
1986	544.36	321.94	402.07	970.78
1987	650.56	244.70	355.63	1022.11
1988	749.51	222.02	313.37	1092.72
1989	601.73	240.39	333.22	989.32
1990	727.20	196.42	280.70	1077.50
1991	955.04	194.37	289.94	1320.98
1992	1330.36	369.57	475.79	1806.72
1993	1732.44	674.24	744.02	2476.46
1994	1693.85	836.00	854.05	2547.90
1995	1837.51	379.06	348.58	2565.15
1996	1695.35	437.02	370.63	2502.99
1997	1281.90	541.79	309.65	2132.64
1998	1190.74	495.41	104.60	1790.75
1999	1382.11	456.91	116.21	1955.23
2000	1628.39	346.18	120.09	2098.66

Note: * Some total export entries are not equal to the sum of mining exports and non-mining exports because of omission of other minor export items and re-exports.

Source: Constructed from Bank of Papua New Guinea, *Quarterly Economic Bulletin* (various issues), AusAID (1996).

Table A3.5
Minerals and agricultural exports of PNG, 1971–2000
(current prices, kina million)

Year	GDP	Mining	Agriculture	Non-mining exports[a]	Total exports*
1971	645.4	0.7	60.5	69.9	127.2
1972	788.8	23.1	51.3	69.9	127.2
1973	1040.6	126.6	53.8	73.9	229.6
1974	1004.0	313.5	99.5	145.7	483.7
1975	1068.4	240.1	131.2	162.5	402.6
1976	1251.3	201.4	104.2	129.0	363.7
1977	1298.5	186.4	288.0	339.1	554.9
1978	1413.3	231.9	208.7	266.7	563.6
1979	1632.5	359.1	276.5	342.8	758.8
1980	1708.1	322.4	230.3	319.4	704.2
1981	1696.9	300.6	165.1	246.1	566.4
1982	1764.7	303.1	164.3	243.4	571.4
1983	2145.4	373.1	231.5	295.3	687.4
1984	2282.2	326.8	380.6	472.3	822.0
1985	2402.2	489.9	330.2	436.3	926.2
1986	2572.4	561.2	331.9	414.5	1000.8
1987	2854.5	714.9	268.9	390.8	1123.2
1988	3169.9	861.5	255.2	360.2	1256.0
1989	3045.7	676.1	270.1	374.4	1111.6
1990	3076.1	758.0	205.0	365.0	1123.0
1991	3605.5	1005.4	204.6	384.6	1390.0
1992	4139.6	1371.5	224.0	491.5	1862.6
1993	5016.0	1767.8	270.0	759.2	2527.0
1994	5411.0	1783.0	375.0	899.0	2682.0
1995	6309.0	2436.0	502.0	899.0	3400.0
1996	6914.0	2245.0	579.0	955.0	3314.0
1997	6824.0	1839.0	777.0	952.0	3059.0
1998	7788.5	2455.0	1020.0	367.0	3688.0
1999	9103.2	3524.0	1165.0	296.3	4985.3
2000	10555.0	4494.6	955.5	342.5	5792.6

Note: a Non-mining exports include the export value of forestry, marine and other re-exports.

   * Some total export entries are not equal to the sum of mining exports and non-mining exports because of omission of other minor export items and re-exports.

Source: Bank of Papua New Guinea, *Quarterly Economic Bulletin* (various issues), AusAID (1996), (1997), (1999).

Table A3.6
Total labour force and wage employment in PNG, 1968–95 (persons)

Year	Total labour force	Formal wage employment*	Public service	Elcom plus PTC	Private employment	Mining
1968	1060704	161540 (15.2)	28093	918	130878	1651
1969	1079456	174648 (16.2)	32796	1411	138245	2229
1970	1098540	182642 (16.6)	33804	1556	144589	2693
1971	1126413	183633 (16.3)	36335	1588	142245	3465
1972	1154993	178594 (15.5)	37452	1716	134263	5163
1973	1184299	176734 (14.9)	40516	1612	130138	4468
1974	1214348	176008 (14.5)	43389	1599	125838	5182
1975	1245160	175429 (14.1)	46465	1760	122081	5153
1976	1262390	174825 (13.9)	49759	1833	118710	4523
1977	1279859	185160 (14.5)	49700	1913	128893	4654
1978	1297570	186943 (14.4)	49742	2288	130053	4860
1979	1315525	194129 (14.8)	50936	2189	136111	4893
1980	1333730	213000 (16.0)	52862	2744	152351	5043
1981	1357762	206816 (15.2)	54728	2659	143328	6101
1982	1382227	196505 (14.2)	52858	4724	130181	8742
1983	1407133	196494 (14.0)	49493	4746	132759	9496
1984	1432488	200871 (14.0)	51460	5001	138023	6387
1985	1458300	204772 (14.1)	51682	4672	142551	5867
1986	1479964	208111 (14.1)	49926	5072	146073	7040
1987	1501951	212908 (14.2)	50099	5363	149427	8019
1988	1524264	218107 (14.3)	49076	5288	154496	9247
1989	1546908	228590 (14.8)	49274	5199	166033	8084
1990	1569890	218957 (14.0)	50309	5143	158174	5331
1991	1587462	213217 (13.4)	50823	4879	152232	5283
1992	1605231	243181(15.1)	72897	8560	156071	5653
1993	1623198	251198 (15.5)	74768	9740	151090	5600
1994	2157200	233255 (10.8)	na	na	162878	7922
1995	2216200	243181 (11.1)	na	na	155241	7599

Note: *   Formal wage employment as percentage of total labour force is given in bracket.
na = not available.

Source: Constructed from World Bank (1995), AIDAB (1993) Table 3.1 and AusAID (1997) Table A11 and *Quarterly Economic Bulletin* (various issues).

Table A3.7
Foreign aid to PNG, 1970–94
(current prices, US dollar million)

Year	1970	1971	1972	1973	1974	1975	1976	1977	1978	1979	1980
Australian Aid	112.4	135.23	148.57	208.57	307.25	322.11	274.18	221.26	242.1	248.2	276.0
Budget support	112.4	115.68	128.81	174.00	220.72	181.05	192.91	221.26	242.10	248.2	259.0
Other		19.55	19.76	34.57	86.52	141.05	81.27	na	na	na	17.0
Bilateral Aid							1.30	2.15	2.82	5.07	11.0
New Zealand							1.30	2.15	2.82	2.82	2.0
United Kingdom							na	na	na	na	na
Japan							na	na	na	2.25	3.0
Germany							na	na	na	na	3.0
Other							na	na	na	na	3.0
Multilateral Aid							8.47	14.55	18.60	17.33	39.0
IDA							3.03	2.53	5.92	5.63	13.0
ADB							1.39	5.44	7.04	6.06	7.0
EEC							na	na	na	na	na
UNDP							1.52	1.52	2.82	2.82	1.0
UNHCR							na	na	na	na	na
Other							2.53	5.06	2.82	2.82	18.0
Total Aid and Grants	112.4	135.23	148.57	208.57	307.25	322.11	283.95	237.96	263.52	270.6	326.0
Population	2.44	2.48	2.54	2.6	2.67	2.73	2.79	2.86	2.93	3.0	3.07
Per capita aid	46.07	54.53	58.49	80.22	115.07	117.99	101.77	83.2	89.94	90.20	106.19
growth of Aid		20.3	9.9	40.4	47.3	4.8	-11.8	-16.2	10.7	2.7	20.5

Continued over

Table A3.7 (continued)
Foreign aid to PNG, 1970–94
(current prices, US dollar million)

Year	1981	1982	1983	1984	1985	1986	1987	1988	1989	1990	1991	1992	1993	1994
Australian Aid	285.0	263.5	264.1	275.2	226.9	222.4	216.7	240.9	254.0	262.2	262.3	242.2	221.8	239.0
Budget support	272.0	251.0	253.1	258.2	210.9	206.3	199.7	215.7	218.0	214.5	214.2	207.3	182.4	145.0
Other	13.0	12.5	11.1	17.0	16.0	16.1	17.0	25.2	36.0	47.7	48.1	34.9	39.4	70.0
Bilateral Aid	19.0	12.8	10.2	19.0	13.7	20.4	37.0	66.6	60.0	57.3	59.4	106.7	43.9	41.0
New Zealand	3.0	2.0	1.6	2.1	2.9	1.7	2.1	2.6	3.4	2.6	3.4	2.9	3.7	4.0
United Kingdom	na	0.1	0.1	0.1	0.1	0.1	6.6	13.1	7.6	5.7	3.0	1.8	-0.5	2.0
Japan	2.0	3.7	3.5	6.2	4.0	10.4	17.7	41.2	39.6	38.0	42.3	87.9	27.4	22.0
Germany	7.0	4.8	2.1	8.9	3.4	5.9	8.6	6.7	6.4	8.0	7.4	10.1	8.7	10.0
Other	6.0	2.3	2.0	1.5	3.3	2.3	2.0	3.0	3.0	3.0	3.3	4.0	4.6	5.0
Multilateral Aid	32.0	34.4	58.7	27.1	18.6	21.1	68.2	67.2	22.5	93.6	75.5	94.5	37.5	50.0
IDA	10.0	8.9	16.6	13.5	3.5	na	-0.4	-1.0	-1.0	-1.0	-1.0	-1.8	-1.7	-2.0
ADB	16.0	4.2	8.7	4.2	4.4	2.4	5.0	9.9	10.7	42.2	54.0	12.9	24.1	25.0
EEC	na	18.0	30.1	4.3	4.2	11.7	58.4	55.6	4.8	45.2	11.5	71.2	4.5	18.0
UNDP	1.8	1.7	1.6	1.3	1.3	1.1	2.0	3.8	5.0	4.9	6.3	6.4	5.5	5.0
UNHCR	1.0	na	na	1.1	2.2	2.9	0.2	2.2	1.9	1.3	1.3	1.2	1.0	1.0
Other	3.2	1.6	2.0	3.0	3.0	3.0	3.0	-3.3	1.1	1.0	3.4	4.6	4.1	3.0
Total Aid and Grants	336.0	310.7	333.0	324.3	259.2	263.9	321.9	374.7	336.5	413.1	397.2	443.4	303.2	326.0
Population	3.14	3.21	3.3	3.38	3.46	3.55	3.63	3.68	3.76	3.84	3.93	4.02	4.11	4.2
Per capita aid	107.01	96.79	100.91	95.95	74.91	74.34	88.68	101.82	89.49	107.58	101.07	110.30	73.77	77.61
Growth of aid	3.1	-7.5	7.2	-2.6	-20.1	1.8	22.0	16.4	-10.2	22.8	-3.8	11.6	-31.6	7.51

Note: na = not available

Source: Constructed from World Bank (1981) and AusAID (1994), (1995), (1996), various tables.

Appendix to Chapter 4

Table A4.1
Nominal and real exchange rate indices, 1970–94 (1990=100)

Year	NEER-import	NEER-export	NEER-trade	RER1-import	RER1-export	RER1-trade
1970	110.10	77.18	93.29	119.1	117.1	122.3
1971	109.95	77.16	93.19	115.6	113.0	118.2
1972	109.44	77.68	92.98	114.8	112.3	117.1
1973	106.47	75.11	89.82	95.2	92.6	96.4
1974	105.61	73.78	88.71	106.7	104.2	108.4
1975	108.13	77.24	92.01	110.3	106.6	111.3
1976	98.27	73.32	85.53	104.3	103.5	106.5
1977	97.14	75.03	85.65	109.5	109.9	111.8
1978	90.82	73.82	81.85	101.2	103.5	103.9
1979	86.90	70.15	78.21	102.8	101.5	103.7
1980	86.59	69.07	77.33	103.9	100.8	103.7
1981	87.06	67.58	76.94	99.4	92.5	97.5
1982	85.15	66.83	75.94	99.4	92.5	97.7
1983	92.81	72.69	82.92	98.8	89.5	95.9
1984	93.33	71.91	83.03	94.0	82.8	90.3
1985	90.35	79.05	85.50	96.0	94.7	97.2
1986	87.86	84.00	86.64	92.8	96.6	96.0
1987	89.71	91.78	91.09	94.3	101.3	98.5
1988	93.31	88.76	91.03	95.3	92.5	94.2
1989	90.23	86.04	88.37	91.6	88.4	90.5
1990	100.00	100.00	100.00	100.0	100.0	100.0
1991	100.18	101.40	101.07	96.2	97.5	97.4
1992	97.23	99.94	99.09	90.3	92.6	92.2
1993	97.66	101.85	100.22	85.5	87.8	87.3
1994	131.21	137.16	134.27	110.3	112.9	112.0

Note: NEER = nominal effective exchange rate and RER1 = trade-weighted real exchange rate. Three different nominal and real exchange rate indices are constructed by using import share, export share and trade share as weights.

Source: Author's computation using data from World Bank, *World Tables*, IMF, *International Financial Statistics*, Bank of PNG, *Quarterly Economic Bulletins*, various issues.

Table A4.2
Test for unit roots

Variables	Data series	DF/ADF Statistics Ho: I(1) versus Ha: I(0)
Real income (real GDP)	Y	−2.25 (1)
Trade-weighted real exchange rate	RER1	−4.25 (0)*
Real exchange rate defined as EPI/CPI	RER2	−3.31 (0)*
Real exchange rate defined as IPI/CPI	RER3	−2.27 (0)
Nominal effective exchange rate	NEER	−1.37 (0)
External terms of trade	TOT	−3.41 (0)*
Openness of trade regime	OP	−1.65 (0)
Money supply	MS	−2.09 (0)
Government expenditure to GDP	GEX	1.00 (0)
Gross investment to GDP	GIY	−4.45 (0)*
Lag net long-term capital inflow	NKI	−2.64 (0)
Foreign aid flow	AID	−14.49 (0)*
Nominal devaluation	NDEV	−96.36 (0)*

Notes: The critical value of null hypothesis of nonstationarity at the 10-per-cent level is −3.13 with total number of observation $n = 23$.

The null hypothesis of rejecting there is no serial correlation lies outside $1.54 < d < 2.46$.

The null hypothesis of rejecting there is no 1st order autocorrelation lies outside $-1.96 < h < 1.96$.

*   indicates the rejection of null hypothesis. Figures in parentheses indicate the number of lags on the differenced variable used in the auxiliary regression to achieve residual whiteness.

Appendix to
Chapter 5

Table A5.1
Test for unit roots

Variables	Data series	DF/ADF Statistics Ho: I(1) versus Ha: I(0)
Per capita GDP	PCY	−1.62(1)
Financial Institutional development	FD	−83.62(0)*
Non-mining GDP	NMY	−1.69 (1)
Domestic absorption	DA	−3.16 (0)*
Government consumption	GC	−1.97 (1)
Gross investment to GDP	GIY	−4.45 (0)*
Net official transfers	OT	−3.14 (0)*
Consumer price index	CPI	−1.25 (1)
GDP deflator	DEF	−1.72 (1)
Nontradable price index	PNT	−2.50 (0)
Agricultural value added	AVA	−2.77 (0)
Manufacturing value added	MVA	−2.54 (0)
Nontradable sector	NT	−3.89 (0)*
Construction sector	CONS	−3.20 (0)*
Gross domestic savings	RDS	−1.85(0)
Private savings	PS	−2.52(0)
Foreign savings	FS	−4.12(0)*
Real interest rate	RIR	−2.06(0)
Expected rate of inflation	INF	−3.73(0)*

Notes: The critical value of null hypothesis of nonstationarity at the 10-per-cent level is −3.13 with total number of observation n = 23.

The null hypothesis of rejecting there is no serial correlation lies outside 1.54<d<2.46.

The null hypothesis of rejecting there is no 1st order autocorrelation lies outside −1.96<h<1.96.

* indicates the rejection of null hypothesis. Figures in parentheses indicate the number of lags on the differenced variable used in the auxiliary regression to achieve residual whiteness.

Appendix
to Chapter 6

Table A6.1
Central government revenues and expenditures, 1971–77
(kina million)

	1971	1972	1973	1974	1975	1976	1977
Total revenue	74.2	85.1	93.3	136.7	179.7	220.2	223.6
Tax revenue	61.8	71.6	74.5	95.1	134.8	178.7	151.5
Non-tax revenue	12.4	13.5	18.8	41.6	44.9	41.5	37.1
Total expenditure	204.7	233.8	250.4	307.5	374.1	415.2	409.4
Current expenditure	162.5	193.7	213.9	277.0	341.0	369.7	362.7
Capital expenditure	42.2	40.1	36.5	30.5	33.1	45.5	46.7

Source: Constructed from World Bank (1981), Table 4.2 and 4.4, Report No. 1150-PNG, 1976, and Table 5.2 and Table 5.6, Report No. 3544a-PNG.

Appendix to Chapter 7

Table A7.1
Index of government consumption and domestic absorption in PNG, Indonesia and Nigeria, 1970-84 (1970=100)

Year	Domestic absorption			Government consumption		
	PNG	Indon-esia	Nigeria	PNG	Indon-esia	Nigeria
1970	100	100	100	100	100	100
1971	111	109	110	113	116	117
1972	107	133	120	125	141	133
1973	105	195	130	144	244	167
1974	122	288	180	173	287	217
1975	141	363	250	201	428	367
1976	152	444	320	210	543	500
1977	168	532	370	195	708	667
1978	183	652	410	204	906	833
1979	209	889	450	214	1162	833
1980	241	1186	510	238	1826	833
1981	259	1560	610	262	2288	1000
1982	277	1736	670	271	2563	1167
1983	299	2072	670	272	2864	1333
1984	314	2301	700	292	3234	1500

Source: Computed from World Bank (1988).

Bibliography

Ady, P. (1976), 'Growth Models for Developing Countries', in A. Cairncross and M. Puri (eds), *Employment, Income Distribution and Development Strategy: Problems of the Developing Countries*, London: Macmillan, pp. 106–19.

AIDAB (Australian International Development Assistance Bureau) (1991), *The Papua New Guinea: Economic Situation and Outlook*, International Development Issues No.16, Canberra: AGPS.

AIDAB (Australian International Development Assistance Bureau) (1993), *The Papua New Guinea Economy: Prospects for Sectoral Development and Broad Based Growth*, International Development Issues No. 30, Canberra: AGPS.

AIDAB (Australian International Development Assistance Bureau) (1994), *The Papua New Guinea Economy: The Role of Government in Economic Development*, International Development Issues No. 33, Canberra: Economic Insights Pty Ltd.

Arndt, H.W. and R.M. Sundrum (1984), 'Devaluation and Inflation: The 1978 Experience', *Bulletin of Indonesian Economic Studies*, **20** (1), 83–95.

Artus, J.R. (1978), 'Methods of Assessing the Long run Equilibrium Value of Exchange Rate', *Journal of International Economics*, **8** (2), 277–99.

Athukorala, P. and J. Menon (1993), 'Pricing to Market Behaviour and Exchange Rate Pass-through in Japanese Exports', *Economic Journal*, **104** (423), 271–82.

Athukorala, P. (1998), 'Interest Rates, Saving and Investment in India', *Oxford Development Studies*.

Athukorala, P. and J. Menon (1995), 'Modelling Manufactured Imports: Methodological Issues With Evidence From Australia', *Journal of Policy Modelling*, **17** (4), 667–75.

Athukorala, P. and S. Jayasuriya (1994), *Crises, Adjustment and Growth: Macroeconomic Policies in Post-Independence Sri Lanka*, Washington, DC: World Bank.

AusAID (Australian Agency for International Development) (1995), *The Papua New Guinea Economy: Improving the Investment Climate*, International Development Issues No. 43, Canberra: ANUTECH Pty Ltd.

AusAID (Australian Agency for International Development) (1996), *The Economy of Papua New Guinea 1996 Report*, International Development Issues No. 46, Canberra: National Capital Printing.

AusAID (Australian Agency for International Development) (1997), *Economic Survey of Papua New Guinea 1996 Report*, International Development Issues No. 46, Canberra: Pirie Printers Pty Limited.

AusAID (Australian Agency for International Development) (1999), *The Economy of Papua New Guinea: Macroeconomic Policies: Implications for Growth and Development in the Informal Sector (1999 Report*, International Development Issues No. 53, Canberra: Economic Insights Pty Ltd.

Balassa, B. (1964), 'The Purchasing Power Parity Doctrine: A Reappraisal', *Journal of Political Economy*, **72** (6), 584–96.

Banerjee, A., J.J. Dolado, D.F. Hendry and G.W. Smith (1986), *Exploring Equilibrium Relationships in Econometrics Through Static Models: Some Monte Carlo Evidence*, Oxford Bulletin of Economics and Statistics, **48** (3), 253–77.

Barro, R. (1991), 'Economic Growth in a Cross-Section of Countries', *Quarterly Journal of Economics*, **106**, 407–43.

Bank of Papua New Guinea, *Quarterly Economic Bulletin*, various issues, Port Moresby.

Beggs, J. J. (1988), 'Diagnostic Testing in Applied Econometrics', *Economic Record*, **64** (4), 81–101.

Benjamin, N.C., S. Devarajan and R.J. Weiner (1989), 'The "Dutch Disease" in a Developing Country: Oil Reserves in Cameroon', *Journal of Development Economies*, **30** (1), 71–92.

Bevan, D., P. Collier and J. Gunning (1987), 'Trade Shocks in Controlled Economies: Theory with an Application to East Africa', *Working Papers in Trade and Development*, 87/1, Canberra: The Australian National University, Research School of Pacific Studies.

Bevan, D., P. Collier and J. Gunning (1990), *Controlled Open Economies: A Newclassical Approach to Structuralism*, Oxford: Clarendon Press.

Bevan, D., P. Collier and J. Gunning (1991), 'The Macroeconomics Of External Shocks', in V.N. Balasubramanyuam and S. Lal (eds), *Current Issues in Development Economics*, Oxford: Oxford University Press.

Bienen, H. (1983), 'Oil Revenues and Policy Choice in Nigeria', *World Bank Staff Working Paper*, No. 592, Washington, DC: The World Bank.

Bird, R.M. (1989), 'Taxation in Papua New Guinea: Backwards to the Future?', *World Development*, **17** (8), 1145–57.

Booth, A. (1989), 'Indonesian Agricultural Development in Comparative Perspective', *World Development*, **17** (8), 1235–54.

Box, G.E.P. and G.M. Jenkins (1970), *Time Series Analysis, Forecasting and Control*, San Francisco: Holden-Day.

Bruno, M. and J. Sachs (1982), 'Energy and Resource Allocation: A Dynamic Model of the Dutch disease', *Review of Economic Studies*, **49** (5), Special Issue, 845–59.

Buiter, W.H. and M. Miller (1981), 'Monetary Policy and International Competitiveness: The Problem of Adjustment', *Oxford Economic Paper*, Supplement July, **33** (0), 143–75.

Buiter, W.H. and D.D. Purvis (1982), 'Oil, Disinflation and Export Competitiveness: A Model of the Dutch Disease', in J. Bhandari and B. Putman (eds), *Economic Interdependence and Flexible Exchange Rate*, Cambridge, Mass.: MIT Press.

Carroll, C. and D. Weil (1993), 'Savings and Growth: A Reinterpretation', *NBER Working Paper*, No. 4470.

Cassing, J.H., C.W. Jerome and E.L. Zamalloa (1987), 'On Resource Booms and Busts: Some Aspects of the Dutch Disease in Six Developing Economies', *Eastern Economic Journal*, **13** (4), 373–87.

Chow, G. (1960), 'Tests of Equality Between Sets of Coefficients in Two Linear Regressions', *Econometrica*, **28** (3), 591–605.

Chowdhury, K. and M. Chowdhury (1993), 'Trade in Labour Services and its Macroeconomic Effects on a Small Economy: Evidence from Bangladesh', *Proceedings of the 14th International Symposium of Asian Studies*, Hong Kong, **4**, 327–34.

Corbo, V. and K. Schmidt-Hebbel (1991), 'Public Policies and Saving in Developing Countries' *Journal of Development Economics*, **36** (1), 89–115.

Collier, P. (1988), 'Oil Shocks and Food Security in Nigeria', *International Labour Review*, **127** (6), 761–82.

Corden, W.M. (1984), 'Booming Sector and Dutch Disease Economics: Survey and Consolidation', *Oxford Economic Papers*. **36** (3), 359–380.

Corden, W.M. (1985), *Inflation, Exchange Rates and the World Economy, Lectures On International Monetary Economics*, Third Edition, Oxford: Clarendon Press.

Corden, W.M. and J.P. Neary (1982), 'Booming Sector and De-Industrialisation in a Small Open Economy', *Economic Journal*, **92** (368), 825–48.

Cottani, J.A., F.C. Domingo and M.S. Khan (1990), 'Real Exchange Rate Behaviour and Economic Performance in LDCs', *Economic Development and Cultural Change*, **39** (1), 61–76.

Curtin, T. (2001), Could Have Done Better?: An Update on Economic Developments in Papua New Guinea Since 1995, http://www.geocities.com/Capitol Hill/Senate/103/better.htm

Daniel, P. (1990), *Economic Policy in Mineral Exporting Countries: What Have We Learned?* Discussion Paper, Sussex: Institute of Development Studies.

Davidson, J., D. Hendry, F. Sbra, and S. Yeo (1978), 'Econometric Modelling of the Aggregate Time Series Relationship Between Consumers' Expenditure and Income in the United Kingdom', *Economic Journal*, **88** (352), 661–92.

Diaz-Alejandro, C.F. (1983), 'Real Exchange Rates and Terms of Trade in the Argentine Republic 1913–76', in M. Syrquin and S. Teitel (eds), *Trade, Stability, Technology, and Equity in Latin America*, New York: Academic Press.

Dickey, D.A. and W.A. Fuller (1979), 'Distribution of Estimates of Autoregressive Time Series with a Unit Root', *Journal of American Statistical Association*, **74** (366), 427–31.

Dolado, J.J., T. Jenkinson and S. Sosvilla-Rivers (1990), 'Cointegration and Unit Roots: A Survey', *Journal of Economic Surveys*, **4** (3), 1–46.

Dornbusch, R. (1976), 'Expectation and Exchange Rate Dynamics', *Journal of Political Economy*, **84** (6), 1161–76.

Dornbusch, R. and A. Reynoso (1989), 'Financial Factors in Economic Development', *American Economic Review Papers and Proceedings*, May, 204–209.

Duncan, R. and T. Lawson (1997), *Cost Structures in Papua New Guinea*, National Centre for Development Studies, Canberra: The Australian National University.

Durbin, J. (1970), 'Testing for Serial Correlation in Least-Squares Regression when Some of the Regressions are Lagged Dependent Variables', *Econometrica*, **38** (3), 410–21.

Durbin, J. and G.S. Watson (1951), 'Testing for Serial Correlation in Least-Squares Regression', *Biometrika*, **38**, 159–71.

Eastwood, R.K., and A.J. Venables (1982), 'The Macroeconomic Implications of a Resource Discovery in an Open Economy', *Economic Journal*, **92** (366), 285–99.

Edwards, S. (1988a), 'Real and Monetary Determinants of Real Exchange Rate Behaviours – Theory and Evidence from Developing Countries', *Journal of Development Economics*, **29** (3), 311–41.

Edwards, S. (1988b), *Exchange Rate Misalignment in Developing Countries, World Bank Occasional Papers*, New Series, No. 2.

Edwards, S. (1989), *Real Exchange Rates, Devaluation, and Adjustment: Exchange Rate Policy in Developing Countries*, Cambridge, Mass.: MIT Press.

Edwards, S. (1992), 'Trade Orientations, Distortions and Growth in Developing Countries', *Journal of Development Economics*, **39** (1), 31–57.

Edwards, S. (1996), 'Why are Latin America's Savings Rates so Low? An International Comparative Analysis', *Journal of Development Economics*, **51** (1), 5–43.

Edwards, S. and M. Aoki (1983), 'Oil Export Boom and Dutch-disease – A Dynamic Analysis', *Resources and Energy*, **5**, 219–242.

Eide, E. (1973), 'Virkninger av Statens Oljeinntekter pa Norsk Okonomi', *Sosialokonomen*, **10**, 12–21; see also Institute of Economics Reprint Series No. 106, University of Oslo.

Elek, A. (1991), *Structural Adjustment in Papua New Guinea 1989–90*, Institute of National Affairs, Discussion Paper No. 47, Port Moresby.

Enders, K. and H. Herberg (1983), 'The Dutch Disease: Causes, Consequences, Cures and Calmatives', *Welwirtschaftliches Archiv*, **119** (3), 473–97.

Engle, R.F. and C.W.J. Granger (1987), 'Co-Integration and Error Correction: Representation, Estimation and Testing', *Econometrica*, **55**, 251–76.

Engle, R.F. and C.W.J. Granger (1991, 'Co-Integration and Error Correction: Representation Estimation and Testing', in R. F. Engle and C. W. J. Granger (eds), *Long Run Economic Relations*, Oxford: Oxford University Press.

Engle, R.F. and B.S. Yoo (1987), 'Forecasting and Testing in Co-Integrated Systems', *Journal of Econometrics*, **35** (1), 143–59.

Engle, R.F. and B.S. Yoo (1991), 'Co-Integrated Economic Time Series: A Survey with New Results', in R.F. Engle and C.W.J. Granger (eds), *Long Run Economic Relations*, Oxford: Oxford University Press.

ESCAP (1990), *Statistical Yearbook for Asia and the Pacific*, Bangkok: ESCAP.

Evans, D. (1986), 'Reverse Dutch Disease and Mineral Exporting Developing Economies', *IDS Bulletin*, **17** (4), 10–13.

Fallon, J. (1992), *The Papua New Guinea Economy: Prospects for Recovery, Reform and Sustained Growth*, Canberra: AGPS.

Fallon, J., T. Kings and J. Zeitsch (1995), 'Exchange Rate Policy In Papua New Guinea', Institute of National Affairs, *Discussion Paper*, No. 64, Brisbane: Economic Insights Pty. Ltd.

Fardamanesh, M. (1991a), 'Dutch Disease Economics and the Oil Syndrome: An Empirical Study', *World Development*, **19** (6), 711–17.

Fardamanesh, M. (1991b), 'Terms of Trade Shocks and Structural Adjustment in a Small Open Economy: Dutch Disease and Oil Price Increase', *Journal of Development Economics*, **34** (2), 339–53.

Feldstein, M. and C. Horioka (1980), 'Domestic Saving and International Capital Flows', *Economic Journal*, **90**, 314–29.

Forsyth, P.J. (1982), 'The Australian Mining Boom and British North Sea Oil: A Comparison of the Economic Effects', Department of Economics, *Discussion Paper*, University of NSW, pp. 1–45.

Fry, M.J. (1980), 'Saving, Investment, Growth and the Cost of Financial Repression', *World Development*, **8** (4), 317–27.

Fry, M.J. (1988), *Money, Interest and Banking in Economic Development*, Baltimore: Johns Hopkins University Press.

Fry, M.J., and A. Mason (1981), *Children, Capital Inflows, Interest and Growth in the Life Cycle Savings Function*, unpublished manuscript (February).

Fuller, W.A. (1976), *Introduction to Time Series Analysis*, New York: John Wiley and Sons.

Garnaut, R. (1991), 'Exchange Rate Regimes in the Asian-Pacific Region', *Asia-Pacific Economic Literature*, **5** (1), 5–26.

Garnaut, R. and P. Baxter (1984), 'Exchange Rate and Macro-Economic Policy in Independent Papua New Guinea', *Pacific Research Monograph*, No. 10, Canberra: Development Studies Centre, Australian National University.

Garnaut, R., M. Wright and R. Curtain (1977), *Employment, Incomes and Migration in Papua New Guinea Towns*, Monograph 6, Papua New Guinea: Institute of Applied Social and Economic Research, Boroko.

Gelb, A.H. (1981), 'Capital-Importing Oil-Exporter: Adjustment Issues and Policy Choices', *World Bank Staff Working Paper No. 475*, Washington, DC: The World Bank.

Gelb, A.H. (1985), 'Adjustment to Windfall Gains: A Comparative Analysis of Oil-Exporting Countries' in J.P. Neary and S. van Wijnbergen (eds), *Natural Resources and Macroeconomy*, Oxford: Basil Blackwell Ltd.

Gelb, A.H. and Associates (1988), *Oil Windfalls: Blessing or Curse?*, Washington, DC: Oxford University Press for The World Bank.

Gibson, B. (1993), 'The Impact of the Exchange Rate on Meat Imports (Where's the Meat?)', *Policy Working Paper No.7*, Port Morseby: Department of Agriculture and Livestock, Papua New Guinea.

Giovannini, A. (1983), 'Interest Elasticity of Savings in Developing Countries: The Existing Evidence', *World Development*, **11**, 601–607.

Giovannini, A. (1985), 'Saving and the Real Interest Rate in LDCs', *Journal of Development Economics*, **18** (2–3), 197–217.

Glassburner, B. (1984), *Oil, Public Policy and Economic Performance: Indonesia in the 1970's*, Report for RPO, Development Research Department, Washington, DC: World Bank.

Goldstein, M. and L.H. Officer (1979), 'New Measures of Prices and Productivity For Tradable and Nontradable Goods', *Review of Income and Wealth*, **25** (4), 413–427.

Goodman, R., C. Lepani, and D. Morawetz (1985), *The Economy of Papua New Guinea: An Independent Rewiew*, Canberra: Development Studies Centre, The Australian National University.

Granger, C.W.J. (1986), 'Developments in the Study of Cointegrated Economic Variables', *Oxford Bulletin of Economics and Statistics*, **48** (3), 213–28.

Granger, C.W.J. (1990), *Modelling Economic Series*, Oxford: Oxford University Press.

Granger, C.W.J. and P. Newbold (1977), 'The Time Series Approach to Econometric Model Building' in C.A. Sims (ed.), *New Methods in Business Cycle Research*, Minneapolis: Federal Reserve Bank of Minneapolis.

Gregory, R.G. (1976), 'Some Implications of the Growth of the Mineral Sector', *Australian Journal of Agricultural Economics*, **20** (2), 71–91.

Gujarati, D.N. (1995), *Basic Econometrics*, Third Edition, Sydney: McGraw-Hill, Inc.

Gylfason, T. (1993), *Optimal Saving, Interest Rates and Endogenous Growth*, Seminar Paper No. 539 (University of Stockholm), September.

Haque, I. (1991), 'International Competitiveness: Public Sector/Private Sector Interface' in Irfan ul Haque (ed.), *International Competitiveness: Interaction of Public and Private Sectors*, Economic Development Institute Seminar Series, Washington, DC: The World Bank.

Harberger, A. (1986), 'Economic Adjustment and the Real Exchange Rate', in S. Edwards and L. Ahamed (eds), *Economic Adjustment and Exchange Rates in Developing Countries*, Chicago: University of Chicago Press.

Harvey, C. (1987), *Successful Macroeconomic Adjustment in Three Developing Countries: Botswana, Malawi, and Papua New Guinea*, The Economic Development Institute, Washington, DC: The World Bank.

Harvie, C. (1994), 'Oil Shocks and the Macroeconomy: A Short and Long Run Comparison', *The Journal of Energy and Development*, **18** (1), 59–94.

Harvie, C. and L. Gower (1993), 'Resource Shocks and Macroeconomic Adjustment in the Short Run and Long Run', *The Middle East Business and Economic Review*, **5** (1), 1–14.

Hendry, D.F. (1986), 'Econometric Modelling with Cointegrated Variables: An Overview', *Oxford Bulletin of Economics and Statistics*, **48** (3), 201–12.

Hendry, D.F. and G. Mizon (1978), 'Serial Correlation as a Convenient Simplification, Not a Nuisance: A Comment on a Study of the Demand for Money of the Bank of England', *Economic Journal*, **88**, 549–63.

Hendry, D.F. and T. Von Ungern-Sternberg (1981), 'Liquidity and Inflation Effects on Consumers' Expenditure', in A.S. Deaton (ed.), *Essays in the Theory and Measurement of Consumer Behaviour*, Cambridge: Cambridge University Press.

Hendry, D.F., A.R. Pagan and J.D. Sargan (1985), 'Dynamic Specification', in Z. Griliches and M.D. Intriligator (eds), *Handbook of Econometrics*, 2, Amsterdam: North Holland.

Hill, C.B. (1991), 'Managing Commodity Booms in Botswana', *World Development*, 19 (9), 1185–96.

Hill, H. (1992), 'Regional Development in a Boom and Bust Petroleum Economy: Indonesia since 1970', *Economic Development and Cultural Change*, 40 (2), 352–79.

Hill, H. (1996), *The Indonesian Economy Since 1966: Southeast Asia's Emerging Giant*, Cambridge: Cambridge University Press.

Holden, K. and J. Thompson (1992), 'Co-Integration: An Introductory Survey', *British Review of Economic Issues*, 14 (33), 1–55.

Inder, B. (1993), 'Estimating Long run Relationships in Economics – A Comparison of Different Approaches', *Journal of Econometrics*, 57 (1–3), 53–68.

International Monetary Fund (IMF), various years, *International Financial Statistics*, Washington, DC: IMF.

Internal Revenue Commission of PNG (1997), *Green Paper on the Tariff Reform Program*, Unpublished Draft, Confidential.

Jappelli, T. and M. Pagano (1994), 'Saving, Growth, and Liquidity Constraints', *Quarterly Journal of Economics*, 109, 83–109.

Jarrett, F. (1985), *Innovation in Papua New Guinea Agriculture*, Port Moresby: Institute of National Affairs.

Jarrett, F.G. and K. Anderson (1989), *Growth, Structural Change and Economic Policy in Papua New Guinea: Implications for Agriculture*, Pacific Policy Paper No. 5, Canberra: National Centre for Development Studies, The Australian National University.

Jarque, C.M. and A.K. Bera (1987), 'A Test for Normality of Observations and Regression Residuals', *International Statistical Review*, 55, 163–72.

Jayasuriya, S. (1994), 'Temporary Shocks, Consumption Smoothing and Economic Adjustment: Sri Lanka (1973–76', *Discussion Paper* No. A.94.10, Victoria, Australia: La Trobe University.

Jazayeri, A. (1986), 'Prices and Output in Two Oil-Based Economies: The Dutch Disease in Iran and Nigeria', *IDS Bulletin*, 17 (4), 14–21.

Johansen, S. (1988), 'Statistical Analysis of Cointegration Vectors', *Journal of Economic Dynamics and Control*, 12, 231–54.

Jones, R.W. (1965), 'The Structure of General Equilibrium Model', *Journal of Political Economy*, LXXIII (6), 557–72.

Kamas, L. (1986), 'Dutch Disease Economics and the Colombian Export Boom', *World Development*, 14 (9), 1177–98.

Keynes, J.M. (1936), *The General Theory of Employment, Interest and Money*, New York: Harcourt Brace.

Kmenta, J. (1986), *Elements of Econometrics*, Second Edition, New York: Macmillan.

Levantis, T. (1997), *The Labour Market of PNG*, unpublished PhD thesis, The Australian National University, Canberra.

Little, I.M.D., R.N. Cooper, W.M. Corden and S. Rajapatirana (1993), *Boom, Crisis, and Adjustment: The Macroeconomic Experience of Developing Countries*, Washington, DC: Oxford University Press for The World Bank.

Lodewijks, J. (1987), *Papua New Guinea: Towards an Employment-Oriented Development Strategy*, Islands/Australia Working Paper No. 87/12, Canberra: National Centre for Development Studies.

Looney, R.E. (1990), 'Oil Revenue and Dutch Disease in Saudi Arabia: Differential Impacts on Sectoral Growth', *Canadian Journal of Development Studies*, 11 (1), 119–33.

Lucas, R. (1988), 'On the Mechanics of Economic Development', *Journal of Monetary Economics*, **22**, 3–42.

MacKinnon, J.G. (1991), 'Critical Values for Cointegrating Tests' in R.F. Engle and C.W.J. Granger (eds), *Long Run Economic Relations*, Oxford: Oxford University Press.

Majd, M.G. (1989), 'The Oil Boom and Agricultural Development: A Reconsideration of Agricultural Policy in Iran', *Journal of Energy and Development*, **15** (1), 125–40.

Mazumdar, D. (1991), 'Import Substituting Industrialization and Protection of the Small-Scale: The Indian Experience in the Textile Industry', *World Development*, **19** (9), 1197–1221.

McGavin, P.A. (1986), *The Labour Market in Papua New Guinea: A Survey and Analysis*, Discussion Paper No. 24, Port Moresby: Institute of National Affairs.

McGavin, P.A. (1991), *Wages, Incomes, and Productivity in Papua New Guinea*, Port Moresby: Institute of National Affairs.

McGavin, P.A. (1993), *Connections: The Process of Enhancing Productivity Change in Papua New Guinea*, Discussion Paper No. 59, Port Moresby: Institute of National Affairs.

McKinnon, R.F. (1991), *The Order of Economic Liberalisation: Financial Control in the Transition to a Market Economy*, Baltimore: Johns Hopkins University Press.

McKinnon, R.I. (1973), *Money and Capital in Economic Development*, Washington, DC: Brookings Institute.

Menon, J. (1992), *Exchange Rates and Prices: The Case of Australian Manufactured Imports*, unpublished PhD thesis, Faculty of Economics and Commerce, University of Melbourne: Melbourne.

Modigliani (1970), 'The Life Cycle Hypothesis of Saving and Inter country Differences in the Saving Ratio' in W.A. Eltis, M.F. Scott and J.N. Wolfe, (eds), *Induction, Growth and Trade: Essays in Honour of Sir Roy Harrod*, Oxford: Clarendon Press, pp. 197–225.

Moreno, R. (1989), 'Exchange Rates and Trade Adjustment in Taiwan and Korea', *Economic Review*, Federal Reserve Bank of San Francisco, **0** (2), 30–48.

Nankani, G. (1979), 'Development Problems of Mineral-Exporting Countries', *World Bank Staff Working Paper No. 354*, Washington, DC: The World Bank.

Nota Keuangan Dan Rancangan Anggaran Pendapatan Negara Republik Indonesia (Income Statement), various issues.

National Center for Development Studies (1993), *Pacific Economic Bulletin*, 8(1): Statistical Annex, Canberra: The Australian National University.

Neary, J.P. and S. Van Wijnbergen (1984), 'Can an Oil Discovery Lead to a Recession? A Comment on Eastwood and Venables', *Economic Journal*, **94** (374), 390–95.

Ogaki, M., J. Ostry and C. Reinhart (1994), 'Saving Behaviour in Low and Middle-income Developing Countries: A Comparison', *Working Paper*, Research Department, International Monetary Fund.

Okonkwo, I.C. (1989), 'The Erosion of Agricultural Exports in an Oil Economy: The Case of Nigeria', *Journal of Agricultural Economics*, **40** (3), 375–84.

Oyejide, T. A. (1986), 'The Effects of Trade and Exchange Rate Policies on Agriculture in Nigeria', *Research Report 55*, Washington, DC: International Food Policy Research Institute.

Oyejide, T.A. (1991), *Trade Shock, Oil Boom and the Nigerian Economy: 1973–1983*, mimeo, Department of Economics, University of Ibadan.

Parsons, D. and D. Vincent (1991), 'High Stakes: Mineral and Petroleum Development in Papua New Guinea', *Island/Australia Working Paper*, No. 91/5, Canberra: National Centre For Development Studies, The Australian National University.

Pagan, A.R. and A.D. Hall (1983), 'Diagnostic Tests as Residual Analysis', *Economic Reviews*, **2** (2), 159–218.

Phillips, P.C.B (1987), 'Time Series Regression with a Unit Root', *Econometrica*, **55**, 277–301.

Phillips, P.C.B. and P. Perron (1988), 'Testing for a Unit Root in Time Series Regression', *Biometrika*, **75**, 335–46.

Pinto, B. (1987), 'Nigeria During and After the Oil Boom: A Policy Comparison with Indonesia', *The World Bank Economic Review*, **1** (3), 419–45.

Ramsey, J.B. (1969), 'Tests for Specification Errors in Classical Linear Least Squares Regression Analysis', *Journal of the Royal Statistical Society*, Series B, **31**, 350–71.

Rao, B.B. (1994), 'Editor's Introduction', in B.B. Rao (ed.), *Cointegration For the Applied Economists*, New York: St Martin's Press.

Romer, M. (1985), 'Dutch Disease in Developing Countries: Swallowing Bitter Medicine', in M. Lundahl, et al. (eds), *The Primary Sector in Economic Development*, Proceedings of Seventh Arne Ryde Symposium, Frostarallen, August 29–30 (1983), New York: St Martins Press.

Romer, P. (1986), 'Increasing Returns and Long run Growth', *Journal of Political Economy*, **94** (5), 1002–1037.

Salehi-Isfahani, D. (1989), 'Oil Exports, Real Exchange Rate Appreciation and Demand for Imports in Nigeria', *Economic Development and Cultural Change*, **37** (3), 495–512.

Salehi-Esfahani, H. (1988), 'Informationally Imperfect Labour Markets and the 'Dutch Disease' Problem', *Canadian Journal of Economics*, **21** (3), 617–24.

Salter, W. (1959), 'Internal and External Balance: The Role of Price and Expenditure Effects', *Economic Record*, **35** (71), 226–38.

Sargan, J.D. (1964), 'Wages and Prices in the UK: A Study in Econometric Methodology', in P. Hart, G. Mills and J. Whittaker (eds), *Econometric Analysis for National Planning*, London: Butterworths.

Sargan, J.D. and A. Bhargava (1983), 'Testing Residuals from Least Squares Regression for being Generated by the Gaussian Random Walk', *Econometrica*, **51** (1) 153–174.

Scherr, S.J. (1989), 'Agriculture in an Export Boom Economy: A Comparative Analysis of Policy and Performance in Indonesia, Mexico and Nigeria', *World Development*, **17** (4), 543–60.

Schwert, G.W. (1989), 'Test for Unit Roots: A Monte Carlo Investigation', *Journal of Business and Economic Statistics*, **7**, 147–60.

Shaw, E. (1973), *Financial Deepening in Economic Development*, Oxford: Oxford University Press.

Schmidt-Hebbel, K., S. Webb and G. Corsetti (1992), 'Household Savings in Developing Countries', *World Bank Economic Review*, **6** (3), 529–47.

Snape, R.H. (1977), 'Effects of Mineral Development on the Economy', *Australian Journal of Agricultural Economics*, **21** (3), 147–56.

Stock, J. H. (1987), 'Asymptotic Properties of Least Squares Estimators of Cointegrating Vectors', *Econometrica*, **55**, 1035–56.

Sundrum, R.M. (1986), 'Indonesia's Rapid Economic Growth: 1968–81', *Bulletin of Indonesian Economic Studies*, **22** (3), 40–69.

Taylor, L. (1983), *Structuralist Macroeconomics: Applicable Models for the Third World*, New York: Basic Books.

Taylor, L. (1988), *Varieties of Stabilisation Experience: Towards Sensible Macroeconomics in the Third World*, Oxford: Clarendon Press.

Taylor, L., K.T. Yurukoglu and S.A. Chowdhury (1985), 'A Macro Model of an Oil Exporter: Nigeria', in J.P. Neary and S.V. Wijnbergen (eds), *Natural Resources and the Macroeconomy*, Oxford: Basil Blackwell Ltd.

Thaha, A. and C. Harvie (1992), *An Analysis of the Economic Effects of the Oil Boom on Indonesia's Agricultural Sector: 1972–91*, Paper presented at the Twenty First Conference of Economists, Economic Society of Australia, University of Melbourne, July 10.

Thomas, R.L. (1993), *Introductory Econometrics: Theory and Applications*, London and New York: Longman.

United Nations Development Program (1995), *Human Development Report 1995*, New York: Oxford University Press.

van Wijnbergen, S. (1982), 'Stagflationary Effects of Monetary Stabilisation Policies: A Quantitative Analysis of South Lores', *Journal of Development Economics*, **10** (2), 133–69.

van Wijnbergen, S. (1984a), 'The Dutch Disease: A Disease After All?' *Economic Journal*, **94** (373), 41–55.

van Wijnbergen, S. (1984b), 'Inflation Employment, and the Dutch Disease in Oil-Exporting Countries: A Short run Disequilibrium Analysis', *Quarterly Journal of Economics*, **99** (2), 233–50.

Warr, P.G. (1984), 'Exchange Rate Protection in Indonesia', *Bulletin of Indonesian Economic Studies*, **20** (2), 53–89.

Warr, P.G. (1986), 'Indonesia's Other Dutch Disease: Economic Effects of the Petroleum Boom', in J.P. Neary and S.V. Wijnbergen (eds), *Natural Resources and the Macroeconomy*, Oxford: Basil Blackwell Ltd.

Woo, W.T., B. Glassburner and A. Nasution (1994), *Macroeconomic Policies, Crises, and Long-term Growth in Indonesia*, Washington, DC: World Bank.

World Bank (1976), *Papua New Guinea: Economic Situation and Development Prospects*, Report No. 1150-PNG, Washington, DC: World Bank.

World Bank (1981), Report No. 3544a-PNG, *Papua New Guinea: Development Policies and Prospects for the 1980s*, Document of the World Bank, Washington, DC: World Bank.

World Bank (1983–84), *World Development Report*, Washington, DC.

World Bank (1984), *World Development Report*, Oxford University Press: New York.

World Bank (1985), *Nigeria: Agricultural Sector* Memorandum Vols. I and II, Report No. 4723–UNI, Washington, DC: World Bank.

World Bank (1988), *World Tables 1988*, Washington, DC: World Bank.

World Bank (1989–90), *World Debt Tables*, Washington, DC: World Bank.

World Bank (1991), *Papua New Guinea: Structural Adjustment, Growth and Human Resource Development*, Report No. 9396–PNG, Country Operations Division, Asia Region, Washington, DC: World Bank.

World Bank (1993), *World Development Report*, Washington, DC: World Bank.

World Bank (1993), *World Tables 1993*, Washington, DC: World Bank.

World Bank (1994), *The World Bank Atlas*, Washington, DC: World Bank.

World Bank (1995), *World Tables 1995*, Washington, DC: World Bank.

World Bank (2002), Development Data Group, http://www.worldbank.org/data/

World Bank (2002a), *World Development Indicators*, CD-ROM, Washington, DC: World Bank.

Yokoyama, H. (1989), 'Export-led Industrialisation and the Dutch Disease', *The Developing Economies*, **27** (4), 427–45.

Young, A. (1994), 'The Tyranny of Numbers: Confronting the Statistical Evidence of the East Asian Growth Experience', NBER Working Paper No. 4680.

Index